Lecture Notes in Computer Science　11276

Commenced Publication in 1973
Founding and Former Series Editors:
Gerhard Goos, Juris Hartmanis, and Jan van Leeuwen

Editorial Board

More information about this series at http://www.springer.com/series/7407

Feng Zhang · Jidong Zhai
Marc Snir · Hai Jin
Hironori Kasahara · Mateo Valero (Eds.)

Network and Parallel Computing

15th IFIP WG 10.3 International Conference, NPC 2018
Muroran, Japan, November 29 – December 1, 2018
Proceedings

 Springer

Editors
Feng Zhang 🄳
Renmin University of China
Beijing, China

Jidong Zhai
Tsinghua University
Beijing, China

Marc Snir
University of Illinois at Urbana-Champaign
Urbana, IL, USA

Hai Jin
Huazhong University of Science
and Technology
Wuhan, China

Hironori Kasahara
Waseda University
Shinjuku-ku, Japan

Mateo Valero
Barcelona Supercomputing Center
Barcelona, Spain

ISSN 0302-9743   ISSN 1611-3349   (electronic)
Lecture Notes in Computer Science
ISBN 978-3-030-05676-6   ISBN 978-3-030-05677-3   (eBook)
https://doi.org/10.1007/978-3-030-05677-3

Library of Congress Control Number: 2018963718

LNCS Sublibrary: SL1 – Theoretical Computer Science and General Issues

This Springer imprint is published by the registered company Springer Nature Switzerland AG
The registered company address is: Gewerbestrasse 11, 6330 Cham, Switzerland

Preface

These proceedings contain the papers presented at the 2018 IFIP International Conference on Network and Parallel Computing (NPC 2018), held in Muroran, Hokkaido, Japan, from November 29 to December 1, 2018. The goal of the conference is to establish an international forum for engineers and scientists to present their ideas and experiences in network and parallel computing.

A total of 72 submissions were received in response to our Call for Papers. These papers originate from Australia, Asia (China, Japan), Europe, and North America (USA). Each submission was sent to at least three reviewers. Each paper was judged according to its originality, innovation, readability, and relevance to the expected audience. Based on the reviews received, 22 full papers (about 30%), including 12 papers published as Special Issue papers of the *International Journal of Parallel Programming*, and ten papers published as LNCS proceedings were retained. A number of strong papers that could not be accepted to the full-paper track were considered for the short-paper tracks. Finally, we selected 12 short papers. These papers cover traditional areas of network and parallel computing, including parallel applications, distributed algorithms, parallel architectures, software environments, and distributed tools.

We share the view that, during the past decade, the tools and cultures of high-performance computing and big data analytics are diverging to the detriment of both, and the international community should find a unified path that can best serve the need of a broad spectrum of major application areas. Unlike other tools, which are limited to particular scientific domains, computational modeling and data analytics are applicable to all areas of science and engineering, as they breathe life into the underlying mathematics of scientific models.

We sincerely appreciate the work and effort of the authors in preparing their submissions for review, and addressing the reviewers' comments before submitting the camera-ready copies of their accepted papers, and attending the conference to present and discuss their work. We also want to thank every member of the NPC 2018 Organizing Committee and Steering Committee for their help in putting together such an exciting program. Finally, we thank all the attendees.

August 2018

Feng Zhang
Jidong Zhai
Marc Snir
Hai Jin
Hironori Kasahara
Mateo Valero

Organization

Organizing Committee

General Co-chairs

Hai Jin	Huazhong University of Science and Technology, China
Hironori Kasahara	Waseda University, Japan
Mateo Valero	Barcelona Supercomputing Center, Spain

Program Co-chairs

Marc Snir	University of Illinois at Urbana-Champaign, USA
Jidong Zhai	Tsinghua University, China

Publications Chair

Feng Zhang	Renmin University of China, China

Local Arrangements Co-chairs

Mianxiong Dong	Muroran Institute of Technology, Japan
He Li	Muroran Institute of Technology, Japan

Publicity Chairs

Bingsheng He	National University of Singapore, Singapore
Keiji Kimura	Waseda University, Japan
Shuaiwen Leon Song	Pacific Northwest National Laboratory, USA
Yunquan Zhang	Institute of Computing Technology, China
Stéphane Zuckerman	University of Cergy-Pontoise, France

Web Chair

Yuyang Jin	Tsinghua University, China

Advisory Committee

Steering Committee

Kemal Ebcioglu (Chair)	Global Supercomputing, USA
Hai Jin (Vice Chair)	Huazhong University of Science and Technology, China
Chen Ding	University of Rochester, USA
Jack Dongarra	University of Tennessee, USA
Guang R. Gao	University of Delaware, USA
Jean-Luc Gaudiot	University of California, Irvine, USA
Tony Hey	Science and Technology Facilities Council, UK

Guojie Li	Institute of Computing Technology, China
Yoichi Muraoka	Waseda University, Japan
Viktor Prasanna	University of Southern California, USA
Daniel Reed	University of Iowa, USA
Weisong Shi	Wayne State University, USA
Ninghui Sun	Institute of Computing Technology, China
Zhiwei Xu	Institute of Computing Technology, China

Program Committee

Yungang Bao	Institute of Computing Technology
Dehao Chen	Google
Wenguang Chen	Tsinghua University, China
Guoyang Chen	Alibaba Group US Inc., USA
Huimin Cui	Institute of Computing Technology
Yufei Ding	University of California, Santa Barbara, USA
Zhihui Du	Tsinghua University, China
Masato Edahiro	Nagoya University, Japan
Keiji Kimura	Waseda University, Japan
Ang Li	Pacific Northwest National Lab
Chao Li	Shanghai Jiao Tong University, China
Dong Li	University of California, Merced, USA
Yun Liang	Peking University, China
Weifeng Liu	Norwegian University of Science and Technology, Norway
Yingwei Luo	Peking University, China
Xiaosong Ma	Qatar Computing Research Institute, Qatar
Daniel A. Orozco	Google
Antoniu Pop	University of Manchester, UK
Xuehai Qian	University of Southern California, USA
Lawrence Rauchwerger	Texas A&M University, USA
Bin Ren	College of William and Mary, USA
Jinglei Ren	Microsoft
Larry Rudolph	Two Sigma Investments
Li Shen	National University of Defense Technology, China
Xuanhua Shi	Huazhong University of Science and Technology, China
Yao Shi	Futurewei Technologies
GuangZhong Sun	University of Science and Technology of China, China
Shanjiang Tang	Tianjin University, China
Dingwen Tao	The University of Alabama, USA
Parimala Thulasiraman	University of Manitoba, Canada
Lei Wang	National University of Defense Technology, China
Zhaoguo Wang	Shanghai Jiao Tong University, China
Zheng Wang	Lancaster University, UK
Bo Wu	Colorado School of Mines, USA

Zhibin Yu   Shenzhen Institutes of Advanced Technology, Chinese
                        Academy of Science, China
Weihua Zhang   Fudan University, China
Zhijia Zhao   University of California Riverside, USA
Amelie Chi Zhou   Shenzhen University, China
Stéphane Zuckerman   University of Cergy-Pontoise, France

Contents

CNLoc: Channel State Information Assisted Indoor WLAN Localization Using Nomadic Access Points

Jiang Xiao[1(✉)], Huichuwu Li[1], He Li[2], and Hai Jin[1]

[1] Services Computing Technology and System Lab,
Cluster and Grid Computing Lab, School of Computer Science and Technology,
Huazhong University of Science and Technology, Wuhan 430074, China
`jiangxiao@hust.edu.cn`
[2] Department of Information and Electronic Engineering,
Muroran Institute of Technology, Muroran, Hokkaido, Japan

Abstract. *Wireless local area network* (WLAN) based indoor localization is expanding its fast-paced adoption to facilitate a variety of *indoor location-based services* (ILBS). Unfortunately, the performance of current WLAN localization systems relying on fixed *access points* (APs) deployment is constrained by the *spatial localizability variance* (SLV) problem that different locations may exhibit significantly distinct localization resolution. Prior approaches tackle this problem through nomadic APs with favorable mobility to dynamically adjust the network topology. However, the lack of prior knowledge of nomadic AP's position has been a challenge for location distinction and will lead to prohibitive performance degradation. In this paper, we propose and develop CNLoc, a novel CSI-based (*Channel State Information*) indoor WLAN localization framework to overcome the location uncertainty of nomadic APs. Our implementation and evaluation show that CNLoc can improve the accuracy with unknown location information of nomadic APs. We also discuss some open issues and new possibilities in future nomadic AP based indoor localization.

Keywords: WLAN · CSI · RSS · Mobility

1 Introduction

The rapid proliferation of *indoor location-based services* (ILBS) has spurred the indoor location market [9], leading to a rash of proposals for developing new localization systems [21]. WLAN-based indoor localization is one of the most efficient methodologies, which applies general WiFi devices in position analysis. Owing to the high availability of infrastructure and low cost, WLAN has become an increasingly attractive choice, ranging from research community [6,8,22] to industry (*e.g.*, Google, Apple, Microsoft, *etc.*).

© IFIP International Federation for Information Processing 2018
Published by Springer Nature Switzerland AG 2018
F. Zhang et al. (Eds.): NPC 2018, LNCS 11276, pp. 1–12, 2018.
https://doi.org/10.1007/978-3-030-05677-3_1

In the deployment of WLAN-based indoor localization services, there are some issues which affect the localization accuracy. An important issue is the placement of WLAN *access points* (APs), which is also very difficult since most APs are deployed for wireless communications. Nomadic APs are those mobile devices that can provide localization services, which brings an opportunity for deployment of WLAN-based indoor localization. In our previous work, we have proposed an indoor localization method based on the nomadic APs, which shows good efficiency in providing localization services.

However, a challenge in the nomadic AP based indoor localization is the location uncertainty of the nomadic APs. In the previous work, we need to know the position of each nomadic AP to estimate the final location. Since the accuracy of the nomadic APs is not always enough and determined, the accumulated error of the estimated location will affect the quality of localization. There are several ways to solve this problem. The first way is to apply some other devices such as microphones or cameras for assistance. Although additional environment information can improve the localization accuracy, the special devices will bring more cost and energy consumption to nomadic APs.

Channel state information (CSI) is another opportunity that improves the localization accuracy by distinguishing the status of different nomadic APs. In the nomadic AP based indoor localization, the location uncertainty is usually brought by moving nomadic APs. Since the mobility of nomadic APs will affect the CSI in WLAN communications, it is possible to distinct static APs and moving APs by analyzing CSI data.

Therefore, in this paper, we propose a new design of CNLoc, to tackle the challenges brought by nomadic APs in indoor WLAN localization. CNLoc leverages the favorable fact that CSI possesses the temporal stability and frequency diversity properties, which makes it capable of inferring the object's status (*i.e.*, moving or static) by the CSI-based location distinction mechanism.

Overall, we summarize the main contributions of our work as:

- We exploit the distinctive capability of CSI to investigate the object's mobility status, which is the crucial premise for better utilizing the nomadic APs' mobility. Due to the advantages of both temporal stability and frequency diversity characteristics, CSI-based location distinction can achieve very high accuracy.
- We overcome the limitation of nomadic APs' location uncertainty by further aggregating the sensor information to the SP-based method which is less sensitive to the nomadic APs' position errors.
- From evaluation results, we observe that CNLoc can achieve great SLV reduction, and outperform the corresponding static AP deployment.

This paper is organized as follows. Section 2 reviews the state-of-the-art researches. Section 3 gives an overview of the technical challenges and then presents the architecture of CNLoc. Section 4 presents our methodology in detail. We present a thorough evaluation in Sect. 5, and demonstrate that it is more accurate compared to the static AP deployment. In Sect. 6 we discuss the practical issues. Finally, we draw our conclusions and indicate some directions for future work in Sect. 7.

2   Related Work

In this section, we introduce some researches in the following categories: (1) deployment of indoor localization infrastructure, and (2) CSI-assisted localization.

2.1   Deployment of Indoor Localization Infrastructure

A localization problem is to transform virtual coordinates of localization infrastructures into physical ones, such as a set of anchors or landmarks. Since the geometric layout of the localization infrastructures significantly affects the localization performance, AP deployment will lead to the SLV problem that the accuracy of indoor localization differs with different layouts. Chen *et al.* [3] first introduced the landmark placement problem in indoor localization with wireless networks and proposed a placement algorithm to minimize the maximum localization error.

Dulman *et al.* [4] focused on the anchor deployment in wireless networks. Meng *et al.* [10] proposed an optimal AP deployment method to improve positioning accuracy in indoor Wi-Fi environments, which maximizes the RSS (*radio signal strength*) euclidean distance between physical locations.

Due to the complex indoor structure, AP deployment inevitably incurs the SLV problem, where the localization accuracy differs at different locations, leading to user experience inconsistence. Lin *et al.* [7] proposed an AP selection mechanism based on AP positioning capabilities to improve WiFi fingerprinting accuracy. Gao *et al.* [5] optimized the placement of landmarks for localization in a warehouse by maximizing the difference degree in each space unit.

2.2   CSI-Assisted Localization

The accuracy of RSS-based indoor localization systems is limited by the multipath effect [1,24]. Bhartia *et al.* [2] measured the frequency diversity of WLAN channels and proposed some methods to harness diversity by leveraging the CSI in WLAN communications. Yang *et al.* [23] first introduced the CSI into WLAN-based indoor localization systems and analyzed the frequency diversity from collected CSI data. Wu *et al.* [18] proposed FILA which is a novel approach that eliminates the multipath effect by leveraging the CSI in indoor scenarios. The CSI is also applied to separate *line-of-sight* (LOS) path in communications, which can assist location estimation in complex indoor environments [14,15].

Building location fingerprints is another way to optimize the multipath effect in indoor WLAN localization. Sen *et al.* [16] proposed an indoor localization system called PinLoc that builds location signatures by harnessing the CSI in WLAN channels. Moreover, since many works focused on the motion detection by using WLAN CSI, it is possible to detect the object position directly with the similar method. Pilot is a device-free indoor localization system that builds different radio maps with CSI data to estimate the positions of entities in the WLAN signal area [19].

3   CNLoc Framework

To deal with the SLV problem due to the static deployment of APs, we leverage nomadic APs to improve localization accuracy and mitigate user experience inconsistence at different locations. This section starts with the challenges to utilize nomadic APs for localization, before presenting the overall framework of our CNLoc system.

To harness nomadic APs to establish a dynamic topology so as to avoid the SLV problem, we need to address the following challenge: how to resolve the location uncertainty of nomadic APs for robust location determination? Since nomadic APs tend to move stochastically within the area of interest, it is difficult to obtain their coordinates accurately. As the location estimation error of nomadic APs accumulates, the localization accuracy also degrades. To deal with this challenge, we design a localization framework that is less sensitive to the location uncertainty of nomadic APs.

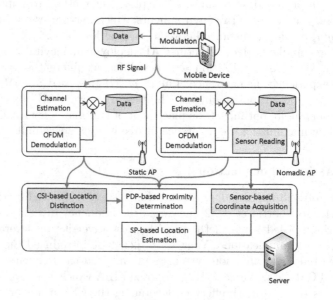

Fig. 1. Architecture of CNLoc

We harness the mobility of nomadic APs via *space partition*. In this way, CNLoc neither requires a pre-collected fingerprint database, which is labor-intensive to construct [24], nor sophisticated calibration to achieve accurate ranging in complex indoor environments [18]. Figure 1 shows the iterative localization framework, which is resilient to location uncertainty of nomadic APs and gradually converges to an accurate location estimate. To enable proximity determination in multipath and NLOS environments, we introduce CSI into the time domain and adopt PDP (*power of direct path*) for distance estimates. PDP filters out signal power from paths with long delays so as to mitigate the impact of multipath on distance estimation. Since CNLoc only needs relative proximity rather than precise distance between each nomadic AP and the object, the adoption of PDP is sufficient to achieve high localization accuracy even in complex indoor environments. Different from the preliminary work NomLoc [20], we do not assume the coordinates of nomadic APs are known, and obtain them using **sensor-based coordinate acquisition**.

4 Methodology

This section presents the detailed design of the three key modules, (1) PDP-based proximity determination, (2) CSI-based location distinction, and (3) Sensor-based coordinate acquisition.

4.1 Proximity Determination

CNLoc uses the maximum power of the power delay profile to approximate PDP of links if there is a strong LOS path. However, it may over-estimate the distance if the LOS path is severely attenuated or even blocked in NLOS propagation situations. To mitigate the impact of NLOS propagation or propagation without a LOS path, CNLoc adopts previous approaches on CSI-based LOS identification schemes for both nomadic and static APs with at least two antennas [17]. As such, we use the PDP as an indicator for proximity determination, which filters out signal power from paths with long delays. Note that CNLoc may still falsely determine the proximity information if there is no LOS path. Nevertheless, since we formulate the localization problem into a space partition problem, which is solved by optimization with redundant measurements, our approach can also tolerate certain extent of errors induced by NLOS propagation.

4.2 CSI-Based Location Distinction

In current CNLoc design, SP-based algorithm is operated under the assumption that the object stays at an identical location. In other words, the status of the object is necessitated to be stationary during the positioning procedure. In this case, we can derive the object's location jointly from the partition results of nomadic APs. It is unlikely to directly apply the proposed SP-based derivation using the measurement of the nomadic AP at multiple positions if the object is walking around in an indoor venue. For example, if an object moves from location A (L_A) to location B (L_B), it is inappropriate to aggregate the SP-based output of L_B with L_A for positioning. This is because the present partition result of L_B only correlates with the preceding ones at L_B, while independent of those at L_A. As a consequence, it raises a prerequisite of detecting the mobility status of the object, *i.e.*, static or moving, which directly bounds up with the outcome of SP-based algorithm. Now that we need to take the object's status into consideration in the design of CNLoc. Because it needs to be guaranteed that the object keeps stationary as long as the nomadic APs fulfil the localization task. To achieve this, we focus our efforts on the location distinction relying on the fine-grained CSI. The basic idea is to exploit the suitable CSI-based feature which can distinguish the statuses between static and moving, taking advantage of both the temporal stability and frequency diversity characteristics. We denote the CSI measurements over sliding window W of length N by $\mathbb{H}$ as,

$$\mathbb{H} = [\mathrm{H}_1, \mathrm{H}_2, \dots, \mathrm{H}_N] \tag{1}$$

For each H_i, it consists of 30 subcarriers and can be expressed as a vector H_i,

$$\mathrm{H}_i = [|H_i^1|, |H_i^2|, \therefore, |H_i^{30}|]^T \tag{2}$$

where $|H_i^k|$ corresponds to the amplitude of k-th subcarrier CSI.

The location distinction feature can then be formulated as the following $\mathbf{C_t}$:

$$\mathbf{C_t} = \frac{1}{N-1} \sum_{j=1}^{N} corr(\mathrm{H}_t, \mathrm{H}_{t-j}) \tag{3}$$

In CNLoc, $\mathbf{C_t}$ is compared to a preset threshold τ. If $\mathbf{C_t}$ is a higher value than the τ, the object is determined to stay stationary in the area of interest without tendency to change position. On the other hand, the movement of the object will be detected when $\mathbf{C_t}$ falls below the τ. Moreover, we can fuse the detection outputs over multiple links to produce a more accurate result.

To summarize, we can employ the CSI-based location distinction feature from multiple static APs deployed in the positioning region. Lying on the benefits of temporal stability and frequency diversity, such feature can be steady in static status while sensitive to the mobility of the object.

4.3   Sensor-Based Coordinate Acquisition

As previously noted in Sect. 3, the uncertainty of nomadic APs' location can result in performance degradation, which is incompatible with our design objective. To confront such difficulty, we assume built-in sensors of nomadic APs become handy tools for identifying the absolute coordinates. In particular, when the prior knowledge of nomadic APs' initial coordinate is available, we suggest a simple yet effective dead reckoning approach based on the sensor information including three phases: (1) leveraging low-pass filter and additional constrains comparing with existing methods for step detection, (2) minimizing the efforts for personalize step length estimation, and (3) direction determination. This method makes it very convenient to ensure accurate nomadic APs' coordinates for optimal preparation of SP-based location estimation.

We start by detecting and counting the number of steps during nomadic APs' movement using the accelerometer sensor reading. A novel AFSM (*augment finite state machine*) algorithm is derived to achieve this goal. AFSM algorithm incorporates the following functionalities:

- to apply the butterworth low pass filter for mitigating the high frequency noise and spikes in raw acceleration magnitudes as to recover the true periodicity of the steps;
- to further remove the erroneous detection by adding two-fold heuristic constrains: (1) for each step, the time duration in respect to the descend and ascend parts of vertical acceleration should be identical; and (2) the maximum time duration of one step is limited.

As the second step, we directly apply the well-known step length model [12, 13] to estimate the step length a as follows,

$$l = a * f + b \qquad (4)$$

where a, b are the parameters need to be estimated, f is the frequency of steps. More specifically, we eliminate the time-consuming calibration efforts with a personalized estimation method. In our experiment, we observe that the nomadic APs with similar variance and average of the vertical acceleration in one step are likely to exhibit similar step length. Relying on this fact, we modify the model for each nomadic AP with minimal efforts required from it. For instance, when a new nomadic AP is tracked for the first step, the model computes the similarly in terms of feature parameters including acceleration variance V, mean M, and frequency f between this new comer and the previous nomadic APs. If it shares the same feature as that of the previous nomadic AP, they presumably share the same a, b. Direction of the nomadic APs' movement is another key factor for acquiring the coordinates. In complex indoor environments, the accuracy of direction determination can be influenced by both ferromagnetic and electrical materials in the vicinity. Fortunately, the gyroscope is decoupled from the geomagnetic sensor, which is insensitive to ambient magnetic fields. Therefore, CNLoc leverages the magnetometer to provide the initial phase as well the gyroscope sensor to obtain the relative angular displacement of the nomadic AP for the purpose of direction determination. This means that CNLoc can detect the orientation of nomadic APs' movement even in the face of the surrounding noises.

5   Performance Evaluation

We evaluate the performance of CNLoc system in this section. We collect CSI measurements from external NICs and sensor readings from smartphones because CSI information is currently unavailable on phones. Each nomadic AP is placed on a wheeled desk and pushed by volunteers to move randomly in the area of interest. To record the ground truth trajectories of each nomadic AP, we record the experiments via video and adopt computer vision based localization scheme to pinpoint the location of each nomadic AP.

5.1 Performance of CSI-based Location Distinction

Next comes to study the performance of location distinction based on CSI in the scenarios Lab and Lobby. In Lab, we first keep the object staying at site L_2 for CSI measurements. Afterwards, the object slightly moves to a close site with around $1m$ distance. By leveraging the CSI-based location distinction feature, we can identify whether the object has changed the location. Figure 2 depicts the results in terms of detection rate (Y-axis) versus false alarm (X-axis). As shown in Fig. 2, the FP rate is negligible which proves the effectiveness of the proposed approach in Sect. 5.1. We further perform the similar measurements at sites L_5 and a position one meter nearby in Lobby. Even in such a considerably large area, the FP rate only increases very slightly. Hence, we show that in practice, the CSI-based location distinction technique makes it effective and reliable enough to imply the mobility status of the object.

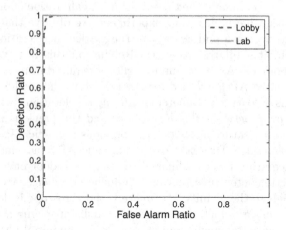

Fig. 2. Location distinction accuracy

5.2 Impact of Nomadic APs' Location Uncertainty

Finally, to provide insights into how the uncertainty of nomadic APs' location influences the overall performance, we show the results in Fig. 3(a) and (b). We can observe in Fig. 3(a) that the sensor information is responsive enough to handle such uncertainty. In general, the smaller coordinate error improves the performance of location estimation in Lab due to the SP-based method barely depends on the AP location which other range-based methods do. We also obtain similar results in Lobby as shown in Fig. 3(b). Thus, it demonstrates the promise of ensuring the overall localization performance by accurately coordinate acquisition with embedded sensors of nomadic APs.

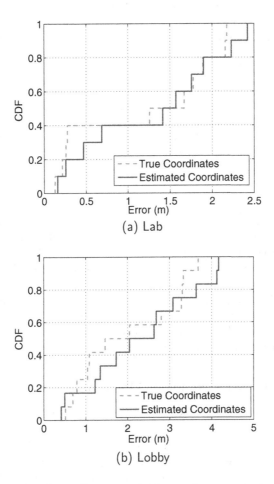

Fig. 3. Sensor-based coordinate acquisition performance in two scenarios

6   Discussion

As an important step forward, CNLoc leaves several open issues and new possibilities for future research. In this section, we briefly comment on the most of important of these here.

6.1   Influence of AP Mobility on CSI Measurement

A possible side-effect of nomadic APs lies in the fact that the dynamic move-ment can give rise to Doppler shift. In particular, nomadic APs move relatively towards or away from an object, resulting in positive or negative Doppler shift as transmission frequency changed. Such Doppler shift may bring in undesirable impact on CSI measurement and degrade the performance of SP-based algo-rithm. We then calculate the Doppler shift frequency Δf as below:

$$\Delta f = \frac{v_{nomAP}}{v_{nomAP} + c} f_0 \tag{5}$$

where c is the speed of light (i.e., 3×10^8 m/sec), v_{nomAP} and f_0 are the speed and frequency of a nomadic AP, respectively. In the typical 2.4 GHz wireless networks, a moving nomadic AP with velocity of v_{nomAP} (i.e., 2 m/sec) results in a maximum Doppler shift of $2\Delta f = 32$ Hz which is very small comparing to the center frequency and can be negligible [11].

6.2   Impact of Diverse APs

Note that CSI is the key to enable proximity determination and location dis-tinction, which is collected at the AP side in our system. All the APs in current prototype are identical. In practice, the WLAN-based localization infrastructure can be consisted of a variety of APs supplied by different manufacturers (e.g., Belkin, D-Link, Linksys). Yet these APs can have diverse antenna gain which is an influential factor for proximity determination. To handle this factor, we suggest that multiple APs mutually measure the transmission power and then proceed to server for calibrating the differences.

6.3   Improvement with Nomadic APs' Moving Pattern

From our evaluation results, CNLoc is capable of improving AP deployment by performing random walk of nomadic APs. Nevertheless, it still leaves upside potential for specifying moving pattern to cover the region of poor localizability. Intuitively, the more the moving traces of nomadic APs approaching an area of dissatisfied localizability, the higher the effectiveness of SP-based scheme. That means optimizing moving pattern can lead to optimum coverage of AP deployment, which ensures to provide users better experience of ILBS at any indoor locations. To this end, we are interested in studying such influence on localization performance resulting from moving pattern of nomadic APs in the future.

7   Conclusion

CSI in WLAN communications provides vast opportunities for indoor localiza-tion. With the help of fine-grained CSI data, the CNLoc framework advocates the use of mobility for addressing the critical SLV problem, and improves the accuracy of the nomadic AP based localization. Our approach is, to the best of our knowledge, the first one to investigate the static AP deployment, and harness the mobility of nomadic APs to adjust the network topology. To be specific, in the mobile environment, CNLoc also shows good performance in monitoring the object's mobility status without calibration efforts. Furthermore, it permits the sensor-based information for resolving the location uncertainty of nomadic APs'. Through extensive experiments, we show the benefits of CNLoc in effectively reducing the SLV and improving the localization accuracy compared to static AP deployment.

In summary, we have taken an important first step towards enabling the mobility of APs for indoor positioning. Our major ongoing work is to arrogate multiple nomadic APs for overall performance enhancement.

Acknowledgment. This work is supported by National Science Foundation of China under Grant No. 61702203, Hubei Provincial Natural Science Foundation General Program No. 2018CFB133.

References

1. Bahl, P., Padmanabhan, V.N.: RADAR: an in-building RF-based user location and tracking system. In: Proceedings of 2000 IEEE Conference on Computer Communications (INFOCOM), vol. 2, pp. 775–784 (2000)
2. Bhartia, A., Chen, Y.C., Rallapalli, S., Qiu, L.: Harnessing frequency diversity in WiFi networks. In: Proceedings of the 17th Annual International Conference on Mobile Computing and Networking (MobiCom), pp. 253–264. ACM, New York (2011)
3. Chen, Y., Francisco, J.A., Trappe, W., Martin, R.P.: A practical approach to landmark deployment for indoor localization. In: Proceedings of the 6th Annual IEEE Communications Society Conference on Sensor, Mesh and Ad Hoc Communications and Networks (SECON), vol. 1, pp. 365–373 (2006)
4. Dulman, S.O., Baggio, A., Havinga, P.J., Langendoen, K.G.: A geometrical perspective on localization. In: Proceedings of the First ACM International Workshop on Mobile Entity Localization and Tracking in GPS-Less Environments (MELT), pp. 85–90. ACM, New York (2008)
5. Gao, X., Wang, J., Chen, W.: Land-mark placement for reliable localization of automatic guided vehicle in warehouse environment. In: Proceedings of 2017 IEEE International Conference on Robotics and Biomimetics (ROBIO), pp. 1900–1905(2015)
6. Gu, Y., Lo, A., Niemegeers, I.: A survey of indoor positioning systems for wireless personal networks. IEEE Commun. Surv. Tutor. (COMST) 11(1), 13–32 (2009)
7. Lin, T.N., Fang, S.H., Tseng, W.H., Lee, C.W., Hsieh, J.W.: A group-discrimination-based access point selection for WLAN fingerprinting localization. IEEE Trans. Veh. Technol. (TVT) 63(8), 3967–3976 (2014)
8. Liu, H., Darabi, H., Banerjee, P., Liu, J.: Survey of wireless indoor positioning techniques and systems. IEEE Trans. Syst., Man, Cybern. (TSMC), Part C (Appl. Rev.) 37(6), 1067–1080 (2007)

9. marketsandmarkets.com: Indoor location market by component (2017). http://www.marketsandmarkets.com/Market-Reports/indoor-positioning-navigation-ipin-market-989.html

10. Meng, W., He, Y., Deng, Z., Li, C.: Optimized access points deployment for WLAN indoor positioning system. In: Proceedings of 2012 IEEE Wireless Communications and Networking Conference (WCNC), pp. 2457–2461 (2012)

11. Pu, Q., Gupta, S., Gollakota, S., Patel, S.: Whole-home gesture recognition using wireless signals. In: Proceedings of the 19th Annual International Conference on Mobile Computing and Networking (MobiCom), pp. 27–38. ACM, New York (2013)

12. Rai, A., Chintalapudi, K.K., Padmanabhan, V.N., Sen, R.: Zee: zero-effort crowd-sourcing for indoor localization. In: Proceedings of the 18th Annual International Conference on Mobile Computing and Networking (MobiCom), pp. 293–304. ACM, New York (2012)

13. Ramirez, L., Dyrks, T., Gerwinski, J., Betz, M., Scholz, M., Wulf, V.: Landmarke: an ad hoc deployable ubicomp infrastructure to support indoor navigation of fire-fighters. Pers. Ubiquitous Comput. (PUC) **16**(8), 1025–1038 (2012)

14. Sen, S., Choudhury, R.R., Nelakuditi, S.: SpinLoc: spin once to know your loca-tion. In: Proceedings of the 13th Workshop on Mobile Computing Systems and Applications (HotMobile), pp. 12:1–12:6. ACM, New York (2012)

15. Sen, S., Lee, J., Kim, K.H., Congdon, P.: Avoiding multipath to revive inbuilding WiFi localization. In: Proceeding of the 11th International Conference on Mobile Systems, Applications, and Services (MobiSys), pp. 249–262. ACM, New York (2013)

16. Sen, S., Radunovic, B., Choudhury, R.R., Minka, T.: You are facing the Mona Lisa: spot localization using PHY layer information. In: Proceedings of the 10th Inter-national Conference on Mobile Systems, Applications, and Services (MobiSys), pp. 183–196. ACM, New York (2012)

17. Wu, C., Yang, Z., Zhou, Z., Qian, K., Liu, Y., Liu, M.: PhaseU: real-time LOS identification with WiFi. In: Proceedings of 2015 IEEE Conference on Computer Communications (INFOCOM), pp. 2038–2046 (2015)

18. Wu, K., Xiao, J., Yi, Y., Gao, M., Ni, L.M.: FILA: fine-grained indoor localization. In: Proceedings of 2012 IEEE Conference on Computer Communications (INFO-COM), pp. 2210–2218 (2012)

19. Xiao, J., Wu, K., Yi, Y., Wang, L., Ni, L.M.: Pilot: passive device-free indoor localization using channel state information. In: Proceedings of 2013 IEEE 33rd International Conference on Distributed Computing Systems (ICDCS), pp. 236–245 (2013)

20. Xiao, J., et al.: NomLoc: calibration-free indoor localization with nomadic access points. In: Proceedings of 2014 IEEE 34th International Conference on Distributed Computing Systems (ICDCS), pp. 587–596 (2014)

21. Xiao, J., Zhou, Z., Yi, Y., Ni, L.M.: A survey on wireless indoor localization from the device perspective. ACM Comput. Surv. (CSUR) **49**(2), 25:1–25:31 (2016)

22. Yang, Z., Wu, C., Zhou, Z., Zhang, X., Wang, X., Liu, Y.: Mobility increases localizability: a survey on wireless indoor localization using inertial sensors. ACM Comput. Surv. (CSUR) **47**(3), 54:1–54:34 (2015)

23. Yang, Z., Zhou, Z., Liu, Y.: From RSSI to CSI: indoor localization via channel response. ACM Comput. Surv. (CSUR) **46**(2), 25:1–25:32 (2013)

24. Youssef, M., Agrawala, A.: The Horus WLAN location determination system. In: Proceedings of the 3rd International Conference on Mobile Systems, Applications and Services (MobiSys), pp. 205–218. ACM, New York (2005)

ALOR: Adaptive Layout Optimization of Raft Groups for Heterogeneous Distributed Key-Value Stores

Yangyang Wang[1,2], Yunpeng Chai[1,2(✉)], and Xin Wang[3]

[1] Key Laboratory of Data Engineering and Knowledge Engineering,
MOE, Beijing, China
ypchai@ruc.edu.cn
[2] School of Information, Renmin University of China, Beijing, China
[3] College of Intelligence and Computing, Tianjin University, Tianjin, China

Abstract. Many distributed key-value storage systems employ the simple and effective Raft protocol to ensure data consistency. They usually assume a homogeneous node hardware configuration for the underlying cluster and thus adopt even data distribution schemes. However, today's distributed systems tend to be heterogeneous in nodes' I/O devices due to the regular worn I/O device replacement and the emergence of expensive new storage media (e.g., non-volatile memory). In this paper, we propose a new data layout scheme called *Adaptive Layout Optimization of Raft groups* (ALOR), considering the hardware heterogeneity of the cluster. ALOR aims to optimize the data layout of Raft groups to achieve a better practical load balance, which leads to higher performance. ALOR consists of two components: *leader migration in Raft groups* and *skewed data layout based on cold data migration*. We conducted experiments on a practical heterogeneous cluster, and the results indicate that, on average, ALOR improves throughput by 36.89%, reduces latency and 99th percentile tail latency by 24.54% and 21.32%, respectively.

1 Introduction

Due to the excellent scalability and efficiency, key-value (KV) stores have been widely adopted by many big data systems (e.g., Cassandra and HBase). Many distributed KV storage systems employ the Raft [1] protocol to ensure data consistency because it is easy to be implemented in practical systems. These distributed KV systems coupled with Raft are usually designed for homogeneous systems. However, today's distributed systems tend to be heterogeneous, especially for nodes' I/O devices. The reason lies in the following two aspects:

- The annual disk replacement rates in large-scale distributed systems are typically 2–4% and can be up to 13% in some systems [2]. The replacement rates of Solid State Drives (SSDs) are usually higher than disks due to the

© IFIP International Federation for Information Processing 2018
Published by Springer Nature Switzerland AG 2018
F. Zhang et al. (Eds.): NPC 2018, LNCS 11276, pp. 13–26, 2018.
https://doi.org/10.1007/978-3-030-05677-3_2

limited write endurance of Flash chips. That is to say, in a large-scale distributed KV system, I/O devices are regularly replaced with new generations of I/O products, and these new products usually have higher performance and cost-efficiency than the old ones.

- The emerging storage devices (e.g., SSDs or non-volatile memory (NVM) [3]) have obvious performance advantages over the traditional ones. However, these new devices are usually much more expensive, so we usually deploy them in only a subset of the clusters for cost efficiency.

In distributed storage systems, the Raft protocol is usually adopted to ensure data consistency by defining the different behaviors of the only leader and the other followers for the same data segment. In consequence, the Raft protocol has the inherent heterogeneous feature, i.e., the leader in a Raft group usually takes more jobs and has greater impact on the performance than the followers do. In a heterogeneous distributed KV storage system based on the Raft protocol, if many leaders locate on slow nodes, the performance of the entire system will be slowed down, because the result is not returned to the client until the corresponding leader completes applying the log into the data set (see Sect. 2.1 for more details). Considering this feature of Raft, the hardware heterogeneity is not necessarily a negative factor. Instead, if we can adapt heterogeneity of Raft to the hardware heterogeneity of distributed KV systems through data layout optimization of Raft groups, the system performance can be improved.

In this paper, we propose a new scheme called *Adaptive Layout Optimization of Raft groups* (ALOR) to match the data layout with the hardware heterogeneity of distributed KV systems for higher performance. ALOR consists of two components: *leader migration in Raft groups* (Sect. 3.1) and *skewed data layout based on cold data migration* (Sect. 3.2). The experiments based on a practical heterogeneous cluster indicate that, on average, ALOR improves throughput by 36.89%, reduces the average latency by 24.54%, and reduces 21.32% tail latency. Furthermore, if we construct hybrid devices with two kinds of different devices (e.g., NVM and SSDs) on each node of the cluster, ALOR can still achieve a 28.57% higher write throughput compared with this homogeneous hybrid device solution coupled with the same hardware resources.

The rest of this paper is organized as follows. Section 2 introduces the background and related work. The detailed design of our proposed ALOR is presented in Sect. 3, followed by the evaluations in Sect. 4. Finally, Sect. 5 concludes this paper with a summary of our contributions.

2 Background and Related Work

2.1 The Raft Protocol

Traditionally, Paxos [4] is a classical protocol to ensure data consistency in distributed systems. However, Paxos was particularly difficult to understand and implement. In this case, the Raft protocol [1], which is readily comprehensible and realized, has been quickly adopted by many practical distributed systems like Etcd [5], TiKV [6], and PolarDB [7] since it was proposed in 2014.

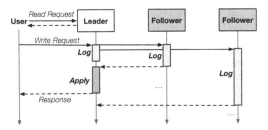

Fig. 1. The main process of serving requests according to Raft.

According to Raft, the main process of serving read and write requests can be found in Fig. 1. We assume a Raft group contains three copies located in three different nodes in the cluster, i.e., one and only one elected leader and two followers.

When a write request arrives at the leader from users, the leader both appends the new contents to the local log and forwards them to the two followers. After more than half of the nodes (i.e., two in this case, including the leader itself) have accomplished the logging action successfully, the leader will proceed to apply the request log, i.e., insert/update the new data into the structured key-value store. Then, the user can get the response of this write request from the leader.

In addition, all read requests are served by the leader alone to ensure the data consistency. In order to ensure linear consistency, Raft will ensure that all the previous logs have been applied before the read request is served.

2.2 Related Work

Raft/Paxos Improvements. In order to reduce the high latency of the Paxos protocol, Wang et al. proposed APUS [15], the first RDMA-based Paxos protocol that aims to be fast and scalable to client connections and hosts. PolarFS [16] implements a parallel Raft to allow parallel submission of logs, breaking Raft's strict limitation that log has to be continuous, with the benefit of increasing concurrency. In order to reduce the latency of distributed systems, Guerraoui et al. proposed Incremental Consistency Guarantees (ICG) [17]. In addition, Alagappan et al. [18] proposed correlated crash vulnerabilities to ensure data security in distributed systems.

Heterogeneous Systems. Zhang et al. developed Mega-KV [19], a high-performance distributed in-memory key-value store system on a heterogeneous CPU-GPU cluster. Dey et al. [20] proposed an approach that gives multi-item transactions across heterogeneous data stores. Strata [21] and OctopusFS [22] designed file systems for heterogeneous storage devices on a single node.

Therefore, few research works consider the heterogeneous I/O performance among nodes in a cluster. This paper will focus on the performance optimization in heterogeneous distributed key-value storage systems.

3   The Design of ALOR

In this section, we will present the detailed design of our proposed *Adaptive Layout Optimization of Raft groups* (ALOR) scheme, which aims to improve the performance of distributed key-value storage systems in case of heterogeneous situations. The two main components of ALOR will be introduced in Sects. 3.1 and 3.2, respectively.

3.1   Leader Migration in Raft Groups

According to the Raft protocol, the performance of service nodes does not affect the leader election. In this case, the leader and the followers in a Raft group are usually randomly and evenly distributed among all the service nodes for the sake of load balance no matter the underlying system is homogeneous or heterogeneous. For example, as Fig. 2 shows, we assume that there are four Raft groups and each group contains three copies of data in a distributed KV storage system with six nodes. According to the original Raft protocol, the data blocks and the leaders are evenly distributed.

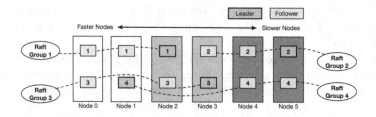

Fig. 2. Raft groups are usually evenly distributed among nodes for load balance.

However, the leader in a Raft group plays the most important role in affecting the performance (e.g., users always read data from leaders and write requests are not confirmed until the leader applies the log). If the leader is placed on a slow node, the performance of accessing this Raft group will be slowed down. Therefore, ALOR gradually migrates leaders to the node with the best performance in Raft groups. The larger the performance gap among the nodes in a Raft group is, the higher priority of migration the corresponding leader will be given in ALOR, as illustrated in Fig. 3. Furthermore, as long as a follower catches up the same status of logging and applying data as the leader, it can be easily set as the new leader with negligible overhead.

For write operations, the leaders and the followers perform the same work (i.e., writing the log first and then applying it). In this case, although the nodes with higher performance undertake more leaders, their average loads are the same as each other. In fact, ALOR just fully utilizes the fast processing of high-performance nodes in a heterogeneous system to reduce the process time of users' write requests.

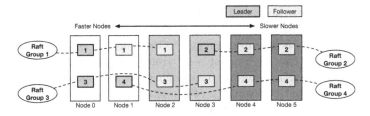

Fig. 3. ALOR migrates the leaders in Raft groups to the faster node as far as possible for higher performance.

For read operations, according to ALOR, the nodes with high performance usually store more leaders than the nodes with low performance. Because users always read data from leaders for strong consistency, the high-performance nodes serving most read requests can reduce the response time of read request processing in most cases. Although the high-performance nodes will undertake more read requests, the read request processing is much more lightweight than the write requests in a key-value storage system due to the significant write amplification of the KV indexes (e.g., B-tree, LSM-tree, etc.).

For a read-write mixed workload, write operations will slow down read operations, because Raft ensures linear consistency, i.e., read operations must be performed after all the previous write operations have been completed. So speeding up the write operations is critical for improving system performance.

3.2   Skewed Data Layout Based on Cold Data Migration

Skewed Data Layout. The idea of promoting system performance in a heterogeneous distributed store is to put appropriate load on nodes according to their ability. Although the aforementioned leader migration mechanism in ALOR puts more leaders on the strong nodes, this is not enough. We should further optimize the data amount distribution during the disk-filling process, i.e., putting more data on the high-performance nodes. The skewed data layout in ALOR can fully utilize the fast processing speed of the high-performance nodes for higher system performance.

However, it also causes two issues: (1) How to set an appropriate data-filling speeds according to the performance of a node? (2) Assuming all nodes have the same storage capacity, some high-performance nodes will be full ahead of others due to the different data-filling speed setting. Thus how to process the new arrival data after some nodes are full is a problem. The solutions to these two problems in ALOR will be presented in the following parts.

Disk-Filling Speed Setting. In ALOR, the disk-filling speed of nodes is set to be proportional to the average performance of writing key-value pairs into the KV store in the node. For example, shown as Fig. 4, assuming there are six nodes and their KV accessing performance is 3:3:2:2:1:1, the proportion of data that they get is similar to this ratio. In this case, the load on a node matches its key-value pairs processing ability.

The next problem is how to estimate the key-value accessing performance of the nodes. The difficulty lies in that a distributed key-value store usually does not supply a KV accessing interface on a single node. Our solution is to automatically measure the I/O performance of a node during its initialization process by calling tools like *fio* [23]. However, the I/O performance is not linear with the node's KV accessing performance. Thus we measured both the I/O and the KV performance of several representative nodes and construct their relationship beforehand. Then we can fit the KV performance of the nodes through their measured I/O performance (See Fig. 10 in the experimental part for reference).

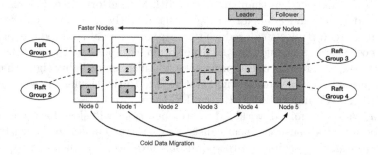

Fig. 4. The distribution of Raft groups in ALOR.

Cold Data Migration. In ALOR, the skewed data layout is achieved through the specially designed data migration mechanism. An important weight, i.e., *Data Weight*, is employed to control the data migration among nodes. The condition of migrating some data in node A to node B can be expressed as Eq. 1, where S_A and S_B are the data volume of node A and B respectively, and S_M is the size of the to-be-migrated data.

$$\frac{S_A - S_M}{DataWeight_A} > \frac{S_B + S_M}{DataWeight_B} \tag{1}$$

If the nodes A and B have the same data weights, Eq. 1 aims to balance the stored data amount between them through data migration. In a heterogeneous system, the strong nodes should have larger data weight values to undertake more data and more requests than weak nodes. In order to reach the above disk-filling speed setting, the data weight values of nodes can be set according to their key-value accessing performance.

When the data volume of a node reaches a specified threshold (e.g., 95% of its capacity), we need to migrate some cold data in this node to others, thus making room for the new arrivals. Then the node's data weight will be set to a very small value (e.g., 10^{-6}), some of its cold data will be migrated to other nodes. When its data volume is lower than the threshold again, the data migration of this node is stopped, avoiding introducing too much overhead.

The advantage of the cold data migration mechanism in ALOR is to promote the hotness of the stored data in high-performance nodes (e.g., Node 0 in Fig. 4), whose side-effect lies in the additional overhead of data migration among nodes. However, the overhead of migrating data is small, because sequential read and write operations of key-value pairs are performed during the data migration process, which are much faster than random GET/PUT operations from users.

4 Implementation and Evaluation

We implemented ALOR based on TiDB [8], one of the most widely used open source NewSQL databases similar to Google Spanner [9]. TiDB is mainly composed of three projects: TiDB (i.e., the SQL Layer), TiKV (i.e., a distributed key-value storage system based on Raft), and the Placement Driver (PD), which is the managing component of the cluster. PD consists of 480K LOC of *Go* and TiKV consists of more than 84K LOC of *Rust*. TiKV has become one of the largest open source projects in the *Rust* community. To implement ALOR, we have added 200+ LOC of *Rust* in TiKV and 400+ LOC of *Go* in PD. The source codes of our implementation of ALOR are on Github now (https://github.com/vliulan/ALOR).

4.1 Experimental Setup

We will compare our proposed ALOR scheme with the widely used scheme which evenly distributing (ED) all the data and leaders of Raft groups in distributed systems. The experiments were performed in a cluster of eight physical nodes; each of them is coupled with Linux Centos 7 3.10.0, 16 GB DRAM and a 16-GB non-volatile memory (NVM) block device, where NVM is emulated by DRAM. Nodes can be equipped with two kinds of Solid State Drives (SSDs), i.e., a 280 GB version of Intel Optane 900p PCIe SSD (a.k.a, high-end SSD) or a 256 GB Intel SATA SSD (a.k.a, plain SSD). Six of the nodes serve as TiKV node, one node as PD, and one node runs the benchmark tool, i.e., go-YCSB [10].

Go-YCSB is a *Go* language version of the widely used YCSB benchmark [11]. In the experiments, the workloads we selected include *Load* (insert-only), *Workload A* (50:50 read/update), *Workload B* (95:5 read/update), and *Workload C* (read-only) of YCSB. Other configurations of the workloads can be found in the specification [12]. Each key-value pair contains a 16-B key and a 1-KB value, and each data block has three copies in TiKV. Although the performance of the storage devices is heterogeneous, the data capacities of all the TiKV nodes are set to be the same (5 GB by default).

In the following experiments, we adopt the system throughput (operations per second, i.e., ops/sec), the average latency, and the 99th percentile latency to evaluate the system performance.

4.2   Overall Results

In the overall experiments, among the six TiKV nodes in the cluster, one node equips the fastest NVM block device, two node equip the high-end SSDs, and the slowest plain SSDs are deployed in the other three nodes. We first load 10 GB of data to fill the cluster (i.e., 30 GB data considering the replicas), and then perform workloads A, B, and C, respectively, accessing 10 GB of data each.

As Fig. 5 plots, ALOR achieves higher throughput than ED in most cases, i.e., 72.6% higher in *Load*, 61.5% higher in *Workload A*, and 13.7% higher in *Workload B*. On average, ALOR promotes the throughput by 36.89%. Compared with the traditional even distribution (ED) solution, which is appropriate in homogeneous distributed systems, ALOR puts properly more data and more leaders on the fast nodes according to nodes' heterogeneous ability. In fact, the practical load balance of a heterogeneous system is improved coupled with ALOR, leading to a higher throughput.

For read operations, ALOR concentrates more leaders, which serve all the read requests, on fast nodes. The benefit is to boost the processing of read requests; the disadvantage lies in that when the load of fast nodes is too high, some requests have to wait a moment. So in the read-only *Workload C*, the throughput of ALOR is a bit lower than, but very close to ED.

For write operations, ALOR certainly boosts the request processing. The reason lies in two aspects: (1) Since a leader has to log and apply the written data before replying the user, the faster nodes can boost these actions of leaders. (2) More than half nodes have to log the written data before replying the user, and more data segments (leader or follower) in a Raft group have the possibility to locate on faster nodes because of the skewed data layout in ALOR.

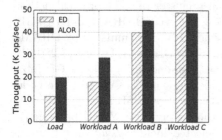
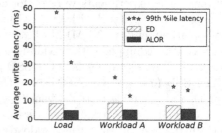

Fig. 5. Overall throughput results.   **Fig. 6.** Overall write latency results.

Figures 6 and 7 exhibit the results of the average latency and the 99th percentile latency. One average, ALOR reduces the latency by 24.54% compared with ED. The average read latency improvement of ALOR in *Workload C* is slightly larger than ED, but those of ALOR *Workload A* and *Workload B* are smaller than ED, because reducing the write processing time leads to less waiting time of read operations in read-write mixed workloads. For both read and write operations, ALOR reduces the tail latency, i.e., 21.32% on average compared with ED.

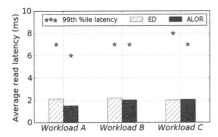
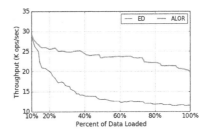
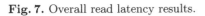

Fig. 7. Overall read latency results.

Fig. 8. Throughput during the data loading process.

Figures 8 and 9 plot the changes of throughput and latency during the data loading process. In the very beginning, three copies of data are written into the three fast nodes first for both ALOR and ED, so the performance of the front ALOR and ED is almost the same. Then, the performance of ALOR and ED both decreased due to the filled cache, but ED dropped more. The overall performance of ALOR is much higher than ED during the whole data loading process in all the aspects of throughput, average latency, and tail latency.

4.3   KV Performance Estimation

Recall Sect. 3.2 that we estimate key-value accessing performance according to I/O performance. The KV engine used by TiKV is RocksDB [13], a famous open source KV engine based on LSM tree developed by Facebook. The granularity of RocksDB writing is megabytes (e.g., 8 MB). Therefore, we first utilize *fio* to measure the I/O performance of randomly writing 8-MB blocks.

We selected three typical devices: NVM block device (emulated by DRAM), high-end SSD, and plain SSD in the measurements, and performed multiple single-point I/O performance tests based on *fio* and KV performance tests based on go-YCSB and RocksDB on the single node. Then we can build the estimated relationship between the two factors through polynomial function fitting.

The measured I/O and KV performance results and the curve of the fitted function are shown in Fig. 10. Taking the red box in the figure as an example, if the disk performance measured by fio is 2 GB/s, we can estimate the nodes' KV performance as 22 MB/s.

4.4   Impacts of Different Heterogeneous Configurations

In this part, we will evaluate ALOR under different heterogeneous configurations, including two high-end SSDs and four plain SSDs (i.e., 2H4P), one NVM block device, two high-end SSDs and three plain SSDs (i.e., 1N2H3P), two NVM block devices, two high-end SSDs and two plain SSDs (i.e., 2N2H2P), and three NVM block devices, two high-end SSDs and one plain SSD (i.e., 3N2H1P). For

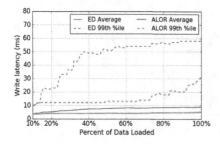

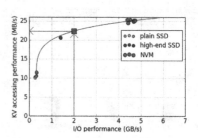

Fig. 9. Latency during the data loading process.

Fig. 10. Relationship between I/O and KV performance.

different settings, we all loaded 10GB data into the cluster to measure the system throughput, latency, and tail latency of ALOR and ED, as shown in Figs. 11 and 12, respectively.

The performance of ALOR is improved compared with ED, but the 2N2H2P and 3N2H1P configurations' enhancements are not as much as the other two. The reason lies in that the heterogeneous situations in the 2N2H2P and 3N2H1P configurations are not as significant as the other two ones.

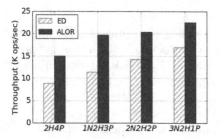

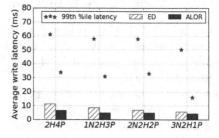

Fig. 11. Throughput under different heterogeneous configurations.

Fig. 12. Latency under different heterogeneous configurations.

4.5   Impacts of System Scale

In order to evaluate the scalability of ALOR, we performed experiments on clusters with different counts of TiKV nodes (i.e., 4, 5, or 6 TiKV nodes). The configuration of the 4 TiKV nodes is one high-end SSD and three plain SSDs, that of the 5 TiKV nodes is one NVM block device, one high-end SSD, and three plain SSDs, and the configuration of the 6 TiKV nodes is one NVM block device, two high-end SSDs, and three plain SSDs.

For the 6 TiKV nodes, we wrote 10 GB data into the cluster; proportionally, we wrote 8.33 GB data into the 5 TiKV nodes, and 6.67 GB data into the 4 TiKV nodes. The throughput and latency results of ALOR and ED are shown in Figs. 13 and 14, respectively. As the cluster's node count increases, the performance of ALOR and ED both increase. ALOR exhibits stable performance advantage compared with ED under various system scales.

4.6 Analysis of ALOR Components

Recall Sect. 3 that ALOR has two components, i.e., the leader migration and the skewed data layout based on cold data migration. In this part, we will evaluate how much the two components of ALOR contribute on the performance improvement. Therefore, we constructed a special version of ALOR with only the leader migration module, i.e., Leader Migration Only (LMO). The comparison among ED, LMO, and ALOR can show us the performance contributions of ALOR's two components.

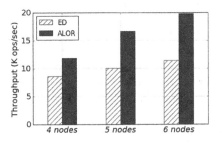

Fig. 13. Throughput under different system scales.

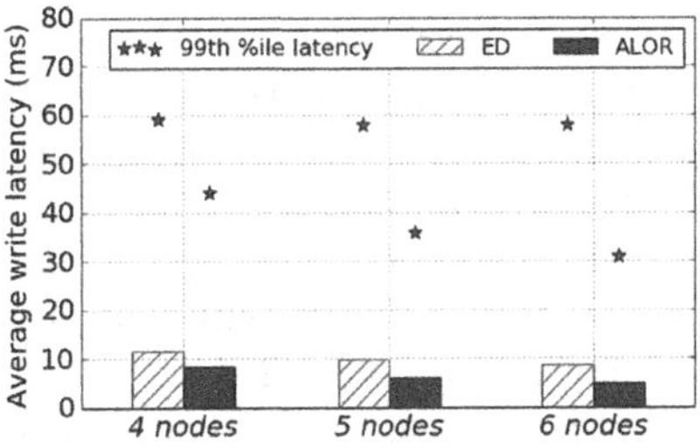

Fig. 14. Latency under different system scales.

As Figs. 15 and 16 plot, we first load (insert-only) 10 GB data to fill the cluster, and then perform *Workload C* (read-only) by reading 10 GB data. The experimental results show that the load performance of LMO is 22.85% higher than ED and ALOR is 40.53% higher than LMO. That means within the 72.64% throughput improvement of ALOR compared with ED, the leader migration module contributes about 31.45% of it, while the skewed data layout contributes

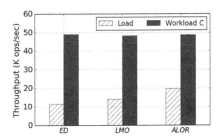

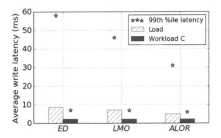

Fig. 15. Throughput comparison among ED, LMO, and ALOR.

Fig. 16. Latency comparison among ED, LMO, and ALOR.

about 68.55%. The average latency and the tail latency of writing are both improved by ALOR's two modules.

The read throughput and average latency of ED, LMO and ALOR are very close to each other, indicating the two modules of ALOR both do not affect the read performance much.

4.7   ALOR vs. Homogeneous Hybrid Device Solution

When both fast storage devices and slow devices are deployed in a distributed system, an alternative solution is to distribute the fast devices evenly among all the nodes and to construct hybrid devices, in which a fast device acts as the cache of a slow device. In this case, although different devices are in the system, the resources and configurations on each node are homogeneous. We use Flashcache [14] to combine NVM block devices and plain SSDs into hybrid devices on each node. The homogeneous hybrid device solution consumes exactly the same resources as ALOR.

In this part, the experiments were performed on 4 TiKV nodes. Both ED and ALOR are deployed in a cluster with one NVM device and three plain SSDs, each of which can hold up to 5 GB data. For the Flashcache solution, it requires four plain SSDs and 4 NVM devices. In order to guarantee the fairness, each plain SSD for Flashcache can only store 3.75 GB data (i.e., 3*5 GB/4), and each NVM device can hold 1.25 GB data (i.e., 5 GB/4).

We first loaded 5GB data into the cluster (i.e., 15GB including replicas), and then performed *Workload C* to read 5GB data. The experimental results are shown in Figs. 17 and 18. Although the Flashcache solution achieves higher write performance compared with ED due to better utilization of fast devices, the write throughput of ALOR is 28.57% higher than Flashcache. This indicates that ALOR coupled with heterogeneous node performance configuration is more appropriate for Raft than the homogeneous hybrid device solution.

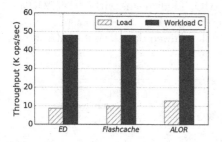
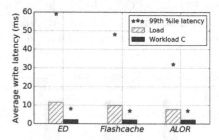

Fig. 17. Throughput comparison among ED, Flashcache, and ALOR.

Fig. 18. Latency comparison among ED, Flashcache, and ALOR.

5 Conclusion

In this section, we conclude this paper with a summary of our contributions:

(1) We found and verified that by matching the inherent heterogeneity of Raft groups and the hardware heterogeneity of distributed key-value stores, the system performance could be promoted.
(2) We proposed a new optimized data layout scheme called ALOR, which achieves an appropriate layout of data and Raft leaders in a heterogeneous distributed key-value storage system through *the leader migration* and *the skewed data layout mechanisms.*
(3) The experiments based on a practical heterogeneous cluster indicate that ALOR can promote the write throughput by up to 72.6% than the even data distribution solution, while achieving similar read performance.

Acknowledgement. This work is supported by the National Key Research and Development Program of China (No. 2018YFB1004401), National Natural Science Foundation of China (No. 61732014, 61472427, and 61572353), Beijing Natural Science Foundation (No. 4172031), the National Science Foundation of Tianjin (17JCYBJC15400), the Fundamental Research Funds for the Central Universities and the Research Funds of Renmin University of China (No. 16XNLQ02), and open research program of State Key Laboratory of Computer Architecture, Institute of Computing Technology, Chinese Academy of Science (No. CARCH201702).

References

1. Ongaro, D., Ousterhout, J.: In search of an understandable consensus algorithm. In: USENIX Annul Technical Conference (2013)
2. Schroeder, B., Gibson, G.A.: Disk failures in the real world: what does an MTTF of 1, 000, 000 hours mean to you? FAST **7**(1), 1–16 (2007)
3. Wikipedia: Non-volatile memory (2018). https://en.wikipedia.org/wiki/Non-volatile_memory
4. Lamport, L.: Paxos made simple. ACM SIGACT News (Distrib. Comput. Column) **32**(4), 18–25 (2001)
5. CoreOS: ETCD Documentation (2018). http://etcd.readthedocs.io/en/latest
6. PingCAP: TiKV (2018). https://github.com/pingcap/tikv
7. Alibaba Cloud: PolarDB. https://www.alibabacloud.com/campaign/polardb-discount-icde-2018?spm=a2c5t.10695662.1996646101.searchclickresult.53f66bd8ztuvrS
8. TiDB PingCAP: TiDB (2018). https://github.com/pingcap/tidb
9. Corbett, J.C., Dean, J., et al.: Spanner: Google's globally-distributed database. ACM Trans. Comput. Syst. **31**(3), 8 (2012)
10. PingCAP: go-ycsb (2018). https://github.com/pingcap/go-ycsb
11. Cooper, B.F., Silberstein, A., Tam, E., Ramakrishnan, R., Sears, R.: Benchmarking cloud serving systems with YCSB. In: ACM Symposium on Cloud Computing, pp. 143–154 (2010)
12. PingCAP: Workloads (2018). https://github.com/pingcap/go-ycsb/tree/master/workloads
13. Facebook: RocksDB (2018). http://rocksdb.org/

14. Facebook: Flashcache (2018). https://wiki.archlinux.org/index.php/Flashcache
15. Wang, C., Jiang, J., Chen, X., Yi, N., Cui, H.: APUS: fast and scalable Paxos on RDMA. In: Proceedings of SoCC 2017, Santa Clara, CA, USA, 24–27 September 2017, 14 p
16. https://www.alibabacloud.com/blog/deep-dive-on-alibaba-clouds-next-generation -database_578138
17. Guerraoui, R., Pavlovic, M., Seredinschi, D.A.: Incremental consistency guarantees for replicated objects. In: The Proceedings of the 12th USENIX Symposium on Operating Systems Design and Implementation (OSDI 2016)
18. Alagappan, R., Ganesan, A., Patel, Y., Pillai, T.S., Arpaci-Dusseau, A.C., Arpaci-Dusseau, R.H.: Correlated crash vulnerabilities. In: The Proceedings of the 12th USENIX Symposium on Operating Systems Design and Implementation (OSDI 2016)
19. Zhang, K., et al.: A distributed in-memory key-value store system on heterogeneous CPU-GPU cluster. The VLDB J. **26**, 729–750 (2017)
20. Dey, A., Fekete, A., Röhm, U.: Scalable transactions across heterogeneous NoSQL key-value data stores. In: The 39th International Conference on Very Large Data Bases (2013)
21. Kwon, Y., Fingler, H., Hunt, T., Peter, S., Witchel, E., Anderson, T.: Strata: a cross media file system. In: ACM Symposium on Operating Systems Principles (2017)
22. Kakoulli, E., Herodotou, H.: OctopusFS: a distributed file system with tiered storage management. In: ACM Conference on Management of Data (2017)
23. Axboe, J.: Flexible I/O Tester. https://github.com/axboe/fio

STrieGD: A Sampling Trie Indexed Compression Algorithm for Large-Scale Gene Data

Yanzhen Gao[1,2]([⊠]), Xiaozhen Bao[1,2], Jing Xing[1], Zheng Wei[1], Jie Ma[1], and Peiheng Zhang[1]

[1] Institute of Computing Technology, Beijing, China
gaoyanzhen@ncic.ac.cn
[2] University of Chinese Academy of Sciences, Beijing, China
http://www.ict.ac.cn/

Abstract. The development of next-generation sequencing (NGS) technology presents a considerable challenge for data storage. To address this challenge, a number of compression algorithms have been developed. However, currently used algorithms fail to simultaneously achieve high compression ratio as well as high compression speed. We propose an algorithm STrieGD that is based on a trie index structure for improving the compression speed of FASTQ files. To reduce the size of the trie index structure, our approach adopts a sampling strategy followed by a filtering step using quality scores. Our experiment shows that the compression ratio of our algorithm increased by approx. 50% over GZip, while being nearly equal to that of DSRC. Importantly, the compression speed of the STrieGD is 3 to 6 times faster than GZip and about 55% faster than DSRC. Moreover, with the increase of compressors, the compression ratio remains stable and the compression speed is nearly linear scalable.

Keywords: Sampling trie · FASTQ file · Data compression

1 Introduction

Analysis of large DNA sequencing datasets is extensively applied to a wide range of research areas, including genetic engineering, medical diagnosis, and forensic biology [1]. Importantly, with the development of next-generation sequencing (NGS) technology, the cost of DNA sequencing has decreased considerably. DNA sequencing data has grown rapidly and had gotten to the petabyte scale until 2017 [2], presenting a considerable challenge for data storage, content access and transfer [3]. Compressing DNA data is an effective way to solve these problems.

In addition, DNA data generated by mainstream high-throughput sequencing platforms, including the SOLiD sequencer independently developed by Illumina GA and ABI [4], are generally stored in the FASTQ format [5]. Therefore, compression of FASTQ is important for computational biology. FASTQ files consist

F. Zhang et al. (Eds.): NPC 2018, LNCS 11276, pp. 27–38, 2018.
https://doi.org/10.1007/978-3-030-05677-3_3

of records, each record has four lines as shown in Fig. 1: title line, genomic sequence, "+" and quality scores. Genomic sequence is the nucleotide sequence obtained by sequencing, containing only five different kinds of characters. The character which is not identified as A, C, G and T, is expressed as the "N". The quality score is the probability of the character being incorrectly identified, which means that the length of Quality scores is the same as that of the genomic sequence. In addition, the length of the title line is shorter than that of the genomic sequence. Therefore, the genomic sequence occupies one-third or more of the entire file, which means that compressing genomic sequence is important for the FASTQ file.

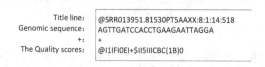

Title line: @SRR013951.81530PT5AAXX:8:1:14:518
Genomic sequence: AGTTGATCCACCTGAAGAATTAGGA
+:   +
The Quality scores: @I1IFIOEI+$II5IIICBC(1B)0

Fig. 1. Format of the FASTQ file

Based on the FASTQ file described above, one can draw a conclusion that compressing four parts of FASTQ data can naturally be processed (almost) independently. Great efforts have been put towards improving compression of gene data with FASTQ format. However, currently used algorithms fail to simultaneously achieve a high compression ratio as well as high compression speed. General compression algorithms do not consider the feature of the FASTQ file, causing a low compression ratio. However, special compression algorithms add judging operations to achieve a high compression ratio, causing a low compression speed. Here, we propose an algorithm STrieGD that is based on trie index structure for improving the compression speed. To reduce the size of the trie index structure, our approach adopts a sampling strategy followed by a filtering step using quality scores, simultaneously aiming at high compression ratio and high compression speed.

The following sections: Sect. 2 describes the related works in compression algorithms. Section 3 describes our algorithms. Section 4 describes the details about the implementation of the distributed compression system. Section 5 presents the evaluation we conducted in the distributed compression system. The last chapter summarizes the paper.

2   Related Research

Genomic sequence occupies one-third or more of FASTQ file. It is redundancy, which dues to the simple structure, great depth of sequencing and large similarity between the same species [6]. How to take full advantage of the peculiar redundancy of genomic sequence is the key to improve compression ratio and compression speed. In recent years, scholars had done in-depth research on the characteristics of genes data and proposed various compression algorithms for the FASTQ file.

G-SQZ algorithm [7] constructs the unit <bases, Quality scores> and adopts the Huffman algorithm to compress. G-SQZ is too simple. The compression ratio and speed are only slightly better than GZip.

The DSRC algorithm [8] moves the character "N" to the quality stream and uses the LZ algorithm [9] to compress the remainder. For the quality scores, the DSRC algorithm records the place of "#" that means the character "N" appears in the genomic sequence and uses RLE algorithm to compress the characters that are repeated with a continuously high rate. However, it achieves a high compression ratio but low compression speed.

KungFQ [10] stores a single bit flag and up to three base calls or a run length for repetitions longer than four bases. The bit flag is necessary to discriminate between these two cases. The quality scores are directly compressed with RLE [11]. This method achieves a high compression ratio, but low compression speed. Moreover, KungFQ wastes space on encoding "N".

LFQC algorithm [2] splits the sequences into non-overlapping $l - mers$ with an empirically decided $l - value$ and counts the frequency of distinct quality scores in each $l - mer$. Assume that the quality score q_i has a frequency of f_i in $l - mer$. LFQC picks the quality score q_i with the largest frequency f_i in $L_j \forall_j$. L_j goes to the q_j^{th} bucket. $l - mers$ where none of the symbols showed a majority of occurrences go to a special bucket called generic bucket B_G. The file is also compressed using Huffman Encoding. The encoding method of genomic sequence is similar to that of the quality score. LFQC is able to achieve a high compression ratio. However, the process of separating buckets slows down the overall compression speed.

Using GZip as a benchmark (compression ratio and compression speed are all set to 1), the compression ratio and compression speed of various compression algorithms are shown in Fig. 2. We found that the compression speed is inversely proportional to compression ratio, which means that to further improve the compression ratio requires more CPU time and memory space. Therefore, it is important to maintain a balance between compression ratio and compression speed in the compressing process.

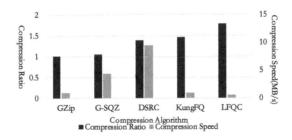

Fig. 2. Comparison of FASTQ file compression algorithms

3   A Trie Index Structure Based Compression Algorithm

Fragments of genomic sequence are highly repeatable in a FASTQ file. How to fully replace repeatable fragments is the key to improve the effect of compression. The most ideal method is to store the repeatable fragment only once. Therefore, we need an index structure to index the repeatable fragments. The index structure is better to support to quickly query and insert data. However, all of the existing algorithms adopted hash table to index data, which needs to traverse all strings before searching. Therefore, to improve the compression speed, we adopt a trie structure to index strings.

3.1   Trie Index Structure

Trie is a tree structure, which only saves the same prefix once. The first step of compressing involves searching a fixed-length sub-string in the trie index structure. If the same fragment is found, the position and length of the matching fragment are recorded. Otherwise, the sub-string will be added into the trie index structure. Query and insert contribute most of the overhead among all the operations. Although the time complexity of the hash table and trie both are O(n), only a trie is able to avoid the collision and support partial matching, thus reducing unnecessary string comparing.

Trie index structure is able to achieve partial matching, which is different from the hash table. If we search string "TCCTA" in the trie shown in Fig. 3, we will obtain the best matching sub-string with the length of four. This matching process reduces the unnecessary character comparison by trie index structure. If we search string "TTACG" in the same trie shown in Fig. 3, we will fail to match the best sub-string on the third character "A" of the string. It is not necessary to match the other characters, which is helpful to query efficiently.

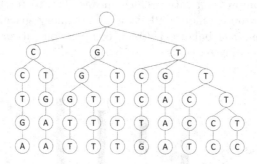

Fig. 3. Trie constructed by the string "GGGTTTTCCTGAAA" with the sub-string's length 5.

Trie is a typical space-time trade-off data structure, which means trie have to consume more memory to achieve efficient query. As the scale of data grows, if the hardware cannot provide enough memory, a query will be less efficient as data will exchange frequently between memory and disk. If the trie index structure only occupies limited memory, the subsequent string will not be added to the index structure, thus decreasing the successful matching rate. In order to reduce excessive memory occupied by the trie, we propose two optimization strategies.

3.2   Optimization of Trie Tree

In order to describe the characteristics of the genomic sequence, we propose two concepts: String coverage calculated by formulas (1), SubString coverage calculated by formulas (2), shown in Fig. 4. As the length of the string grows, the SubString coverage drops from 50% to 27% and the String coverage increases to 82%, indicating that the repeated substring is relatively concentrated.

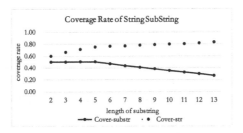

Fig. 4. String coverage and substring coverage.

M_{length} indicates the number of substring types whose length is $length$, N_{M_i} indicates the number of substrings M_i, $Sum\,(M_{length})$ indicates the number of substrings that are generated in length, $Cover_{str}$ indicates the coverage of the string and $Cover_{SubStr}$ indicates the coverage of the substring.

$$Cover_{SubStr} = \frac{\sum_{i=1}^{M_{length}} a}{M_{length}}, N_{M_i} > \frac{sum(M_{length})}{M_{length}} \tag{1}$$

$$Cover_{Str} = \frac{\sum_{i=1}^{M_{length}} N_{M_i}}{sum(M_{length})}, N_{M_i} > \frac{sum(M_{length})}{M_{length}} \tag{2}$$

Therefore, it is not necessary to store all the strings to obtain a higher compression ratio in the trie. However, how to choose the right string to save and how many strings to save are problems.

Sampling. Sampling is mainly used to reduce the scale of referenced objects to a certain size that is covered by the processing system. We still take the string in Fig. 3 as an example. Several strings are inserted into the trie structure when the sampling rate is 1/3. Figure 5(a) shows substrings and Fig. 5(b) shows the trie. The occupied space greatly reduces. However, the sampling rate has a great influence on matching. If the sampling rate is too high, the problem of excessive memory space will still exist. If the sampling rate is too low, the matching will often fail, causing the compression ratio to decrease. Therefore, when we select the sampling rate, we need to consider occupied memory space and the compression ratio.

The trie is a perfect structure for a partial matching. For the Trie structure in Fig. 5, we obtain the best matching sub-string with the length of 4 to compress the string of "TCCTA". This matching reduces unnecessary character comparisons as much as possible and achieves efficiently query.

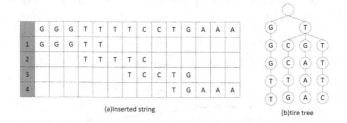

(a)Inserted string   (b)tire tree

Fig. 5. String coverage and substring coverage.

However, not all substrings are inserted into the trie structure, causing a problem in the matching process. For the string "GTTTT", the matching length is one (matching to the insert string one) and the matching length is too short. If we ignore the first character "G" and starts to match from the second character "T", we will obtain a matching length of four (matching to the insert string 2). In the actual process, the normal matching will be done first. If the substring is not completely matched, the first character will be ignored. Then compare the two ways and select a longer matching length. This process is called "lazy match".

Filtering by Quality Scores. The quality score is the probability of the base being incorrectly identified. It is known that if a sequence's quality score is too low, it indicates that the accuracy of the sequence obtained by sequencing is low, meaning that the sequence is next to impossible to be matched in the future. Therefore, the quality score is used to decide whether the string deserves to be inserted into the trie index structure. Strings with low quality score will be filtered out, which ensures high speed.

4 Implementation of Distributed Compression System

4.1 Compression of Quality Portion and Identification Portion

Each identification field of the record is highly similar. Therefore, we divide the identification field into four fields according to the feature of each field.

1. The data remains unchanged in different record. (Field 1)
2. Integer values vary monotonically over consecutive records. (Field 2)
3. Integer values vary in a certain range. (Field 3)
4. The data does not belong to any of the above-mentioned types. (Field 4)

StrieGD stores Field 1 only once and uses RLE algorithm to encode Field 2. In addition, StrieGD stores Field2 with a minimum of bits and stores Field 4 without compressing.

4.2 Compression of Quality Portion

Since the quality scores range from 33 to 126, it is possible to restore the character of "N" according to its Quality scores during the decompression process. Therefore, we add the score 128 representing "N" of sequence portion to the quality scores, achieving to delete the character of"N" from sequence portion. Although the length of the quality scores is equal to that of the sequence portion, quality scores contain much more variety of characters than sequence portion, causing that to improve the compression performance of the quality score is more difficult. Therefore, we did not take much effort to improve the compression performance of the quality score. Our STrieGD adopts the RLE algorithm to encode characters with high repeatable and Huffman algorithm to encode others. STrieGD stores a single bit flag to discriminate between these two cases.

4.3 Implementation of Distributed Compression System

It is impractical to support compressing a large volume of DNA files for a single server. To compress large-scale genetic data, we designed and implemented a distributed compression system, Dic-DNA. Dic-DNA includes client, server and compressor shown in Fig. 6.

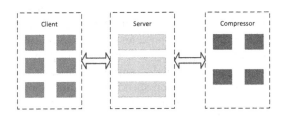

Fig. 6. String coverage and substring coverage.

In the distributed system, the client asks to write (compress), read (decompress), search, and delete genomic sequence. In addition, the client will send the genomic sequence to the server if the server allows the client to write.

The server plays a bridge role, connecting the client and the Compressor and maintains a request queue to receive requests. The server extracts the request from the queue and selects the appropriate processing according to the type of request. In addition, requests of compression and decompression are forwarded to the compressed node. The server maintains a file-block map that stores file-block mapping information, including block offsets, target compression nodes and other useful information. The server make it possible to compress and decompress the same file in different clients.

The compressor compresses and decompresses the files. Each compressor employs individual block-location to map information, thus the distributed system is more scalable.

5   Evaluation

The distributed system includes eight clients, four servers and eight compressors. Each node runs on 64-bit CentOS 6.3 operating system with 16-core 2.00 GHz Intel(R) Xeon(R) CPU and memory 16 G. The test data is from the NCBI, ENA and other sites. The size of files ranges from 3 GB to 15 GB and the length of each sequence is between 45 and 120.

5.1   Performance of Compressing Single FASTQ File

In order to verify whether our optimization strategy is effective, we evaluated the compression speed and compression ratio in different sampling rates and different thresholds of quality scores.

Firstly, Fig. 7 shows compression speed and compression ratio at different sampling rates. The compression ratio is the highest when the sampling rate is 1. However, the compression speed is very slow, only 1 MB/s or so, due to that the size of the trie structure is quite large. With the decrease of the sampling rate, the compression ratio gradually decreases but without great fluctuation, because the repeated fragments are relatively concentrated. In addition, with the decrease of the sampling rate, the compression speed increases. When the sampling rate is 1/8, the compression speed reaches the maximum value. As the sampling rate further decreases, both the compression speed and the compression ratio begin to decrease quickly. The lower sampling rate, the more sub-string adopts Huffman encoding, affecting the compression speed and compression ratio. Therefore, the data shows that our sampling strategy considerably improves the compression speed and simultaneously obtain a high compression ratio.

Secondly, we evaluated compression speed and compression ratio at different threshold values shown in Fig. 8. Only the sequence, whose the average value of quality scores reaches the threshold, was inserted into the Trie. With the increase of the threshold, the compression speed increases, because a number of strings with the lower quality score than the threshold are filtered out. When the threshold value is 62, the compression speed reaches the maximum. As the threshold further increase, less and less strings are inserted into the trie structure, causing that many strings are encoded with Huffman and compression speed and compression ratio decrease. Therefore, the data shows that our filter strategy considerably improves the compression speed and simultaneously obtain a high compression ratio.

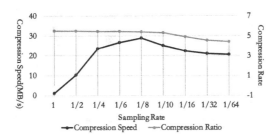

Fig. 7. Effects of different sampling rates trie index structure for compression speed and compression ratio.

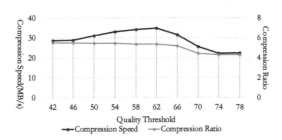

Fig. 8. Trie indexing structures of different effects on the quality scores threshold speed and compression ratio values.

Moreover, in order to compare our STrieGD with other compression algorithms, we evaluated the compression speed and compression ratio of four algorithms: GZip, Bzip2, DSRC and STrieGD. The compression speeds and compression ratios of two files (SRR608881 and ERR217195) are respectively shown in Figs. 9 and 10.

Compared to other compression algorithms, the compression speeds of both test files in STrieGD are the highest and reach 40 MB/s or more shown in Fig. 9. However, the compression speeds of two general algorithms (GZip, Bzip2) are both below 10 MB/s and the compression speeds of the DSRC algorithm are below 30 MB/s. Therefore, our STrieGD achieves a high compression speed. In addition, we found that the compression speed fluctuates greatly in different files, due to that the levels of file redundancy are different. Moreover, we found that the compression ratio of our STrieGD is 50% higher than that of GZip, 18% higher than that of Bzip2 and nearly equal to that of DSRC shown in Fig. 10. Therefore, our STrieGD is able to achieve high compression speed and high compression ratio.

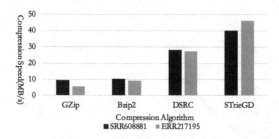

Fig. 9. FASTQ file compression speed comparison stand-alone case.

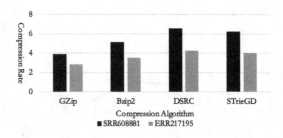

Fig. 10. FASTQ file compression ratio vs. stand-alone case.

5.2   Performance of System

In order to test the scalability of our STrieGD, we evaluated the compression speed and compression ratio at 1–8 different compressors. The testing environment includes eight clients, four servers with four threads. As shown in Fig. 11, with the number of compressors increases, the compression ratio linearly grows and the compression ratio is stable, which shows that the distributed system has a good scalability.

Moreover, we test the bandwidth of the system with the number of compressors from one to eight. As shown in Fig. 12, the system bandwidth is about 200 MB/s when the compressed node is 1, because the system spent many sources in compressing, causing the actual disk write rate in the compressor is much lower than the rate of data received. With the number of node increasing, the system's bandwidth linearly grows. Therefore, our data shows that our STrieGD is highly scalable.

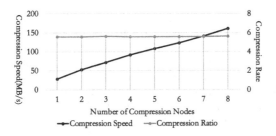

Fig. 11. FASTQ file compression ratio vs. stand-alone case.

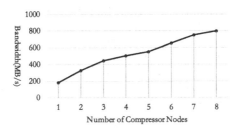

Fig. 12. FASTQ file compression ratio vs. stand-alone case.

6 Conclusions

The advance of NGS produces huge volume of data, presenting a big challenge for gene data storage. To address this challenge, we proposed a sampling trie indexed compression algorithm to compress FASTQ files. It adopts tried indexed structure to accelerate compression speed, and employ a sampling strategy to reduce the size of tried index structure to support large scale gene data. Through evaluation on our distributed compression system, the results show that STrieGD is able to gain a high compression ratio as well as the highest compression speed compared with other related works. With its features of high compression speed and high compression ratio, STrieGD is able to be used on the filed of online processing for gene data.

Acknowledgments. We thank the anonymous reviewers for their insightful comments. We thank Xueqi Li for providing data sets and Torsten Juelich for his helpful advices in writing. We would also like to thank Hougui Liu and Huajie Zheng for the implementation of our deduplication systems. This work was supported by the National Natural Science Foundation of China (Grant No. 601502454).

References

1. Clinton, R.D.: The Selfish Gene. Oxford University Press, Oxford (2006)
2. Nicolae, M., Pathak, S., Rajasekaran, S.: LFQC: a lossless compression algorithm for FASTQ files. Bioinformatics **31**(20), 3276–3281 (2015)

3. Roguski, L., Ribeca, P.: CARGO: effective format-free compressed storage of genomic information. Nucleic Acids Res. **44**(12), 114 (2016)
4. Stuart, M.B.: Sequencing-by-synthesis: explaining the illumina sequencing technology. BitesizeBio (2012). https://bitesizebio.com/13546/sequencing-by-synthesis-explaining-the-illumina-sequencing-technology/
5. Cock, P.J., Fields, C.J., Goto, N., Heuer, M.L., Rice, P.M.: The sanger FASTQ file format for sequences with quality scores, and the solexa/illumina FASTQ variants. Nucleic Acids Res. **38**(6), 1767–1771 (2010)
6. WIKIPEDIA. Genetic testing (2017). https://en.wikipedia.org/wiki/Genetic_testing
7. Waibhav, T., James, L., Suh, E.: G-SQZ: compact encoding of genomic sequence and Quality scores. Bioinformatics **26**(17), 2192–2194 (2010)
8. Deorowicz, S., Grabowski, S.: Compression of DNA sequence reads in FASTQ format. Bioinformatics **27**(6), 860–862 (2011)
9. Ziv, J., Lempel, A., Lempel, A.: A universal algorithm for sequential data compression. IEEE Trans. Inf. Theory **23**(3), 337–343 (1977)
10. Grassi, E., Gregorio, F.D., Molineris, I.: KungFQ: a simple and powerful approach to compress FASTQ files. IEEE/ACM Trans. Comput. Biol. Bioinform. **9**(6), 1837–1842 (2012)
11. Golomb, S.W.: Run-length encodings. IEEE Trans Inf. Theory **12**(3), 399–401 (1966)

On Retargeting the AI Programming Framework to New Hardwares

Jiacheng Zhao[1,2], Yisong Chang[1,2], Denghui Li[1], Chunwei Xia[1,2],
Huimin Cui[1,2(✉)], Ke Zhang[1,2], and Xiaobing Feng[1,2]

[1] SKL Computer Architecture, Institute of Computing Technology, CAS,
Beijing, China
{zhaojiacheng,changyisong,lidenghui,xiachunwei,cuihm,
zhangke,fxb}@ict.ac.cn
[2] University of Chinese Academy of Sciences, Beijing, China

Abstract. Nowadays, a large number of accelerators are proposed to increase the performance of AI applications, making it a big challenge to enhance existing AI programming frameworks to support these new accelerators. In this paper, we select TensorFlow to demonstrate how to port the AI programming framework to new hardwares, i.e., FPGA and Sunway TaihuLight here. FPGA and Sunway TaihuLight represent two distinct and significant hardware architectures for considering the retargeting process. We introduce our retargeting processes and experiences for these two platforms, from the source codes to the compilation processes. We compare the two retargeting approaches and demonstrate some preliminary experimental results.

Keywords: Retarget · AI programming framework · FPGA · Sunway

1 Introduction

In recent years, AI has moved from research labs to production, due to the encouraging results when applying it in a variety of applications, such as speech recognition and computer vision. As the widespread deployment of AI algorithms, a number of AI processors [1,2] and FPGA accelerators [3,4] are proposed to accelerate AI applications meanwhile reducing power consumption, including DianNao [1], EIE [2], ESE [4], etc. Therefore, it is a significant issue for retargeting AI programming frameworks to different hardware platforms.

Some popular AI programming frameworks, e.g., TensorFlow/MXNet, have enhanced the fundamental infrastructure for retargetability using compiler technologies. In particular, TensorFlow introduces XLA [5] to make it relatively easy to write a new backend for novel hardwares. It translates computation graphs into an IR called "HLO IR", then applies high-level target-independent optimizations, and generates optimized HLO IR. Finally, the optimized HLO IR is compiled into a compiler IR, i.e., LLVM IR, which is further translated to

F. Zhang et al. (Eds.): NPC 2018, LNCS 11276, pp. 39–51, 2018.
https://doi.org/10.1007/978-3-030-05677-3_4

machine instructions of various architectures using the compiler of the platform. Similarly, MXNet introduces NNVM compiler as an end-to-end compiler [6].

The evolving compiler approach significantly enhances the retargetability of AI programming frameworks. However, it still has a number of challenges. First, the non-compiler version is of the essence since it guarantees performance via directly invoking underlying high performance libraries. Therefore, maintaining the TensorFlow non-XLA and MXNET non-NNVM versions are necessary when retargeting the frameworks to a new platform. Second, the existing compiler approaches rely on LLVM backend of the AI processors, since the final binary code generation is implemented by the backend compiler. But for emerging AI processors especially designed for inference, vendors typically provide only library APIs without compiler toolchains. Therefore, it requires us to consider retargetability of non-compiler approaches for AI programming frameworks.

In this paper, we select one representative AI programming framework, TensorFlow, to present our experience of retargeting it to FPGA and Sunway TaihuLight. For FPGA, the architecture is the X86 CPU equipped with FPGA as an accelerator, thus we discuss how to add a new accelerator in TensorFlow. Meanwhile, we also design a set of software APIs for controlling FPGA in high-level C/C++ languages. For Sunway TaihuLight, the processor is a many-core architecture which has 260 heterogeneous cores. All these cores are divided into 4 core groups (CG), with each CG including a big core and 64 little cores. Sunway can be regarded as a chip integrating CPUs (big cores) and accelerators (little cores), thus we discuss how to change the CPU type in TensorFlow. In this paper, we respectively discuss how to retarget TensorFlow to these two distinct architectures, and present some preliminary experimental results on FPGA and Sunway TaihuLight. We wish this paper can be helpful for programming framework developers to retarget TensorFlow to other newly designed hardwares.

The rest of this paper is organized as follows: Sects. 2 and 3 discuss how to retarget TensorFlow to FPGA and Sunway TaihuLight respectively. Section 4 demonstrates experimental results. Section 5 discusses differences of retargeting to FPGA and Sunway. Section 6 discusses the related work. Section 7 concludes.

2   Retargeting TensorFlow to FPGA

2.1   FPGA Execution Model

A representative approach to utilizing FPGA is Amazon EC2 F1 [3], which is a compute instance with FPGA that users can program to create custom accelerators for their applications. The user-designed FPGA can further be registered as an Amazon FPGA Image (AFI), and be deployed to an F1 instance.

We also follow the design rule for leveraging FPGA in AI programming frameworks. In particular, we create an abstract execution model for FPGA, and provide a set of APIs for the developers to register an FPGA into the system. In this paper, we use the naive first-in-first-out policy (FIFO) to model the FPGA execution, shown in Fig. 1a. Furthermore, the task execution on our FPGA is

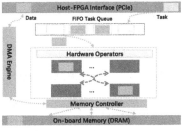
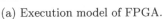

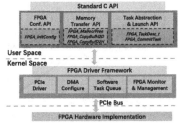

(a) Execution model of FPGA.   (b) APIs of FPGA.

Fig. 1. Abstract execution model and APIs of target FPGA accelerators.

non-preemptive. Our current execution model is similar with GPU kernel execution (without streams). Certainly designers can create different execution models for FPGA, and TensorFlow runtime shall be adjusted correspondingly.

2.2   FPGA APIs and Implementation

Furthermore, we also provide a set of abstract APIs for accessing FPGA accelerators. The abstract APIs are designed to be standard C functions and data structures, as shown in the top part of Fig. 1b. The APIs are:

- *FPGA_InitConfig*. FPGA resource initialization and configuration.
- *FPGA_Malloc/Free*. FPGA memory management.
- *FPGA_CopyBufH2D*. Copy data from host to device, using DMA.
- *FPGA_CopyBufD2H*. Copy data from device to host, using DMA.
- *FPGA_TaskDesc_t*. Data structure for FPGA task description.
- *FPGA_CommitTask*. Commit a task to FPGA.

The APIs are implemented in the operating system (middle part of Fig. 1b) and user-space libraries (top part of Fig. 1b) coordinately. User-space libraries encapsulate the FPGA accelerators into APIs, based on interfaces provided by the FPGA driver framework. The FPGA driver framework interacts with FPGA hardware via PCIe bus, and consists of four functional components: "PCIe Driver" for handling PCIe device registration and interrupts, "DMA Configure" for DMA memory transfer requests, "Software Task Queue" for FIFO execution model and "FPGA Monitor & Management" for monitoring and managing FPGA devices, such as querying FPGA states and task status.

2.3   TensorFlow Architecture for Supporting Retargetability

Figure 2a illustrates how TensorFlow executes user-defined dataflow graphs. When the session manager receives a message of *session.run()*, it starts the "computational graph optimization and execution" module, which automatically partitions the dataflow graph into a set of subgraphs, and then assigns the subgraphs to a set of worker nodes.

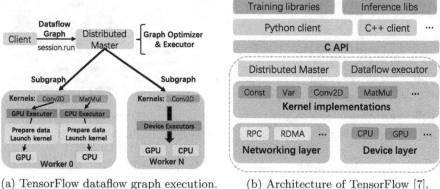

(a) TensorFlow dataflow graph execution.   (b) Architecture of TensorFlow [7].

Fig. 2. TensorFlow architecture and its execution of user-defined dataflow graphs.

The execution of subgraphs is managed by "dataflow executor", which is local to one worker node where the subgraphs are assigned to. The dataflow executor schedules operations in subgraphs to the underlying devices. Dataflow executor prepares the input and output data for each kernel invocation, launches the specific kernel via device executor (e.g. CPU/GPU Executor in Fig. 2a).

Figure 2b further depicts the overall architecture of TensorFlow framework. The modules related to retargeting are: "Device Layer", "Dataflow Executor" and "Kernel Implementation". "Device Layer" aims to provide proper abstraction of FPGA resources and launching FPGA tasks. "Dataflow Executor" should be aware of the FPGA devices and be able to assign operations to them, and "Kernel Implementation" is the fundamental operation kernels on the FPGA.

2.4   Supporting FPGA in TensorFlow

Step 1. FPGA Device Abstraction. First, we add the FPGA device into the device layer. Two important issues are addressed here:

Memory Management: FPGA accelerators are commonly equipped with DDR memory to hold input/output features and/or weights. This memory is treated as a memory pool in our work and C-style memory management scheme is provided. Thus, four critical routines: *memcpyDeviceToHost*, *memcpyHostToDevice*, *malloc*, and *free* are implemented using APIs provided in Sect. 2.2.

Execution Model: Execution model determines how TensorFlow runtime interacts with underlying devices and must match the nature of corresponding devices. The abstracted FPGA in this paper is a synchronous FIFO device. An FPGA executor is implemented using APIs defined in Sect. 2.2.

Step 2. FPGA Device Runtime. Second, runtime support for the new FPGA device will be implemented, including the kernel launching and high level memory management wrapper.

Kernel Launching. In TensorFlow, the dataflow executor assigns operations to specific device by invoking the *Compute* method of corresponding device, which is set to launch the *Compute* function of the given kernel.

High-Level Memory Management Wrapper. The device abstraction provides low-level C-style memory management API. And TensorFlow runtime requires high-level APIs to deal with tensor data. In particular, a 'best-fit with coalescing' memory allocator, *FPGABFCAllocator*, is provided to serve the tensor data allocation/free of TensorFlow runtime. Furthermore, two high-level APIs, *CopyCPUTensorToDevice* and *CopyDeviceTensorToCPU*, are implemented to manipulate tensor data, instead of raw data.

Besides, a factory class, namely "FPGADeviceFactory" is provided to create and instantiate instances of "FPGADevice".

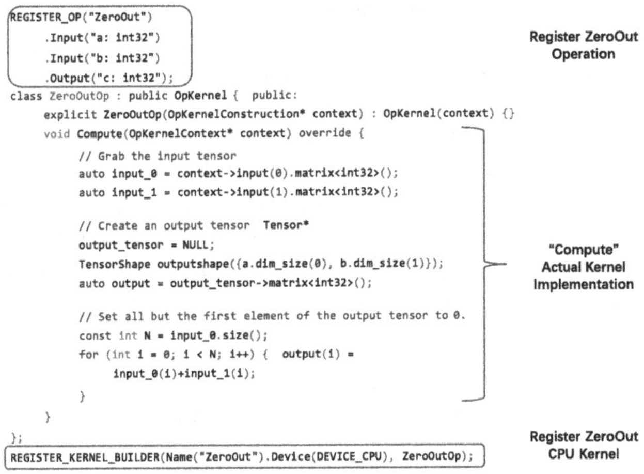

```
REGISTER_OP("ZeroOut")
    .Input("a: int32")                                      Register ZeroOut
    .Input("b: int32")                                      Operation
    .Output("c: int32");
class ZeroOutOp : public OpKernel {  public:
    explicit ZeroOutOp(OpKernelConstruction* context) : OpKernel(context) {}
    void Compute(OpKernelContext* context) override {

        // Grab the input tensor
        auto input_0 = context->input(0).matrix<int32>();
        auto input_1 = context->input(1).matrix<int32>();

        // Create an output tensor  Tensor*
        output_tensor = NULL;                               "Compute"
        TensorShape outputshape({a.dim_size(0), b.dim_size(1)});   Actual Kernel
        auto output = output_tensor->matrix<int32>();       Implementation

        // Set all but the first element of the output tensor to 0.
        const int N = input_0.size();
        for (int i = 0; i < N; i++) {  output(i) =
            input_0(i)+input_1(i);
        }
    }
};                                                          Register ZeroOut
REGISTER_KERNEL_BUILDER(Name("ZeroOut").Device(DEVICE_CPU), ZeroOutOp);   CPU Kernel
```

Fig. 3. An example of implementing an operation in TensorFlow.

Step 3. FPGA Kernel Implementation. Figure 3 shows an example operation in TensorFlow, where the `Compute` function takes the input tensor parameters, the target device, and the context. All the input parameters are encapsulated into the data structure of `OpKernelContext`.

When defining an operation, its specific implementation on a device is called a *kernel*, which is typically implemented as libraries. For example, most CPU kernels are implemented via Eigen libraries [8], and most GPU kernels are implemented via CUBLAS or CUDNN libraries. Therefore, when we introduce FPGA for acceleration, we first define the implementation of operations on FPGA, which translates to function calls to *FPGA_CommitTask* defined in FPGA APIs. After implementing an operation on a new device, we should register the new implementation into TensorFlow, using the `REGISTER_OP` and `REGISTER_KERNEL_BUILDER`.

Figure 3 shows an example for registering a new operation `ZeroOut`, which has two input tensor parameters `a` and `b`, and generates one output tensor `c`. We specify these information in `REGISTER_OP` and implement the operation in `OpKernel`. Finally, `REGISTER_KERNEL_BUILDER` is used for registering the kernel.

3   Retargeting TensorFlow to Sunway

In this section, we first briefly introduce the architecture of Sunway processor, and then present our retargeting process.

3.1   Sunway Architecture

Sunway 26010 processor [9] is composed of 4 core groups (CGs) connected via an NoC. Each CG includes a Management Processing Element (MPE) and 64 Computing Processing Elements (CPEs) arranged in an 8 by 8 grid. MPE and CPE cluster in one CG share same memory space. All the MPEs and CPEs run at the frequency of 1.45 GHz.

On the software side, Sunway uses a customized 64-bit Linux with a set of compilation tools, including native C/C++ compiler and cross compiler.

Aiming at Sunway processor, we regard MPEs as CPUs and leverage CPEs for acceleration. However, the MPEs and CPEs share same memory space, making it pointless to transfer data between them. Thus, we firstly retarget the TensorFlow framework which runs on CPUs to the Sunway MPEs, and then CPEs for acceleration in the retargeted TensorFlow.

3.2   Compiling TensorFlow for Sunway MPEs

We have two ways to compile TensorFlow for Sunway. The first is to use the native compiler of Sunway nodes by submitting compilation process as a job for Sunway. The second is to cross-compiler TensorFlow on an X86 server. We select cross-complication, since the native compiler is too restricted to compile the large-scale complex TensorFlow source codes. We met a series of obstacles during the retargeting process, and we discuss them here for providing some experience of porting a large scale software package to Sunway TaihuLight.

Static Linked Library. First, Sunway TaihuLight does not support dynamic linked library when CPEs are expected to be used. Therefore, we choose to cross-compile TensorFlow into a static linked library, i.e., libtensorflow.a.

The Bazel Compilation Tool. TensorFlow is configured to use Bazel as its default compilation tool, which can generate dynamic linked library, but does not work well for generating static linked library. Meanwhile, a number of unexpected problems raised when using the cross compiler `swgcc` in Bazel. Therefore, we switch to use Makefile as our compilation tool.

The Python Support. TensorFlow is tightly coupled with the language of Python, which is not supported on Sunway TaihuLight. A number of modules utilize

Python-based tools, such as *tf.train* and *tf.timeline*. Therefore, we decouple these modules from the TensorFlow framework. As a result, our retargeted TensorFlow on Sunway TaihuLight only supports C++ programming interface, without support for the Python binding.

Processing Protobuf. The Protobuf tool `protoc` is used both during the compilation of TensorFlow (on X86 platform), and during the execution of TensorFlow (on Sunway TaihuLight platform). For such purpose, `protoc` is required to be compiled on x86 platform using X86 native `gcc` and cross compiler `swgcc`.

Two-Phase Compilation. The compilation of TensorFlow is a two-phase compilation. In the first phase, the X86 `gcc` compiler is used to generate some tools for X86 platform, e.g., the X86 `protoc`, which reads the *.pb files in TensorFlow source code and generates the corresponding C++ files. In the second phase, the cross compiler `swgcc` is used to generate the final libtensorflow.a. During this phase, all dependent libraries should be switched to the static linked versions, e.g., protobuf, libstdc++, libm, etc.

After TensorFlow is cross-compiled successfully, it can run on the MPEs of Sunway TaihuLight. Since Python module like *tf.train* is disabled, the ported TensorFlow does not support training.

Now we have had a baseline TensorFlow which completely runs on the MPEs of Sunway. The operations can be implemented following steps in Sect. 2.4. Next we add CPEs for acceleration. Specially, MPEs are responsible for graph creation and optimization, together with task creation and scheduling. Meanwhile CPEs can execute the computation-intensive kernels, e.g. convolutions.

3.3 Using CPEs for Acceleration

We have two approaches for using CPEs. First, we can force the CPU kernel implementation to invoke CPE libraries, which means MPEs and CPEs are considered together as one device. Alternatively, we can consider CPEs as individual accelerators, similar with GPUs and FPGAs. In this paper, we select first approach as the second approach has been discussed in Sect. 2.

To use CPEs in an operation, consider the steps described in Fig. 3. Take `matmul` for example, the original implementation will use Eigen as the math library in *Compute* part. We will change the math library from Eigen to SWCBLAS library, i.e. from Eigen call *MatMul< CPUDevice>* to *sgemm/dgemm* call in SWCBLAS. As SWDNN library is being developed, we only use SWCBLAS for implementing the operations in this work. When SWDNN is released, we can use the same approach to change the library from SWCBLAS to SWDNN.

4 Evaluation

We select four DNN models, i.e., Cifarnet [10], Lenet [11], Inception-V3 [12] and Resnet-50 [13], to evaluate our retargeted TensorFlow on FPGA and Sunway

TaihuLight. The trained models are obtained from TensorFlow model zoo. We only focus on inference phase. Our experimental results demonstrate that our retargeted TensorFlow can run correctly on FPGA and Sunway platforms.

The functionality of retargeted TensorFlow relies on underlying operation kernels. For the aforementioned four DNN models, CPU and Sunway MPE support all seven main operations: *Conv2D*, *BiasAdd*, *Pooling*, *Relu*, *Softmax*, *Matmul*, *FusedBatchNorm*. Our FPGA doesn't implement *FusedBatchNorm*, which means it can't support Inception-V3 and Restnet-50. Sunway CPE supports only *Conv2D*, *Softmax* and *Matmul*. Other operations can be easily supported once SWDNN is deployed.

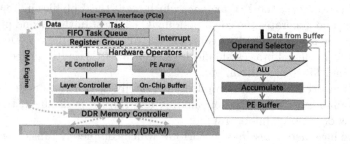

Fig. 4. Evaluated hardware of target FPGA accelerator.

4.1   Hardware Platforms

FPGA Implementation: We implement a custom PCIe-attached acceleration card based on a Xilinx Virtex-7 690T FPGA chip as shown in Fig. 4. The card communicates with host CPU via the standard PCIe Gen 3 × 8 interconnect. We leverage dual off-chip DDR3-1600 SODIMMs with total capacity of 8 GB as device memory. Xilinx Vivado 2016.4 toolset is used and the synthesized core accelerator logic and DMA engine operate at the frequency as high as 200 MHz.

Figure 4 further illustrates the design of our FPGA accelerator. For details, we implement a unified hardware template of DNN accelerator with a configurable number of processing elements (PEs) for per layer specific operations, like convolution and full-connection. The processing element is composed of a 1-D array of multiply-and-accumulation (MACC) units, loop tiling and unrolling are leveraged to partition computation into specific PEs. An on-chip buffer is also implemented to hold tiled input feature map. To reduce the external memory bandwidth, temporary results are pushed into the PE buffer. Data movements between PE array and on-chip buffer is elaborately controlled by the PE controller according to the loop unrolling and tiling strategies.

Sunway TaihuLight: The Sunway TaihuLight is described in Sect. 3, and we use one node for evaluation. As we focus on the inference, the number of nodes does not matter.

Baseline Platforms: For comparison, we also run these models on a CPU and nVIDIA GPU. In particular, the CPU is Intel Xeon E5-2620 which runs at 2.0 GHz and has a main memory of 32 GB. The nVIDIA GPU is Tesla K40c which has the frequency of 745 MHz, and the global memory is 12 GB.

4.2 Results on FPGA Platform

With our retargeted TensorFlow, programmers can use the "with tf.device ("fgpa:0")" statements to use the FPGA, with no modifications in their source codes.

Figure 5 shows the overall execution time (data transfer time included) of Cifarnet and Lenet on FPGA, CPU and GPU. In this paper, we focus on retargeting process, thus the underlying FPGA implementation is not optimized.

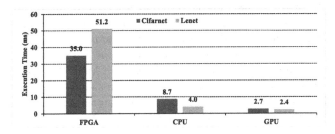

Fig. 5. Overall execution time of Cifarnet and Lenet on FPGA, CPU and GPU.

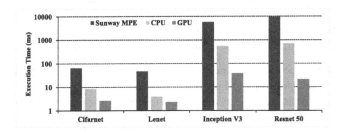

Fig. 6. The overall execution time on Sunway MPE, CPU and GPU.

4.3 Results on Sunway TaihuLight Platform

As we treat Sunway MPE and CPEs as a CPU, the source codes needs no modification and the models can be directly executed on the ported TensorFlow.

Figure 6 shows the overall execution time when using only MPE, in comparison with CPU and GPU. Note that the vertical axis is in log scale. Besides, we use only one core of Sunway and CPU, frequency of which are 1.45 GHz and 2.0GHz respectively. Therefore, Sunway MPE performs worse than CPU.

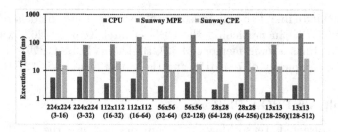

Fig. 7. Performance of convolution with 3 × 3 filter size.

Figure 7 demonstrates the execution time of one convolution operation (with the filter size of 3 × 3) on Sunway MPEs and CPEs, in comparison with CPU. We don't evaluate the overall execution as some operations are not supported on CPEs. The horizontal axis marks different scales of input feature sizes and input/output channel numbers, e.g. $224 * 224 * (3 - 16)$ means input feature size is $224 * 224$ while input channel is 3 and output channel is 16. The vertical axis is execution time in log scale. The results show that CPEs can obtain significant performance improvement, up to 45 times than MPE. Furthermore, in our experiments, only one core group is leveraged (the reason is that the SWCBLAS interface is designed for one core group). The performance is expected to be improved when all core groups are utilized and SWDNN is released.

5   Discussion and Future Work

We have discussed two types of TensorFlow retargeting processes, i.e., FPGA and Sunway TaihuLight. In particular, FPGA represents the approach of introducing a new accelerator into TensorFlow while Sunway TaihuLight represents the approach of changing the CPU architecture in TensorFlow.

Retargeting to a New AI Accelerator. Most of emerging AI processors will be deployed as accelerators. Thus, our experience of retargeting to FPGA can apply for such scenarios. The modification for the device layer is the same with the process for FPGA. The runtime support shall be designed by vendors of AI processors, in corresponding to their execution model. Furthermore, amount of work is needed for implementing hundreds of operation kernels. Even if most AI processors will provide machine learning libraries, porting these operation kernels are still time-consuming. We will further explore automatic kernel generation.

Exploiting the Computation Ability of Sunway TaihuLight. Sunway TaihuLight exhibits performance potential for machine learning, e.g., some preliminary work on SWDNN [14] has been released. To enable more machine learning programs, especially model training, to run on Sunway TaihuLight, a more robust TensorFlow is necessary. Thus, we will further consider following issues, i.e., Bazel compilation tool, Python support, and stable SWDNN library.

Data Layout Issue. Moreover, the data layout is a significant issue for the framework developers. For example, TensorFlow stores the tensor with the default format of NHWC. But NCHW is the default format for GPU libraries, e.g. cudnn [15], making it the framework's burden to transform between them. Sunway TaihuLight has not finally determined its data layout in SWDNN. When TensorFlow is retargeted to a new platform, data format shall be designed by taking hardware and/or library into consideration.

6   Related Work

In recent years, AI has drawn many interest from both researchers and industry, especially DNNs (Deep Neural Networks [12,13,16,17]). Despite the enormous advance in AI algorithms, researchers have also done extensive work to meet the performance/energy/programming requirements of DNN applications.

First, from the aspect of software, a huge number of software tools are proposed to enable flexible programming of DNN applications, such as Tensor-Flow [18], Caffe [19], and MXNet [20]. All these tools support general purpose CPU and high performance nVIDIA GPU, both of which have mature compiler toolchains [21] and highly optimized libraries [15].

Second, from the aspect of hardware, a series of domain specific accelerators [1,2,22,23] are explored. DianNao [1] leverages loop tiling to efficiently reuse data and supports both DNNs and CNNs. EIE [2] focus on inference for compressed DNN models. Furthermore, researchers also explore FPGA as accelerators [4,24,25] for DNN applications. And to the best of our knowledge, all these accelerators lack mature compiler toolchains, for example, a C compiler.

At last, it is becoming a big challenge to utilize these diverse hardware accelerators in software tools. TensorFlow proposes XLA [5], which leverages compiler technology to transform high-level dataflow graph to compiler intermediate representation, i.e. LLVM IR, relies on hardware-specific backend to generate binary code, e.g., NVPTX for nVIDIA GPU. Similarly, MXNET introduces NNVM [6], which also makes use of compiler backend. However, these compiler-based approaches require a mature compiler backend, which is rarely seen in AI processors. Thus, this work explores non-compiler approach of retargeting software frameworks to diverse AI hardwares. Besides, [26] proposes a NN compiler to transform a trained NN model to an equivalent network that can run on specific hardwares, which sheds some light on automatic retargeting of AI frameworks.

7   Conclusion

We have presented our experience of retargeting TensorFlow to different hardwares, e.g. FPGA and Sunway, together with some preliminary evaluation results using popular DNN models. We have investigated the differences between FPGA and Sunway with respect to retargeting.

Acknowledgments. This work is supported in part by the National Key R&D Program of China (2016YFB1000402), the National Natural Science Foundation of China (61802368, 61521092, 61432016, 61432018, 61332009, 61702485). The authors would like to thank all the anonymous reviewers for their valuable comments and helpful suggestions.

References

1. Chen, T., et al.: DianNao: a small-footprint high-throughput accelerator for ubiquitous machine-learning. In: ASPLOS 2014, NY, USA. ACM, New York (2014)
2. Han, S., et al.: EIE: efficient inference engine on compressed deep neural network. In: ISCA 2016 (2016)
3. Amazon EC2 F1. https://aws.amazon.com/cn/ec2/instance-types/f1/
4. Han, S., et al.: ESE: efficient speech recognition engine with sparse LSTM on FPGA. In: FPGA 2017 (2017)
5. Tensorflow XLA. https://www.tensorflow.org/performance/xla/
6. Li, M.: Introducing NNVM compiler: a new open end-to-end compiler for AI frameworks (2017)
7. Tensorflow architecture. https://www.tensorflow.org/extend/architecture
8. Guennebaud, G., Jacob, B., et al.: Eigen v3 (2010). http://eigen.tuxfamily.org
9. Lin, H., et al.: Scalable graph traversal on sunway taihulight with ten million cores. In: IPDPS 2017 (2017)
10. Krizhevsky, A.: Learning multiple layers of features from tiny images (2009)
11. Lécun, Y., Bottou, L., Bengio, Y., Haner, P.: Gradient-based learning applied to document recognition. In: Proceedings of the IEEE (1998)
12. Szegedy, C., Vanhoucke, V., Ioffe, S., Shlens, J., Wojna, Z.: Rethinking the inception architecture for computer vision. CoRR vol. abs/1512.00567 (2015)
13. He, K., Zhang, X., Ren, S., Sun, J.: Identity mappings in deep residual networks. CoRR vol. abs/1603.05027 (2016)
14. Fang, J., Fu, H., Zhao, W., Chen, B., Zheng, W., Yang, G.: swDNN: a library for accelerating deep learning applications on sunway taihulight. In: IPDPS 2017 (2017)
15. Chetlur, S., et al.: cuDNN: efficient primitives for deep learning. CoRR vol. abs/1410.0759 (2014)
16. Lecun, Y., Bottou, L., Bengio, Y., Haner, P.: Gradient-based learning applied to document recognition. In: Proceedings of the IEEE, pp. 2278–2324, November 1998
17. Krizhevsky, A., Sutskever, I., Hinton, G.E.: ImageNet classification with deep convolutional neural networks. In: NIPS 2012 (2012)
18. Abadi, M., et al.: TensorFlow: a system for large-scale machine learning. In: OSDI 2016 (2016)
19. Jia, Y., et al.: Caffe: convolutional architecture for fast feature embedding. In: MM 2014, pp. 675–678 (2014)
20. Chen, T., et al.:, MXNet: a flexible and efficient machine learning library for heterogeneous distributed systems. CoRR vol. abs/1512.01274 (2015)
21. Nvidia Corporation: Nvidia cuda C programming guide. Nvidia Corporation (2011)
22. Chen, Y.-H., Emer, J., Sze, V.: Eyeriss: a spatial architecture for energy-efficient dataflow for convolutional neural networks. In: ISCA 2016 (2016)
23. Parashar, A., et al.: SCNN: an accelerator for compressed-sparse convolutional neural networks. In: ISCA 2017 (2017)

24. Suda, N., et al.: Throughput-optimized OpenCL-based FPGA accelerator for large-scale convolutional neural networks. In: FPGA 2016 (2016)
25. Qiu, J., et al.: Going deeper with embedded FPGA platform for convolutional neural network. In: FPGA 2016 (2016)
26. Ji, Y., Zhang, Y., Chen, W., Xie, Y.: Bridge the gap between neural networks and neuromorphic hardware with a neural network compiler. In: ASPLOS 2018 (2018)

An Efficient Method for Determining Full Point-to-Point Latency of Arbitrary Indirect HPC Networks

Chengchun Liu[1], Zhang Yang[2]($\boxtimes$), Limin Xiao[1]($\boxtimes$), Baicheng Yan[1], Zhihao Wang[1], and Hongyun Tian[2]

[1] School of Computer Science and Engineering, Beihang University, Beijing 100191, China
xiaolm@buaa.edu.cn
[2] Institute of Applied Physics and Computational Mathematics, No. 2 East Fenghao Road, Haidian District, Beijing 100094, China
yang_zhang@iapcm.ac.cn

Abstract. Point-to-point latency is one of the most important metrics for high performance computer networks and is used widely in communication performance modeling, link-failure detection, and application optimization. However, it is often hard to determine the full-scale point-to-point latency of large scale HPC networks since it often requires measurements to the square of the number of terminal nodes. In this paper, we propose an efficient method to generate measurement plans for arbitrary indirect HPC networks and reduces the measurement requirements from $O(n^2)$ to m, which is often $O(n)$ in modern indirect networks containing n nodes and m links, thus significantly reduces the latency measure overhead. Both analysis and experiments show that the proposed method can reduce the overhead of large-scale fat-tree networks by orders of magnitudes.

1 Introduction

Point-to-point latency is a fundamental metric of high performance computer networks, and is widely used in network performance modeling [1,2], communication performance optimization [3], and high performance computer maintenance. The first and formost step to make use of the latency is to measure the latency. A common method to get the latency is to measure the round-trip time (RTT) between any pair of nodes. While one measurement of RTT is quick enough, obtaining the full-network point-to-point latency can be extremly time-consuming since it involves $n(n-1)/2$ (or $O(n^2)$) measurements, where n is the number of terminal nodes. One may use parallel measurements to reduce the round of measurements, but parallel measurements can interfere with each other and reduce the accuracy of the results. Thus, it is essential to reduce the total

© IFIP International Federation for Information Processing 2018
Published by Springer Nature Switzerland AG 2018
F. Zhang et al. (Eds.): NPC 2018, LNCS 11276, pp. 52–63, 2018.
https://doi.org/10.1007/978-3-030-05677-3_5

number of measurements, so as to make it possible to use these latency-based methods on modern super-computers with tens of thousands of computer nodes.

In this paper, we propose a minimal and parallel method for full-scale point-to-point latency measurements on super-computers with indirect networks (such as fat-tree, dragonfly and slimfly networks), abbreviated as *PMM*. Our method first construct a minimal set of node pairs between which the RTT is measured, given the network topology and the routing table, then compute a measurement plan to make use of the parallelism between the measurements with the gurantee that concurrent measurements will not interfere with one another. The minimal set of node pairs goes from $n(n-1)/2$ to m, where m is the number of links connecting the network interface and the routers, which is often proportional to the number of nodes, thus reduces the number of measurements from $O(n^2)$ to $O(n)$. The parallel measurement plan can further reduce the round of measurements, for example, by 33.3% in our experimental settings.

The reset of this paper is organized as follows. In Sect. 2, we introduce some related works on network latency measurement. In Sect. 3, we present our latency measurement method in detail. In Sect. 4, we prove the effectiveness of our methods by theoretical analysis and experiments. We also present performance analysis of the method itself. In Sect. 5, we discuss the possible applications of our proposed method. In the last section comes the conclusions.

2   Related Works

Communication latency or distance measurement are investigated in some literatures. Authors in [4] proposed a latency system based on GNP for fast obtaining latency information between arbitrary web client pairs distributed in wide area networks. This method has been used in the Google's content distribution network which helps to find the nearest data center for a web client. This method can estimate latency results quickly only with a small number of CDN modifications and decouples with web client, but is not suitable for the dense network such as HPC network or data center network. The literatures [5,6] also aim to obtain the latency in wide area network environment in different ways, but those methods are not suitable for dense networks.

Authors in [7] proposed a system called Pingmesh for latency measurement and analysis in large scale data center networks. The latency measurement system represents the network topology as three complete graphs, namely the server complete graph, the switch complete graph, and the data center complete graph. The method needs to select some representative node pairs and measure the latency information between those nodes. With these information, the method can approximately estimate the latency between different nodes in the same switch, in different switches, or in different data centers. But this method measures only partially the network and can not be used in full-network measurements.

The work [8] is the most similar to our work. They proposed a method to measure the communication distance between nodes on the Internet. This method also needs to construct the communication distance equations through a large number of measurements and then solve the least squares solution of the equations, which is considered as the distance. The main concern of the method is whether the calculation result of the communication distance is accurate without considering the time cost caused by the inappropriate measurement set. In contrast, our method carefully selects a minimal measurement set and then measures the latency between node pairs in the set in parallel to reduce the total time cost.

3   The PMM Method

3.1   Definitions

In order to simplify the introduction of our measurement method, we introduce some definitions, mathematical symbols and necessary assumptions in this section. Data transmission in the network is a complex process, which is affected by communication protocol, network topology, and hardware architecture. Since point-to-point latency on direct networks can be easy, we only focus on indirect networks in this paper. The data is transmitted from the source NIC, through the links, to routers, and direct to other routers, and finally to the destination NIC, as shown in Fig. 1. The NIC is connected to a computing node, which is called a terminal node. We also assume the network uses static routing instead of adaptive routing.

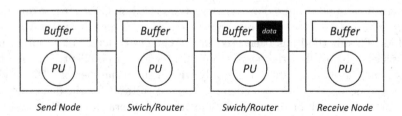

Fig. 1. Data transmission in indirect networks. The data is transmitted from the source terminal node to the destination through links and routers.

Definition 1. *a single link refers to a physical link between any adjacent devices in an indirect network. The latency of a single link refers to the time for a measuring packet to pass through the link from the buffer of the device at one end of the link to the buffer of the device at another end.*

Definition 2. *a measuring path refers to the entire path contained in the transmission of data between two communication nodes in an indirect network, which passes through some middle routing devices and physical links. The latency of the measuring path refers to the sum of latency of all single links in the path.*

Definition 3. *an aggregated link refers to a subpath of a measuring path which consists of one or more adjacent links. The method is not able to calculate the latency of any single link in an aggregated link, but is able to calculate the latency of the aggregated link.*

We provide some mathematical symbols to represent the elements in the method, as shown in Table 1.

Table 1. All mathematical symbols used in the method

Symbol	Description
k_x	Computing node
$P_{x,y}$	The measuring path from node x to node y
$P_{x,y}^{rtt}$	The round-trip measuring path between node x and node y
l_x	Single link
$a_{<x,y>,z}$	The times the single link z appears in the path $P_{x,y}^{rtt}$
$\alpha_{<x,y>}$	The vector form of a path whose elements are $a_{<x,y>,z}$
o_x	The latency of link x
O_x	The latency of path x
S	The set of path whose elements are $\alpha_{<x,y>}$
S_x'	A maximal linearly independent subset of S

3.2 Method

Now we describe our latency measurement method in detail. Our method assumes that one can get the route of arbitrary node pairs. Through our paper, we use a simple network as shown in Fig. 2 for illustration. The network consists of 3 switches, 6 nodes and 8 single links. We can find many redundant measurements when we measure the latency between all node pairs. We take the 4 nodes connected by r_1 as an example. When measuring all pairs, we need to measure the latency of 6 paths, i.e., $P_{k_1,k_2}^{rtt}, P_{k_1,k_5}^{rtt}, P_{k_1,k_6}^{rtt}, P_{k_2,k_5}^{rtt}, P_{k_2,k_6}^{rtt}, P_{k_5,k_6}^{rtt}$. But if we just measure $P_{k_1,k_2}^{rtt}, P_{k_1,k_5}^{rtt}, P_{k_1,k_6}^{rtt}, P_{k_2,k_5}^{rtt}$ for latency, and make use of the fact link latency is additive, we can get Eq. 1.

$$\begin{cases} o_{l_1} + o_{l_2} = 1/2 \cdot O_{P_{k_1,k_2}^{rtt}} \\ o_{l_1} + o_{l_7} = 1/2 \cdot O_{P_{k_1,k_5}^{rtt}} \\ o_{l_1} + o_{l_8} = 1/2 \cdot O_{P_{k_1,k_6}^{rtt}} \\ o_{l_2} + o_{l_7} = 1/2 \cdot O_{P_{k_2,k_5}^{rtt}} \end{cases} \tag{1}$$

By solving Eq. 1, we can obtain $o_{l_1}, o_{l_2}, o_{l_7}, o_{l_8}$ and calculate $O_{P_{k_2,k_6}^{rtt}} = 2 \cdot (o_{l_2} + o_{l_8}), O_{P_{k_5,k_6}^{rtt}} = 2 \cdot (o_{l_7} + o_{l_8})$. Further more, there are redundant measurements between the nodes connected to different switches. Suppose we have measured the path latency between some nodes directly connected to the same switch. We need to measure $P^{rtt}_{k_1,k_3}, P^{rtt}_{k_1,k_4}, P^{rtt}_{k_2,k_3}, P^{rtt}_{k_2,k_4}, P^{rtt}_{k_5,k_3}, P^{rtt}_{k_5,k_4}, P^{rtt}_{k_6,k_3}, P^{rtt}_{k_6,k_4}$ for latency when measuring one by one. In fact, we can only measure $P^{rtt}_{k_1,k_3}$ to get $o_{l_1} + o_{l_3} + o_{l_4} + o_{l_5} = O_{P^{rtt}_{k_1,k_3}}$ and calculate $o_{l_3} + o_{l_4}$. In addition, we can measure node pairs which do not share any link in parallel. For example, we can measure the latency of $P^{rtt}_{k_1,k_2}$ and $P^{rtt}_{k_3,k_4}$ in parallel.

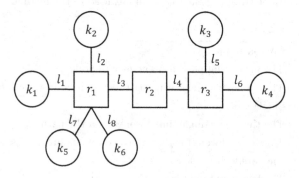

Fig. 2. A sample network with 6 nodes, 8 single links and 3 switches. Only 7 rather than 15 measurements are necessary for full-network point-to-point latency.

The example above illustrates the core idea of our method. By assuming the node-to-node latency is the addition of link latencies, we can select a number of node pairs which covers all links in the network and measure the node-to-node latencies, then recover the link latencies by solving a linear equation. The measurement can further be done in parallel. Although we only consider link latency here, our method applies to cases where both link and router latency are included, since they only add more variables and does not change the additive nature of latency.

Concretely, for a network containing n nodes and m links, the method includes the following steps.

a. Construct full measurement path set S, which contains all measuring paths.

By querying routing information, we can get the single link set of any path between node k_i and k_j. The latency of path $P^{rtt}_{k_i,k_j}$ can be expressed as $Latency(P^{rtt}_{k_i,k_j}) = a_{<i,j>,1} \cdot o_{l_1} + a_{<i,j>,2} \cdot o_{l_2} + \cdots + a_{<i,j>,m} \cdot o_{l_m} = \alpha_{<i,j>} \cdot \beta$ where $\alpha_{<i,j>} = (a_{<i,j>,1}, a_{<i,j>,2}, \cdots, a_{<i,j>,m-1}, a_{<i,j>,m})$, $\beta = (o_{l_1}, o_{l_2}, \cdots, o_{l_{m-1}}, o_{l_m})$. The full measuring path set $S = \{\alpha_{<1,2>}, \alpha_{<1,3>}, \cdots, \alpha_{<n-2,n>}, \alpha_{<n-1,n>}\}$ which consists of $n(n-1)/2$ measuring paths. For the network shown in Fig. 2, $S = \{\alpha_{<k_1,k_2>}, \alpha_{<k_1,k_3>}, \alpha_{<k_1,k_4>}, \alpha_{<k_1,k_5>}, \alpha_{<k_1,k_6>}, \alpha_{<k_2,k_3>}, \alpha_{<k_2,k_4>}, \alpha_{<k_2,k_5>}, \alpha_{<k_2,k_6>}, \alpha_{<k_3,k_4>}, \alpha_{<k_3,k_5>}, \alpha_{<k_3,k_6>}, \alpha_{<k_4,k_5>}, \alpha_{<k_4,k_6>}, \alpha_{<k_5,k_6>}\}$. Taking $\alpha_{<k_1,k_2>}$ as an example. $\alpha_{<k_1,k_2>} = (2,2,0,0,0,0,0,0)$ means that the measuring path $P^{rtt}_{k_1,k_2}$ consists of l_1, l_2, l_2, l_1.

b. Select the minimal measurement path set S', which is the subset after removing redundant measurement path in S.

By linear algebra theory, any element in S can be expressed as a linear combination of the maximal linearly independent subset of S. Thus, we choose the maximal linearly independent subset of S as the minimal measurement path set S', and name it as *MMSets*. The maximal number of elements in any *MMSet* is never greater than the dimension of the linear space, which is the number of single links m. Thus, if we can find the MMSets, we can reduce the number of measurements from $n(n-1)/2$ to m. Given the fact that HPC networks contain links only proportional to the number of terminal nodes, $m = O(n)$, we reduce the total number of measurements from $O(n^2)$ to $O(n)$, which is very significant.

The *MMSets* can be found using the Gaussian elimination method. Due to different order of elements in S, the Gaussian elimination method can result in different valid *MMSets*. This suggests we have different minimal measurement path sets. For the previous sample network, we can obtain three different *MMSets* which are:

$$S_1' = \{\alpha_{<k_1,k_2>}, \alpha_{<k_1,k_3>}, \alpha_{<k_1,k_4>}, \alpha_{<k_1,k_5>}, \alpha_{<k_1,k_6>}, \alpha_{<k_2,k_5>}, \alpha_{<k_3,k_4>}\},$$

$$S_2' = \{\alpha_{<k_1,k_2>}, \alpha_{<k_1,k_3>}, \alpha_{<k_1,k_4>}, \alpha_{<k_1,k_5>}, \alpha_{<k_1,k_6>}, \alpha_{<k_2,k_6>}, \alpha_{<k_3,k_4>}\},$$

$$S_3' = \{\alpha_{<k_1,k_2>}, \alpha_{<k_1,k_3>}, \alpha_{<k_1,k_4>}, \alpha_{<k_1,k_5>}, \alpha_{<k_1,k_6>}, \alpha_{<k_5,k_6>}, \alpha_{<k_3,k_4>}\}$$

c. Measure the latency of paths in S' in parallel.

We can simultaneously measure the latency of paths that do not contain the same single link. We define a measuring path graph $MPG <V, E>$ in which each vertex represents a measuring path and edge between the two vertexes indicates that the two measuring paths represented by these two vertex share at least one simple link. We propose an innovative method based on graph coloring to divide the graph into a number of subsections and simultaneously measure the latency of all paths in the same subsections. The method stipulates that adjacent vertexes can not have same color. Finally, according to the graph coloring results, we can determine the number of parallel measurements and the path set to be measured in each measuring round. For graph coloring is essentially NP-Hard problem, we use an adaptive coloring algorithm, such as the Welch Powell algorithm, when the graph is large. Only when the measurement set is small enough, we make use of the divide algorithm to get an optimal scheme.

It should be noted that there are often multiple S' for the same S. Although different S' have the same number of measuring paths, the layout of measuring paths in those set are different, which bring different coloring results. For small networks, we determine an optimal S' as the final *MMset* by comparing the coloring results of all S'. For large scale networks, we randomly select some sets from all S' and find out the one with best dyeing scheme as the final optimized *MMSet*. In the previous network, we select S_1' as the final *MMSet* because there are same coloring results for all three S'. The $MPG <V, E>$ colored is shown in Fig. 3. Five rounds of measurement will be carried out finally.

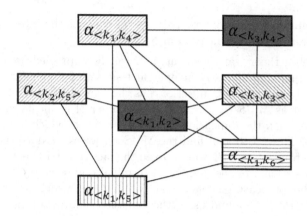

Fig. 3. A coloring result of *MMSet*. Five instead of 7 rounds of measurement is needed finally. (Color figure online)

d. Construct single link latency equations to calculate the latency of all paths in S.

Let $O' = (O_1, O_2, \cdots, O_x)$ be the latency of all paths in *MMset* after parallel measuring. We construct a matrix C which contains x rows and m columns whose rows correspond to the single link composition of measuring paths in *MMset*. We can get a general solution by solving equation $C \cdot \beta^T = O'$. Any solution can be used to calculate the unique latency of all measuring paths in S', which means that we can also calculate the unique latency of all measuring paths in S. For the previous network, suppose that the real latency of each path in the network are $O_{p_{k_1,k_2}^{rtt}} = 16$, $O_{p_{k_1,k_3}^{rtt}} = 37$, $O_{p_{k_1,k_4}^{rtt}} = 36$, $O_{p_{k_1,k_5}^{rtt}} = 18$, $O_{p_{k_1,k_6}^{rtt}} = 17$, $O_{p_{k_2,k_3}^{rtt}} = 39$, $O_{p_{k_2,k_4}^{rtt}} = 38$, $O_{p_{k_2,k_5}^{rtt}} = 20$, $O_{p_{k_2,k_6}^{rtt}} = 19$, $O_{p_{k_3,k_4}^{rtt}} = 25$, $O_{p_{k_3,k_5}^{rtt}} = 41$, $O_{p_{k_3,k_6}^{rtt}} = 40$, $O_{p_{k_4,k_5}^{rtt}} = 40$, $O_{p_{k_4,k_6}^{rtt}} = 39$, $O_{p_{k_5,k_6}^{rtt}} = 21$. After only measuring the latency of x paths in S', we get a solution $o_{l_1} = 3.5$, $o_{l_2} = 4.5$, $o_{l_3} = 8.5$, $o_{l_4} = 0$, $o_{l_5} = 6.5$, $o_{l_6} = 6$, $o_{l_7} = 5.5$, $o_{l_8} = 5$ which can be used to calculate the latency of all paths in S.

Although it is not necessary to calculate all aggregated links' latency for getting path latency, the latency of the aggregated link reflects the characteristics of the network in more detail. It is useful in some application scenarios, such as link fault detection. According to step b, we know $rank(C) \leq m$. When $rank(C) = m$, the equation has unique solution. When $rank(C) < m$, the equation has countless solutions which means that some single links' latency in the network can not by accurately calculated. We propose a method of link aggregation, which can merge several single links into an aggregated link to ensure all aggregated links' latency in network is accurate and unique. We construct augmented matrix $(C|O')$ and transfer it into row canonical form matrix G. All non-zero columns in a row correspond to all single links in aggregated link and the last column represents the latency of the aggregated link. In our example, the matrix $(C|O')$ and G are shown in Eq. 2. The latency of all aggregated links are

$o_{l_1} = 3.5, o_{l_2} = 4.5, o_{l_3} + o_{l_4} = 8.5, o_{l_5} = 6.5, o_{l_6} = 6, o_{l_7} = 5.5, o_{l_8} = 5$. l_3 and l_4 make up an aggregation link, which is reasonable for that they always transmit the data at the same time.

$$(C|O') = \begin{bmatrix} 2 & 2 & 0 & 0 & 0 & 0 & 0 & 0 & 16 \\ 2 & 0 & 2 & 2 & 2 & 0 & 0 & 0 & 37 \\ 2 & 0 & 2 & 2 & 0 & 2 & 0 & 0 & 36 \\ 2 & 0 & 0 & 0 & 0 & 2 & 0 & 18 \\ 2 & 0 & 0 & 0 & 0 & 0 & 2 & 17 \\ 0 & 2 & 0 & 0 & 0 & 2 & 0 & 20 \\ 0 & 0 & 0 & 0 & 2 & 2 & 0 & 0 & 25 \end{bmatrix}, G = \begin{bmatrix} 1 & 0 & 0 & 0 & 0 & 0 & 0 & 0 & 3.5 \\ 0 & 1 & 0 & 0 & 0 & 0 & 0 & 0 & 4.5 \\ 0 & 0 & 1 & 1 & 0 & 0 & 0 & 0 & 8.5 \\ 0 & 0 & 0 & 0 & 1 & 0 & 0 & 0 & 6.5 \\ 0 & 0 & 0 & 0 & 0 & 1 & 0 & 0 & 6 \\ 0 & 0 & 0 & 0 & 0 & 1 & 0 & 5.5 \\ 0 & 0 & 0 & 0 & 0 & 0 & 1 & 5 \end{bmatrix} \tag{2}$$

4 Validation and Analysis

4.1 Exprimental Settings

Since our method is based on rigorous mathematical process, the method is applicable to arbitrary indirect networks. Thus as a validation, we only evaluate the effectiveness of our method in synthesised fat-tree networks. We implement a source routing fat tree network simulator using the topology described in [9], to simulate fat-tree networks commonly used in data centers and supercomputers. $p - port\ q - tree$ InfiniBand network which contains $2 \times (p/2)^q$ nodes and $2 \times q \times (p/2)^q$ single links are simulated. To simulate typical fat-tree networks, we choose 7 different fat-tree configurations as shown in Table 2.

Table 2. Fat-tree configurations used in the experiments

Configuration	Number of terminal nodes	Number of links
$4 - port2 - tree$	8	16
$4 - port3 - tree$	16	48
$6 - port3 - tree$	54	162
$8 - port3 - tree$	128	384
$10 - port3 - tree$	250	750
$12 - port3 - tree$	432	1296
$16 - port3 - tree$	1024	3072

4.2 Accuracy of the Measurement

We first show our method can recover the link latency of the network. We design the following experiments: Firstly, We set every link in the network a random latency. Secondly, we compute a parallel measurement plan using our method. We carry out the measurement by simply aggregating the link latencies along the measuring path. Thirdly, we calculate the latency of all measuring paths and aggregated links in the network. Finally, we check those calculated link latency with the preset values. Our method finds the correct values for all the links. Table 3 shows that the calculated latency of all measuring paths is the same as the actual values in 4-port 2-tree network separately. In fact, we get the same conclusion as this example in the other 6 networks.

Table 3. Actual latency and calculated latency of all measuring paths in $4 - port$ $2 - tree$ network

(a) Actual latency of all measuring paths

Node	1	2	3	4	5	6	7	8
1	0	25	54	51	67	49	58	54
2	25	0	55	52	68	50	59	55
3	54	49	0	25	61	53	52	58
4	57	52	25	0	64	56	55	61
5	67	55	61	61	0	31	65	64
6	62	50	56	56	31	0	60	59
7	58	53	52	59	65	57	0	30
8	60	55	54	61	67	59	30	0

(b) Calculated latency of all measuring paths

Node	1	2	3	4	5	6	7	8
1	0	25	54	51	67	49	58	54
2	25	0	55	52	68	50	59	55
3	54	49	0	25	61	53	52	58
4	57	52	25	0	64	56	55	61
5	67	55	61	61	0	31	65	64
6	62	50	56	56	31	0	60	59
7	58	53	52	59	65	57	0	30
8	60	55	54	61	67	59	30	0

4.3   Measurement Reduction

We then show that our method can greatly reduce the number of measurements in full-network point-to-point latency measurements. We compute the measurement plan for 6 different network configurations, and compute the round of measurements required. Each round of measurements involves a collection of measurements can be done concurrently. We assume one measurement takes T seconds, and compare the total measurement execution time in Fig. 4. We compare our method with the brute-force one-by-one measurement of all node pairs. In the brute-force method, it takes us $(n \times (n-1)/2)T$ seconds to measure the latency of all paths serially. In our measurement method, it takes about m T seconds to serially measure the latency of all paths in *MMset*. In the network with 3-tree, the total measurement time can be further reduced by 33.3% compared with the serial measurement. With parallel measuring the latency of paths in the same *MMset*, only n T seconds are needed. We can conclude that the proposed methods can reduce the overhead of large-scale fat-tree networks containing thousands of nodes by three orders of magnitude.

4.4   Complexity Analysis of the PMM Method

Although the proposed method reduces the time costed in measuring the latency, it brings additional computing overhead. We analyze the complexity of the extra computing here. We choose the time during which CPU completes an arithmetic operation or access a variable in memory as the unit.

The first part of the computing overhead comes from generating the measurement scheme. We use *Gaussian elimination* to transfer matrix A into row echelon form for getting all maximal linear independent subsets of S, during which about m eliminations are required. In each elimination, we need to look up an main row from $n(n-1)/2$ rows firstly, and then carry out $n(n-1)/2$ elementary transformations. Thus the average time overhead of *Gaussian elimination* is T_1.

$$T_1 = m(mn(n-1)/2 + mn(n-1)/2) = m^2n(n-1). \tag{3}$$

The second part of the computing overhead comes from deriving $MPG <V, E>$ to get parallel measurement scheme. We use Welch Powell algorithm to get an optimized solution of the NP-Hard Graph Dying problem in large-scale network. The time complexity of the algorithm is $O(m^3)$.

The third part of the computing overhead comes from calculating the latency of all paths and links. Our method use *Gaussian elimination* to solve m linear equations for getting the latency of all aggregated links, and then calculate the latency of all paths. The average time overhead is T_2

$$T_2 = 2m^3 + n(n-1)/2 \tag{4}$$

For $p - port\ q - tree$ network, $n < m < n(n-1)/2$. As a result, a loose time complexity of our method is $O(n^2 \cdot m^2)$.

We further investigate reducing the computing overhead by parallel computing. We substitute the Gaussian elimination with a MPI based implementation and run the computing of a $12 - port\ 3 - tree$ with 432 nodes and 1296 links on Tianhe-2 super computer. The timing results are shown in Fig. 5 and it shows than we can compute the measurement plan in less than $30\,s$ with 116 MPI processes, which is pretty acceptable in HPC environments.

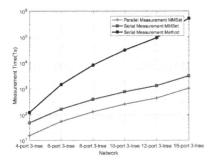

Fig. 4. The measurement time of two methods. Each measurement takes T seconds.

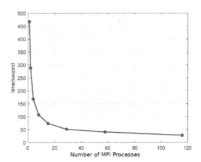

Fig. 5. The computing overhead of generating measurement plan and calculating the latency of all paths and links in $12 - port\ 3 - tree$ network in parallel settings

5   Applications

Being a low level method, our *PMM* method can be used in many application scenarios where full point-to-point latency is required. We discuss some of these applications in this section.

5.1   Communication Performance Modeling and Prediction

In many cases we want to model the communication network, so as to predicate the application performance on given supercomputers, to inspect the communication bottlenecks of parallel applications, and to compare design alternatives of network parameters. For example, when we optimize the application communication performance, we can use trace simulators such as LogGOPSim [10] to simulate the communication and find the bottlenecks. The LogGOPSim relies on point-to-point latency to make an accurate predication for small messages, which often require one to measure the full-network point-to-point latency of a given super-computer. Our methods can greatly reduce the number of measurements and thus improve the model accuracy by being able to incorporate the difference of per node pair latencies.

5.2   Transitional Link Failure Detection

Transitional link failures happens a lot on large scale high performance computer networks, which often results in downgraded communication performance, and gradual system failures. Extra hardware can be built into the network to moniter each link to detect these problematic states, but this is not practical on many networks. Our method provides a software-based alternative. One can generate a measurement plan for any suspecting subnet and measure the point-to-point latency quickly to obtain per-link latency, and flag links with larger latency than expected as problematic for further investigation.

5.3   Parallel Communication Optimization

Automatic optimization of communication performance often requires knowing the inter-node message latency of the running nodes, which can only be measured online. For example, in topology-aware process mapping algorithms, one often needs to model the per-note message latency, and accurate online modeling of these latency is essential for real-world parallel applications. Our method can help by generating the measurement plan and measure the point-to-point latency on the fly quickly, thus make the optimization applicable to any indirect networks.

6   Conclusion

In this paper, we propose an efficient method, namely *PMM*, to generate full-network point-to-point latency measurement plans for arbitrary indirect HPC networks. Our method reduces the measurements required from $O(n^2)$ to $O(n)$ for modern high performance computer networks such as fat-tree based infiniband networks, and can be extremely useful in communication performance modeling, transitional link failure detection, and parallel communication optimization.

Although being effective, there are still aspects to improve in our methods. We go through some or all *MMsets* to find out an optimized one in our method, which is ineffective. We also consider find out heuristics to locate measurement plans with the maximal parallelism. We can also make the measurement additive to allow for continuously monitoring link latencies.

Acknowledgement. This work in this paper is supported by the National Key R&D Program of China under Grant NO. 2018YFB0203901, Science Challenge Project, NO. TZ2016002, and the National Natural Science Foundation of China under Grant No. 61772053. The authors would like to thank the reviewers for their valuable comments.

References

1. Alexandrov, A., Ionescu, M.F., Schauser, K.E., Scheiman, C.: LogGP: incorporating long messages into the LogP model. J. Parallel Distrib. Comput. **44**, 71–79 (1995)
2. Ino, F., Fujimoto, N., Hagihara, K.: LogGPS: a parallel computational model for synchronization analysis. ACM SIGPLAN Not. **36**, 133–142 (2001)
3. Bhanot, G., Gara, A., Heidelberger, P., Lawless, E., Sexton, J.C., Walkup, R.: Optimizing task layout on the Blue Gene/L supercomputer. IBM J. Res. Dev. **49**, 489–500 (2005)
4. Szymaniak, M., Presotto, D., Pierre, G., Steen, M.V.: Practical large-scale latency estimation. Comput. Netw. **52**, 1343–1364 (2008)
5. Sen, S., Wang, J.: Analyzing peer-to-peer traffic across large networks. In: Proceedings of the 2nd ACM SIGCOMM Workshop on Internet measurement, no. 2, pp. 137–150 (2002)
6. Liu, J., Zhang, X., Li, B., Zhang, Q., Zhu, W.: Distributed distance measurement for large-scale networks. Comput. Netw. **41**, 177–192 (2003)
7. Guo, C., et al.: Pingmesh: a large-scale system for data center network latency measurement and analysis. In: ACM SIGCOMM Computer Communication Review, vol. 45, pp. 139–152 (2012)
8. Shavitt, Y., Sun, X., Wool, A., Yener, B.: Computing the unmeasured: an algebraic approach to Internet mapping. IEEE J. Sel. Areas Commun. **22**, 67–78 (2004)
9. Lin, X,Y., Chung, Y,C., Huang, T,Y.: A multiple LID routing scheme for fat-tree-based InfiniBand networks. In: Parallel and Distributed Processing Symposium, 18, p. 11 (2004)
10. Hoefler, T., Schneider, T., Lumsdaine, A.: LogGOPSim: simulating large-scale applications in the LogGOPS model. In: Proceedings of ACM International Symposium on High Performance Distributed Computing, 19, pp. 597–604 (2010)

KT-Store: A Key-Order and Write-Order Hybrid Key-Value Store with High Write and Range-Query Performance

Haobo Wang[1,2], Yinliang Yue[1,2(✉)], Shuibing He[3], and Weiping Wang[1,2]

[1] Institute of Information Engineering, Chinese Academy of Sciences, Beijing, China
{wanghaobo,yueyinliang,wangweiping}@iie.ac.cn
[2] School of Cyber Security, University of Chinese Academy of Sciences, Beijing, China
[3] School of Computer Science, Wuhan University, Wuhan, China
heshuibing@whu.edu.cn

Abstract. With the data volume increasing, key-value (KV) store plays an important role in today's storage systems due to its flexible architecture and good scalability. There are two types of data organization in current KV stores: *key-order* layout and *write-order* layout, which organize records according to key order and write sequence, respectively. While the former and the latter layouts deliver high throughput for range-query and write operations respectively, neither of them can perform well for both write and range-query operations. In this paper, we propose a hybrid KV store, KT-Store, which combines the key-order and write-order layout together to improve performance. More specifically, KT-Store stores keys and value metadata into a LSM-tree, and stores values into multiple tables called TrieTables. By inserting the value among multiple TrieTables in a key-order fashion leveraging a trie, and into a specific TrieTable in a write-order fashion, KT-Store can obtain the advantages of existing two layout types and avoid their shortcomings. We implement KT-Store in RocksDB 5.7.2. Extensive evaluations demonstrate that KT-Store can simultaneously obtain encouraging write and range-query performance: compared with key-order based RocksDB, the write performance is improved by $4.3 \times -12.6\times$ on HDDs; compared with write-order based Wisckey, KT-Store has $54.2 \times -112.6\times$ range-query performance on HDDs. Besides, KT-Store also has encouraging performance on SSDs.

1 Introduction

Key-value stores play a critical role in today's large-scale, high-performance, data-intensive applications in recent years. Compared with conventional SQL databases and other NoSQL data stores, key-value stores have stronger horizontal scalability, more flexible architectures, and more portable supports of different types of applications [1]. Due to their importance and benefits, KV

© IFIP International Federation for Information Processing 2018
Published by Springer Nature Switzerland AG 2018
F. Zhang et al. (Eds.): NPC 2018, LNCS 11276, pp. 64–76, 2018.
https://doi.org/10.1007/978-3-030-05677-3_6

stores are widely used in distributed storage systems, such as BigTable, HBase and local storage systems, such as LevelDB and RocksDB.

Similar to traditional databases, KV stores need to support basic system workloads, such as data inserts, data updates, and range-queries. Data-intensive applications often run with massive data. These operations involve a large number of I/O read and write activities on hard disk drives (HDDs), which are the dominate media in current KV storage systems. As different workloads exhibit various data access characteristics, previous KV stores use different index structures to organize the key-value items, such that the system can provide desirable performance for different workloads.

There are two main types of data layouts in the data organization of current KV systems. The first type is the *key-order* layout that organizes the key-value items according to lexicographical order. Typical systems include conventional LSM-tree, its variants [2–4], B$^+$-tree [5], and its variants [6,7]. As all the key-value items are organized in key-order, such data layout can greatly improve range-query performance by utilizing the sequential read I/Os on HDDs. The second type is the *write-order* layout that organizes the key-value items based on the order of write sequence, which is inspired by the idea of Log-structured file system [8]. The typical systems applying this policy are Wisckey [9] and LSM-Trie [10]. By performing the append operations, random write I/O operations are translated into sequential ones on the HDDs, which means high I/O efficiency, thus such data layout can bring high throughput for write operations.

While the above approaches show decent performance for write and range-query workloads respectively. Unfortunately, to the best of our knowledge, none of them can perform well for write and range-query simultaneously. For example, while write-order layout can get high write throughput, it has inherent shortcoming of poor random read performance in the range-query operations; the key-order layout would cost lots of time to sort the key-value items like LSM-tree or to search the targeted storage location like B$^+$-tree, which results in limited write throughput.

To bridge this gap, we propose a hybrid KV store, which combines the key-order and write-order layout together to organize key-value items in the systems. KT-Store consists of three parts, one LSM-tree, one trie and multiple TrieTables. These components are used to store the keys and the metadata of values, to index the TrieTables according to a given key, and to store the values, respectively. In KT-Store, the values among multiple TrieTables are organized by the key-order while the values within each TrieTable are organized by the write-order. Thus, such hybrid structure can achieve high performance for both write and range-query operations.

KT-Store separates values from keys and stores them into different locations to eliminate the unnecessary compaction of values for enhanced write performance. While this design is inspired by the idea of Wisckey [9], it differs from Wisckey in that it stores the values into multiple tables while Wisckey [9] stores them into a single table. By leveraging a trie and organizing all the TrieTables in a key-order fashion, KT-Store can also achieve high throughput for range-query.

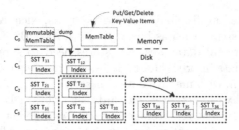

Fig. 1. LSM-tree data structure.

We implement KT-Store in RocksDB 5.7.2. Extensive evaluations demonstrate that KT-Store can simultaneously obtain encouraging write and range-query performance: it significantly outperforms RocksDB with $4.3 \times -12.6\times$ write performance and Wisckey with $54.2 \times -112.6\times$ range-query performance.

The proposed hybrid data layout scheme creates a better balance between write performance and range-query throughput. It can be applied in both HDDs and SSDs.

The following of this paper is organized as follows. Section 2 describes the related work. Section 3 describes the system design and implementation. Section 4 presents and discusses the evaluation results. Finally, we conclude this paper in Sect. 5.

2   Related Work

Key-order layout organizes key-value pairs ordered by the key. Log-Structured Merge-Tree (LSM-tree) is the typical structure, which was proposed by Patrick O'Neil et al. in 1996 [11]. LSM-tree is composed of multiple components, generally including one memory resident component and multiple disk resident components, as shown in Fig. 1. The key-value pairs in each component is sorted and arranged in lexicographical order. Each component size is limited to a predefined threshold, which grows exponentially. LSM-tree first uses an in-memory buffer, called MemTable, to hold the incoming KV items and keeps them sorted. When an MemTable exceeds its capacity threshold, it will be dumped into the hard disk as an immutable SSTable, such as T_{12}. Every disk component consists of multiple SSTables. Each SSTable contained the sorted KV items which have been sorted in the compaction procedure. During compaction procedure, KV items are merged and sorted. KV items of both C_i and C_{i+1} within the same key-range are firstly read into memory, then merged and sorted, and finally written back to C_{i+1} as the fix-sized SSTables. The compaction procedure is extremely I/O-intensive for repeated reads and writes, and dominates the disk I/Os of LSM-tree [2]. As a result, compactions that keep the key-value pairs in key-order layout bring write throughput decrease seriously. Several methods have been adopted to improve the write throughput key-order layout LSM-tree-based systems. First, fully utilizing the available hardware/software resources. PCP [12] makes use of the parallelism of CPUs and I/O devices. LOCS [13] leverages the multiple channels of an SSD. Second, reducing the unnecessary data blocks moving. Skip-tree [2] skips some compaction procedures. PebblesDB [14], VT-tree [3] reduce the data rewrite. Third, accelerating the data flow. bLSM [15] and PE [16] partition the key range into multiple sub-key range and confine compactions in hot data key ranges. Others, like [17] applies LSM-tree to non-volatile memories, and GTSSL [18] uses layered mix of storage devices such as Flash SSDs and magnetic disks.

Write-order layout organizes key-value pairs ordered by the write sequence like LSM-trie [10] and Wisckey [9]. LSM-trie [10] stores data in a hierarchical structure by sacrificing the supporting of range-query operations. Wisckey organizes values in a value-log file, named vLog. The values in vLog is ordered by the write sequence. When a key-value pair is inserted, Wisckey first separates the key and the value, and append the value to the vLog. Then Wisckey inserts the key and the value metadata into LSM-tree. The values are appended to vLog as the insert procedure goes on. The write throughput keeps a high level because Wisckey spends no time to sort the values. As the value are arranged in vLog by write-order, Wisckey implements the range-query operations by parallel search the targeted key-value pairs. Under SSD environment, Wisckey could get comparable range-query performance as RocksDB [9]. Although SSDs are widely used nowadays, hard disks are still the main devices for conventional data stores. The range-query operations of Wisckey performs undesirable in hard disks for the reason that the search procedure is through random I/Os and can't utilize the sequential I/Os.

Key-order data layout can obtain attractive range-query performance but bad write performance, while write-order data layout can obtain attractive write performance but bad range-query performance. In RocksDB, we insert 100 GB data volume with value size as 4 KB by random order and by sequential order. The result shows that random insert performance only reaches about 30% of sequential insert performance. In Wisckey, the range-query performance with the values is randomly arranged only reaches about 22% of that with the value is sorted when the value size is 4 KB [9] with SSDs. There remains a need to well balance the write performance and range-query performance. Consequently, we are motivated to propose a hybrid KV store, KT-Store, to obtain attractive write and range-query performance simultaneously in one typical key-value store.

3   Design and Implementation

3.1   The Basic Idea of KT-Store

For effective balancing write and range-query throughput, we suggest KeyTrie-Store (KT-Store), which is designed as a replacement of RocksDB or Wisckey. The major distinction of KT-Store is that it uses a new key-and-write hybrid data layout to organize values. Figure 2 depicts the overall architecture of KT-Store. Each KT-Store instance consists of three parts, one LSM-tree, one trie, and multiple TrieTables. The basic concept of organizing keys and light-weighted

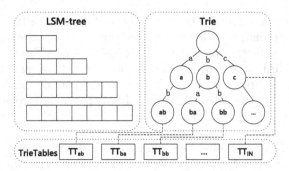

Fig. 2. The overall architecture of KT-Store (the strings in circles present the path from the root node to the child node or leaf node).

Table 1. The data structure of the trie node

Type	Property	Value
Internal node	ID	Denote the trie node and corresponding to one TrieTable
	Leaf flag	False
	Children mapping	Map to the child node with a mapping of <Character, Trie Node> (the character is the edge value in Fig. 2)
Leaf node	ID	Denote the trie node and corresponding to one TrieTable
	Leaf flag	True

value metadata into LSM-tree is similar to Wisckey. But different from Wisckey arranging values to one vLog, KT-Store leverages trie to split the input values into multiple TrieTables. Trie divides the whole key-range into multiple sub-ranges and sorts the sub-ranges in key-order. Every sub-range is correspond to a TrieTable, while trie keeps track of TrieTable locations in memory. TrieTables are in key-order among multiple TrieTables. Within a specific TrieTable, values are organized by write-order. Each leaf node of trie is correspond to a TrieTable, while all the internal nodes are correspond to one TrieTable TT_{IN}. In the write operation, all incoming values are appended at the end of the corresponding TrieTable to get the desirable write performance. In the range-query operation, the required values are stored in TrieTables under the key-and-write layout for the random I/Os can be avoided.

3.2 The Three Parts of KT-Store

The LSM-tree, which is originated from the conventional LSM-tree structure, is designed to store the key-metadata pairs. The value metadata includes its corresponding TrieTable ID, the offset in TrieTable, and the value size. We could locate the value based on the metadata.

One index structure of KT-Store, trie, is one of the most popular search trees, where keys are arranged in order. As shown in the Fig. 2, the root node

Fig. 3. The key-and-write hybrid order layout.

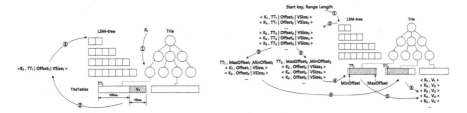

Fig. 4. The insert procedure of KT-Store.

Fig. 5. The range-query procedure of KT-Store.

is associated with empty string and each edge presents one character. The path from the root node to the child node contributes to a key prefix or a key. Hence, the child nodes of one common node share the same key prefix. When one key-value pair is inserted, trie nodes are searched to match the key prefix and the matched node determines the TrieTable.

The two node formats of trie, also shown in Table 1, are: (1) internal node; and (2) leaf node. For example, the leaf node 'ab' in Fig. 2 has the properties of $<ab, true, TT_{ab}>$. If there exists one key-value pair with key as 'b', its value would be appended to TrieTable TT_{IN}, since all the internal nodes are corresponding to one TrieTable TT_{IN}.

TrieTables are used to store the values. The values are organized by key-and-write hybrid order as shown in Fig. 3. For example, TT_{ab}, TT_{ba} and TT_{bb} are in lexicographical order which denote the key prefix of 'ab', 'ba' and 'bb' respectively. In a specific TrieTable, the values are arranged by write-order which is in key random sequence.

3.3   The Main Procedures in KT-Store

Write Procedure. When a insert request of a key-value pair K_1V_1 arrives, KT-Store would separate K_1V_1 into the key and the value. Figure 4 presents the insert procedure. First, search the trie nodes to match the key prefix. A node and corresponding TrieTable are created when the node doesn't exist. Second, the value of K_1V_1 would be appended at the end of corresponding TrieTable. Third, original key and value metadata are bounded as $<key, TrieTable\ ID|offset|value\ size>$ to be stored into LMS-tree. For example, for a key-value pair $<abh, Value>$, we search trie to get the 'ab' node first. Next, the value 'Value' will be append to TrieTable TT_{ab}. We presumes that the start offset is 500. Then the $<abh, T_{ab}|500|6>$ would be inserted into LSM-tree as one key-value pair. Since disk writes are performed sequentially for appending to the TrieTable, the write performance of KT-Store is much better than that of RocksDB.

Range-Query Procedure. A range-query operation first does the range-query operation in the LSM-tree to get the LSM-values in ② of Fig. 5. Then parse the LSM-values and group them by the TrieTable ID and compute the minimal offset and the maximal offset for each TrieTable in ③. Contiguously Read each TrieTable and get the data from the minimal offset to the maximal offset. This makes that every TrieTable would be read no more than once in one range-query operation. As known that disk I/Os cost a lot of time, KT-Store utilizes the sequential I/Os to decrease the range-query latency. Then, we pick the data that is read from TrieTables into key-value pairs according to their metadata. Last, aggregate the key-value pairs from TrieTables as output and return them in ⑤. For the TrieTable, we contiguously read the part rather than the whole TrieTable. Values are arranged on TrieTable by time sequence. Thus, in small length range-query operations or sequential insert, the targeted values only locate in part of one TrieTable.

Read Procedure. The read procedure begins with searching LSM-tree to find the key and the metadata, then it gets the value according to the metadata. KT-Store first searches the targeted TrieTable through the TrieTable ID, then it reads the targeted TrieTable to obtain the value. The beginning location is the offset address and the length is the value size. As this procedure is relatively straightforward and the page space is limited, here we ignore the detailed procedure.

3.4   Implementation

We build KT-Store with insert, update, read, delete and range-query interfaces. We integrate RocksDB 5.7.2 into KT-Store as the LSM-tree part. As RocksDB is written by C++, we develop KT-Store by C++. Except RocksDB, we implement all the other structures without utilizing other existing code. We implement the range-query API through the iterator in RocksDB referred to the RocksDB wiki in GitHub. We implement Wisckey also by integrate RocksDB 5.7.2 and develop it by C++ according its design.

3.5   Discussion

Reliability Mechanisms. When the system crashed, KT-Store needs to restore two types of data during the recovery procedure. One type is the key-value pairs that have been written into the TrieTables but have not been written into LSM-tree. The other is the key-value pairs that stored in MemTable of LSM-tree. For the former type, we utilize the write-ahead log to rerun the operations and ignore the data that have been appended to the TrieTable. For the latter one, we utilize the existing LSM-tree reliability mechanism to recover the LSM-tree. Trie works as an index of the TrieTable in the insert procedure. As the trie changes infrequently, we persist the trie to the disk when the trie changes. When the storage server crashed, we recover trie from the disk.

Trie Scalability. In the current implementation, we only use fixed levels in trie part of KT-Store. We acknowledge that dynamic level numbers that varies with data volume would further improve the performance of KT-Store and adapt to the workloads with un-uniform key distribution. However, the focus of this study is to balance the write and range-query performance well. Thus, we believe the fixed levels do not hurt the conclusions and contributions of this study. We will develop adaptive policy in the future work.

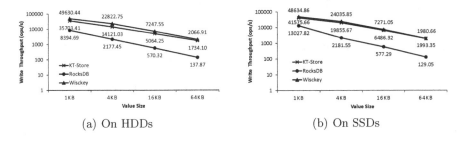

(a) On HDDs   (b) On SSDs

Fig. 6. The average write throughput of KT-Store, RocksDB and Wisckey for the value sizes vary from 1 KB to 64 KB for a 100 GB dataset.

4   Evaluation

4.1   Experiment Setup

We evaluate KT-Store and RocksDB, Wisckey on one Linux servers with hard disk devices and Solid State Drives. RocksDB is a persistent key-value store based on LSM-tree, started by Facebook. In every evaluation, we compare KT-Store with RocksDB and Wisckey. Except the compression type, which we set it as non-compression, the parameter values of RocksDB are applied to its defaulted settings as described following. The compaction style is level compaction which is the same as LSM-tree designed to be. The SSTable size is 64 MB and the ratio of C_{i+1} size to C_i size is 10. We use YCSB to generate workload traces, which are replayed in a light-weight workload generator. YCSB generates synthetic workloads with various degrees of read/write ratio, statistical distribution and value size. We configure YCSB to generate different datasets that are described in following subsections.

4.2 Write Performance

We load datasets with different value sizes and different scales into KT-Store, RocksDB and Wisckey to evaluate the write performance. The YCSB workload is set to 100% insert operations and insert key-value pairs randomly with uniform key distribution. We use the parameter of insert operations per second to evaluate the write performance.

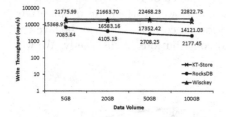

Fig. 7. The average write throughput of KT-Store, RocksDB and Wisckey for the data volumes vary from 5 GB to 100 GB for a 4 KB value size on HDDs.

Fig. 8. The average range-query latencies of KT-Store, RocksDB and Wisckey for different range length with the value size as 4 KB on HDDs.

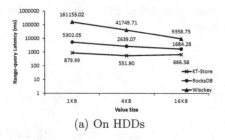

(a) On HDDs

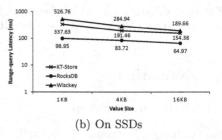

(b) On SSDs

Fig. 9. The average range-query latencies of KT-Store, RocksDB and Wisckey for different value sizes with querying 40 MB data from a 100 GB database.

We conduct experiments on KT-Store, RocksDB and Wisckey with the value size grows from 1 KB to 4 KB, 16 KB and 64 KB, and the data volume is 100 GB. Figure 6(a) shows the write throughput of KT-Store is about $4.3 \times -12.6\times$ of that of RocksDB with HDDs. With the value size increasing, KT-Store obtain better write throughput than RocksDB. Moreover, KT-Store has comparable write throughput with Wisckey, which is about 16% decrease in best case. For SSDs, KT-Store outperforms RocksDB in all the cases and has almost the same performance with Wisckey in the best case as Fig. 6(b) depicts. To evaluate the write performance under different scales, we conduct experiments with the data volumes are 5 GB, 20 GB, 50 GB and 100 GB and the value size as 4 KB as

Fig. 7 shows. With the data volume increasing, KT-Store outperforms RocksDB further. KT-Store matches Wisckey for about only 23% decrease. Without sorting every key-value pairs, KT-Store obtain attractive write performance than RocksDB, and get comparable write performance than Wisckey.

4.3   Range-Query Performance

YCSB supplies the range-query interface required two parameters, the 'startkey' and the 'recordcount'. The former denotes the first key searched in range-query operation. The latter denotes the number of key-value pairs that this range-query operation requires, that is, the range length. We measure range-query performance for workloads with different range length of 2000, 3000, 5000, 15000 and 20000, and with different value sizes of 1 KB, 4 KB and 16 KB respectively. The data that already in the store is with uniform key distribution and inserted randomly. And the data volume is 100 GB.

Figure 8 presents the comparison of average range-query latencies in KT-Store, RocksDB and Wisckey with HDDs. It can be found that the range-query performance of KT-Store is $54.2 \times -112.6 \times$ of that of Wisckey. And is $3.42 \times -5.81 \times$ of that of RocksDB. Figure 9(a) and (b) depict the range-query latencies of KT-Store, RocksDB and Wisckey for querying 40 MB data from a 100 GB database on HDDs and on SSDs. KT-Store outperforms Wisckey in all our cases. The range-query operation in RocksDB is complemented by the iterator, and the index block and data block have iterators respectively. First, the data block of targeted key-value pair is determined by the index block iterator. Then according to the index which contains the offset information, RocksDB reads the targeted key-value pairs. KT-Store utilizes the sequential I/Os to read the parted TrieTable into the memory. Then KT-Store matches each key with its value and returns the range-query result.

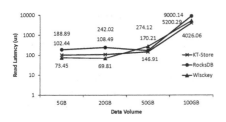

Fig. 10. The average read latencies of KT-Store, RocksDB and Wisckey for the different data volume with the value length of 4 KB.

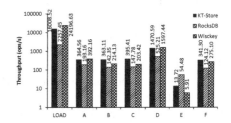

Fig. 11. The throughput of KT-Store, RocksDB and Wisckey in terms of the load and the six standard workloads with the key distribution is Zipf.

We attribute the difference of above evaluation to the following observations. First, RocksDB reads key-value pairs one by one with the key-order, but multiple versions of a same key can exist in different components in the same time.

Multiple component searches make that RocksDB can't fully utilize the sequential I/Os of hard disk and affects the range-query performance seriously. Second, KT-Store reads TrieTables one by one to fully utilize the sequential I/Os. The key-and-write hybrid order layout of TrieTables decreases the number of TrieTables that need to be read. As for Wisckey, the range-query operation relies on multiple read operations which results in massive random I/Os.

4.4   Read Performance

We conduct read operations on 5 GB, 20 GB, 50 GB and 100 GB YCSB datasets and evaluate the average read latencies on KT-Store, RocksDB and Wisckey on HDDs. We set the number of read operations as 1000 in each experiment and the value size as 4 KB. The dataset that already in the store is inserted randomly. Figure 10 shows the average read latencies of KT-Store, RocksDB and Wisckey. We can see that KT-Store shows a average read performance with RocksDB and Wisckey.

4.5   YCSB Standard Workload Evaluation

Our final set of experiments compares the performance with YCSB standard workloads, which can be treated as a basic benchmark for storage systems. Each of the six standard workload combines one or two operation types and can make us understanding the performance of the system. All the standard workloads are based on the Zipf distribution of key-value pairs.

Workload A is an update heavy workload. Workload B is a read mostly workload. Workload C is a read only workload. Workload D is a read latest workload which has 95% reads of the most recently inserted KV pairs. Workload E is a short ranges workload which does the short range-query operations. In Workload E, the max range-query length is 100 and the range-query length is under uniform distribution. Workload F is a read-modify-write workload. In Workload F, the key-value pairs will be read first, be modified next, and then be written back to the storage system.

We perform the six workloads on KT-Store, RocksDB and Wisckey with the 4 KB value size on HDDs. For each value size, we load 100 GB dataset with Zipf key distribution, then perform each workload and evaluate the throughput.

Figure 11 presents the operations throughput of KT-Store, RocksDB and Wisckey. In load stage, Workload A-D and F, KT-Store outperforms RocksDB by $1.8 \times -7.0\times$ throughput and obtains comparable performance with Wisckey. In Workload E, KT-Store performance is about $2.32\times$ of that of Wisckey. As have been discussed in Subsect. 3.5, each range-query almost read the whole TrieTable since the key-value pairs are organized by write-order in every TrieTable. In short range-query, KT-Store would only read one TrieTable in most case, while RocksDB maybe only read several blocks. Since the I/Os cost most time, reading the TrieTable in KT-Store would take much more time than reading several blocks in RocksDB. As a consequence, KT-Store performs a little worse than RocksDB in short range-query, but outperforms RocksDB in normal or long range-query as described in Subsect. 4.3. Moreover, KT-Store gets attractive performance compared with Wisckey in Workload E.

5   Conclusion

In this paper, we propose KT-Store, based on a key-and-write hybrid order data layout. KT-Store well balance the write and range-query performance. Extensive evaluations demonstrate that KT-Store can simultaneously obtain encouraging write and range-query performance: compared with key-order based RocksDB, write performance is improved by $4.3 \times -12.6\times$; compared with write-order based Wisckey, KT-Store has $54.2 \times -112.6\times$ range-query performance. The YCSB standard workload evaluation shows that KT-store balances RocksDB and Wisckey well in various workload. In the future, we will dynamically extend the trie and limit each TrieTable in a threshold size, which would make KT-Store adapted to more workloads. We will also do some research to collect garbage.

Acknowledgments. This work was partially supported by Youth Innovation Promotion Association of Chinese Academy of Sciences No. 2016146, the National Science Foundation of China under Grant No. 61303056, No. 61572377, No. 61602467 and No. 6173396, and the Natural Science Foundation of Hubei Province of China under Grant No. 2017CFC889.

References

1. Beaver, D., Kumar, S., Li, H.C., Sobel, J., Vajgel, P., et al.: Finding a needle in haystack: Facebook's photo storage. In: OSDI, vol. 10, pp. 1–8 (2010)
2. Yue, Y., He, B., Li, Y., Wang, W.: Building an efficient put-intensive key-value store with skip-tree. IEEE Trans. Parallel Distrib. Syst. **28**(4), 961–973 (2017)
3. Shetty, P., Spillane, R.P., Malpani, R., Andrews, B., Seyster, J., Zadok, E.: Building workload-independent storage with VT-trees. In: FAST, pp. 17–30 (2013)
4. Yao, T., et al.: A light-weight compaction tree to reduce I/O amplification toward efficient key-value stores. In: Proceedings of the 33rd International Conference on Massive Storage Systems and Technology (MSST 2017) (2017)
5. Comer, D.: Ubiquitous B-tree. ACM Comput. Surv. (CSUR) **11**(2), 121–137 (1979)
6. Olson, M.A., Bostic, K., Seltzer, M.: Berkeley DB. In: Conference on USENIX Technical Conference, p. 43 (1999)
7. Frühwirt, P., Huber, M., Mulazzani, M., Weippl, E.R.: InnoDB database forensics, pp. 1028–1036 (2010)
8. Rosenblum, M., Ousterhout, J.K.: The design and implementation of a log-structured file system. In: Thirteenth ACM Symposium on Operating Systems Principles, pp. 1–15 (1991)
9. Lu, L., Pillai, T.S., Gopalakrishnan, H., Arpaci-Dusseau, A.C., Arpaci-Dusseau, R.H.: WiscKey: separating keys from values in SSD-conscious storage. ACM Trans. Storage (TOS) **13**(1), 5 (2017)
10. Wu, X., Xu, Y., Shao, Z., Jiang, S.: LSM-trie: an LSM-tree-based ultra-large key-value store for small data. In: 2015 Proceedings of the 2015 USENIX Conference on USENIX Annual Technical Conference, pp. 71–82. USENIX Association (2015)

11. O'Neil, P., Cheng, E., Gawlick, D., O'Neil, E.: The log-structured merge-tree (LSM-tree). Acta Informatica **33**(4), 351–385 (1996)
12. Zhang, Z., et al.: Pipelined compaction for the LSM-tree. In: IEEE International Parallel and Distributed Processing Symposium, pp. 777–786 (2014)
13. Wang, P., et al.: An efficient design and implementation of LSM-tree based key-value store on open-channel SSD. In: Proceedings of the Ninth European Conference on Computer Systems, p. 16. ACM (2014)
14. Raju, P., Kadekodi, R., Chidambaram, V., Abraham, I.: PebblesDB: building key-value stores using fragmented log-structured merge trees. In: Proceedings of the 26th Symposium on Operating Systems Principles, pp. 497–514. ACM (2017)
15. Sears, R., Ramakrishnan, R.: bLSM: a general purpose log structured merge tree. In: Proceedings of the 2012 ACM SIGMOD International Conference on Management of Data, pp. 217–228. ACM (2012)
16. Jermaine, C., Omiecinski, E., Yee, W.G.: The partitioned exponential file for database storage management. VLDB J.- Int. J. Very Large Data Bases **16**(4), 417–437 (2007)
17. Kannan, S., Bhat, N., Gavrilovska, A., Arpaci-Dusseau, A., Arpaci-Dusseau, R.: Redesigning LSMs for nonvolatile memory with NoveLSM. In: 2018 USENIX Annual Technical Conference (USENIX ATC 18), pp. 993–1005. USENIX Association (2018)
18. Spillane, R.P., Shetty, P.J., Zadok, E., Dixit, S., Archak, S.: An efficient multi-tier tablet server storage architecture. In: Proceedings of the 2nd ACM Symposium on Cloud Computing, p. 1. ACM (2011)

GRAM: A GPU-Based Property Graph Traversal and Query for HPC Rich Metadata Management

Wenke Li[1], Xuanhua Shi[1(✉)], Hong Huang[1], Peng Zhao[1], Hai Jin[1],
Dong Dai[2], and Yong Chen[2]

[1] Services Computing Technology and System Lab,
Big Data Technology and System Lab,
Huazhong University of Science and Technology, Wuhan 430074, China
`xhshi@hust.edu.cn`
[2] Department of Computer Science, Texas Tech University,
Lubbock, TX 43104, USA

Abstract. In HPC systems, rich metadata are defined to describe rich information about data files, like the executions that lead to the data files, the environment variables, and the parameters of all executions, etc. Recent studies have shown the feasibility of using property graph to model rich metadata and utilizing graph traversal to query rich metadata stored in the property graph. We propose to utilize GPU to process the rich metadata graphs. There are generally two challenges to utilize GPU for metadata graph query. First, there is no proper data representation for the metadata graph on GPU yet. Second, there is no optimization techniques specifically for metadata graph traversal on GPU neither. In order to tackle these challenges, we propose GRAM, a GPU-based property graph traversal and query framework. GRAM uses GPU to express metadata graph in *Compressed Sparse Row* (CSR) format, and uses *Structure of Arrays* (SoA) layout to store properties. In addition, we propose two new optimizations, parallel filtering and basic operations merging, to accelerate the metadata graph traversal. Our evaluation results show that GRAM can be effectively applied to user scenarios in HPC systems, and the performance of metadata management is greatly improved.

Keywords: Rich metadata management · Property graph
Graph traversal · GPU

1 Introduction

Graph structures are widely used in various domains to solve real problems, such as friend recommendation in social networks where people are vertices and their relationships are edges, or shortest path selection in digital maps where locations

© IFIP International Federation for Information Processing 2018
Published by Springer Nature Switzerland AG 2018
F. Zhang et al. (Eds.): NPC 2018, LNCS 11276, pp. 77–89, 2018.
https://doi.org/10.1007/978-3-030-05677-3_7

are vertices and routes connecting them are edges. Among all the graph structures, property graph [3] is one commonly used one, whose vertices and edges are associated with arbitrary properties. Because of its richness in expressing the graph entities and their relationships, the property graph has been used widely in graph computing frameworks [13] and graph storage systems [1].

Recently, property graphs have been used in modeling metadata of large-scale parallel computing systems [7–9]. Unlike traditional metadata management [24] that relies on directory trees and *inode* data structure [22], property graph can utilize graph structure to represent and manage various entities and their complex relationships. This is particularly useful for the case where rich metadata like provenance is recorded and managed. In addition, using graph model, complex metadata queries can be easily expressed as graph traversal. To accomplish that, GraphTrek [7], an asynchronous graph traversal engine providing high access speed and supporting flexible queries, has been proposed and evaluated to show the effectiveness of property graph in managing rich metadata in HPC systems.

Because of the large volume of information contained in rich metadata, storing and querying them in property graph is still challenging. Although many property graph databases have been proposed and developed in recent years [2,4,17,23], they have limitations regarding speed and throughput during managing rich metadata in performance critical usage scenarios, such as user audit [9] and provenance query [21,25]. In these two scenarios, efficient rich metadata querying is needed, which brings significant burden on modern CPUs, particularly in computation speed and memory bandwidth. Harish et al. [14] have found that many graph algorithms run faster on GPU, for example, the *Single Source Shortest Paths* (SSSP) algorithm and *Breadth-first search* (BFS) algorithm implemented on GPU can provide more than 100 times speedup. As we have described before, queries on graph-based rich metadata can be easily mapped to level-synchronous graph traversal operations, with extra filtering and path selection. This inspires us to cooperate GPU to further enhance the performance of rich metadata management.

It is non-trivial to use GPU to accelerate graph-based rich metadata management. On the model side, it lacks a proper metadata graph representation on GPU. On the algorithm side, the parallelism of graph traversal is largely limited by the super-step in level-synchronous traversal. In order to fully utilize the potentials of GPU, new optimization techniques are required for graph traversal.

To this end, we propose GRAM, a GPU-based property graph traversal and query framework for HPC rich metadata management. Our design focuses on reducing memory access overhead and improving procedure efficiency and utilization of GPU. Specifically, the amount of data processed by rich metadata graph traversal could be very large due to the attached arbitrary properties. Hence, GPU's high memory bandwidth helps significantly in reducing the memory access latency and improving the efficiency of memory access. Furthermore, since the data unit processed by property graph is independent, we can make full use of GPU's parallelism and storage resources to further improve the performance.

In GRAM, we arrange data using the *Structure of Arrays* (SoA) layout. Specifically, the graph topological data (vertices and their connecting edges) are represented using *Compressed Sparse Row* (CSR) which consists of three arrays; the property data attached to vertices and edges are put separately in other arrays. Through our property graph representation and layout, the metadata management activities are translated into arrays operations. The property graph traversal to query rich metadata is becoming a n-step iterative process. There are two array operations in each step: detecting whether one of the properties conforms to the filter criteria and gathering the vertices/edges with a qualified label. In GRAM, these two operations on arrays are optimized by GPU, while the complex relationships between the arrays are suitable for CPU to process. In addition, we use parallel filtering and basic operations merging to optimize the performance of GRAM. Our contributions in this study are three-fold:

- To the best of our knowledge, we are the first to utilize GPU for managing graph-based rich metadata generated in HPC systems.
- We propose metadata graph representation on GPU, combining CSR graph structure and SoA layout to represent graphs to represent and store rich metadata information.
- We parallelize filtering and merge basic operations in GRAM, and experimental results show that our design improves the performance of property graph traversal and query in metadata management usage scenarios.

The rest of the paper is organized as follows. The design and implementation details of GRAM are presented in Sect. 2, including overall architecture, metadata graph representation on GPU, metadata graph operations model on GPU, metadata operations translating and GRAM's optimizations. We evaluate the performance of GRAM, and present the results in Sect. 3. Related work is given in Sect. 4. Section 5 concludes the paper.

2   Design and Implementation

GRAM is designed to manage HPC rich metadata using GPU. In GRAM, the rich metadata graphs are stored in arrays and the queries on rich metadata, i.e., the graph traversal operations are mapped to GPU operations on these arrays. More design and implementation details will be discussed in this section. Specifically, Sect. 2.2 introduces rich metadata graph representation on GPU. After that, Sect. 2.3 states how rich metadata graph operations are modeled on GPU. In addition, Sect. 2.4 presents the translation details of rich metadata management and property graph traversal and query. Finally, Sect. 2.5 describes two optimizations proposed in GRAM to enhance the rich metadata query performance.

2.1   Overall Architecture

We design and implement GRAM, a GPU-based framework for HPC rich metadata management. GRAM is designed to support HPC rich metadata query through property graph traversal on GPU. The overall architecture of GRAM is shown in Fig. 1. It includes four modules internally: Query Interface, Metadata Translating, Query Engine, and Storage. Query Interface module receives user's metadata management requests, and forwards the requests to Query Engine module. Query Interface module interacts with Metadata Translating module through basic query operations. Metadata Translating module translates the representation of the property graph and maps metadata to Storage module. In this way, Query Engine can directly operate on arrays stored in the Storage module. Storage return results to Query Engine for further processing. These four parts work together to perform rich metadata graph traversal and query.

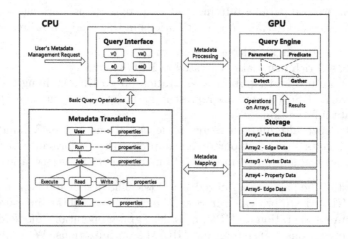

Fig. 1. Overall architecture of GRAM

The four components are designed in both GPU and CPU. Query Interface and Metadata Translating module are expected to run on CPU. They prepro-cess the rich metadata graphs before executing any operation on GPU. Users submit their queries through a sequence of API calls to Query Interface mod-ule. Query Interface module works as a coordinator with necessary functional APIs to translates users' queries into a sequence of basic query operations. These basic query operations are then dispatched to the Metadata Translating module. The Metadata Translating module handles the relationships between the entities of the property graph. The Metadata Translating module and Query Interface module collaborate together to translate the sequence of queries into metadata operations on the two modules (Query Engine and Storage) running on GPU.

Storage module and Query Engine module are running on GPU, which play a key role in reducing memory access overhead and improving procedure efficiency. The Storage module uses arrays to describe information of rich metadata. In addition, these arrays are abstracted by metadata graph representation on GPU, which are arranged together in a contiguous memory chunk to reduce the time of memory allocation, initialization, and management. In Query Engine module, the HPC rich metadata queries are turned into two basic array operations: the detecting operation and the gathering operation, which are performed on arrays stored in Storage module.

2.2   Metadata Graph Representation on GPU

As GRAM manages rich metadata by GPU-based property graph traversal and query, a suitable graph representation is needed. In GRAM, we design metadata graph representation with the GPU's benefits in mind. It is well known that, to take full advantage of GPU's high memory bandwidth, a coalesced memory access pattern is necessary, by which each cache line transmission contains more data required by the concurrent threads and then transferred to register files other than discarded. In other words, the data access instructions require less data traffic from memory to cache and register files. Considering the efficient and beneficial coalesced memory access pattern for GPU, we choose *Structure of Arrays* (SoA) instead of *Array of Structure* (AoS) as the layout of the property graphs, in which multiple arrays are used to hold the property values attached to vertices and edges of the graph. Comparing with AoS, SoA allows coalesced global memory accesses, which benefit GPU-based system. For the topological data of the graph, the commonly used *Compressed Sparse Row* (CSR) format is applied, simply because CSR format is easy to implement many graph algorithms (i.e., metadata graph traversal) in our vertex-centric programming model. Only CSR format can not meet our requirements for storing the properties of metadata, so more arrays are required in our graph representation.

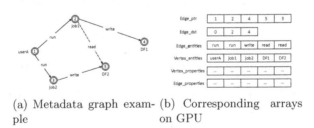

(a) Metadata graph exam- (b) Corresponding   arrays
ple   on GPU

Fig. 2. Metadata graph representation on GPU

Figure 2 shows a detailed example of the metadata graph representation. The topology of the graph is described by array *Edge_ptr* and array *Edge_dst* which construct the CSR structure. The property data including the IDs, names, types, values for vertices and edges are grouped into the other arrays that each array stores one simple data item for every vertice/edge. Importantly, these multiple arrays in Storage module are arranged together in a contiguous memory chunk to reduce the time of memory allocation, initialization, and management.

Algorithm 1. Detect(Frontier, PropertySet, Predicate and Marks)

1: Marks ← empty
2: **for** each Item in Frontier **do**
3:     **if** Marks.get(Item) == 0 **then**
4:         P ← PropertySet.read(Item)
5:         **if** Predicate(P) > 0 **then**
6:             Marks.set(Item)
7: return Marks

Algorithm 2. Gather(Frontier, Marks, NextFrontier, Collector)

1: NextFrontier ← empty
2: ResultMarks ← empty
3: **for** each Item in Frontier **do**
4:     **if** Marks.get(Item) > 0 **then**
5:         Coll ← Collector(Item)
6:         **for** each Result in Coll **do**
7:             **if** ResultMarks.get(Result) == 0 **then**
8:                 ResultMarks.set(Result)
9:                 NextFrontier.put(Result)
10: return NextFrontier

2.3   Metadata Graph Operations Model on GPU

As described above, the HPC rich metadata queries are translated into property graph traversals and finally mapped to array operations on GPU, which offers significantly better performance due to its high parallelism. In this section, we will introduce the array operations in GRAM's Query Engine module. Specifically, traversal and query in metadata graph are generalized into two basic array operations. By utilizing the array-based data layout, we focus on how the operations are performed on the arrays. Two types of basic operations are as follows:

- *Detect whether properties conform to the filter criteria:* During the detection of entities, one or more properties need to be filtered based on whether they conform to the criteria. Algorithm 1 presents the filter method. Different properties are filtered in a parallel or sequential manner. In addition, multiple filter criteria of properties can form a step of detection. Whether to parallelize the filtering depends on the procedure's efficiency. In addition, the multiple filters in each step is called combined filters. As shown in Fig. 3, combined filters of 1-step detection consist of two filters, and combined filters of 2-step detection consist of three filters.
- *Gather the vertices/edges with a qualified label:* The gathering operation collects all vertices conformed to the filter criteria into a new frontier queue. Algorithm 2 shows how it works. The frontier queue may be a set of edges or a set of vertices. The whole process is iterative and convergent, the frontier queue is either the intermediate results to process in next iteration or the correct results.

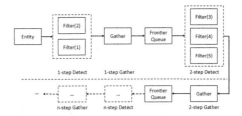

Fig. 3. The processing of n-step iterations

(a) The processing of vertex frontier array operations

(b) The processing of edge frontier array operations

Fig. 4. The processing of frontier array operations: detection and gathering on vertex/edge frontier

It is an iterative process to query metadata by operations on arrays. Furthermore, each step is composed of a detection operation and a gathering operation. Each iteration gets a new vertex/edge frontier queue. The detection and gathering operation of each iteration are shown in the Fig. 4a and b. There may be dependencies between steps of different iterations, but the data processed inside each iteration are independent. The synchronization step is achieved in BSP model. BSP operations leverage the parallelism of the GPU without any lock operations.

2.4 Metadata Operations Translating

GRAM manages rich metadata in a new fashion by introducing two basic operations on arrays. In Dai's previous research, GraphTrek [7] uses an asynchronous property graph traversal to query metadata. It defines property graph traversal operations based on an iterative query-building language. Several core methods in Query Interface module are applied to manage rich metadata. Query Interface module and Metadata Translating module cooperate to translate Graph-Trek's main traversal methods into corresponding operations on arrays mentioned above. This section describes the translation in detail.

– *Vertex/Edge selector: v(), e()*. The vertex selector $v()$ selects a specific set of vertices by setting a specific parameter, which represents the entry of property graph traversal to manage metadata in HPC systems. The edge selector $e()$ selects a specific edge set from all the edges of a vertex by a specific label. Both of these two methods are very important and can select a specific subset based on the label of the vertex/edge. In the implementation of GRAM, these two selection methods are transformed to gather the vertices/edges with a qualified label on vertex/edge frontier.

- *Property filters: va(), ea().* These two property filters have three parameters, property key, property values, and type of filter. Three types of filter include EQ, IN, and RANGE. Because each entity can have more than one property, multiple properties can be filtered by different property filters at the same time. In the implementation on the GPU, each filter turns to detect whether one of the properties conforms to the filter criteria.

Overall, metadata management is processed as graph traversal query, which in turn is translated into a series of operations on the corresponding arrays on GPU. The relationships between different entities and the storage schema for entities and properties are maintained on the CPU and then queried during the translation. After that, the main part of the query process which requires a large amount of data accesses and computation is dispatched to the GPU as a number of kernel functions launch that correspond to each operation on arrays. The CPU part manipulates a small amount of data structures that would involve dozens of to hundreds of successive random memory accesses, which could perform poorly on the CPU due to the low parallelism. The remaining part is suitable for GPU cause it can read and process the massive amount of data concurrently with its high bandwidth and computation power.

2.5 GRAM's Optimization

In this section, we describe two optimizations applied to the metadata management in property graph traversal and query fashion. The experimental results show that these two methods are effective. The design details are described as follows:

- *Parallel filtering.* In the detection phase, there are multiple types of filter criteria, which means that multiple properties of an entity are to be filtered. The filter criteria can be chosen to process serially or concurrently. Multiple filters are combined to detect concurrently. It is proved by our evaluations that the efficiency of concurrently detecting on combined filters is higher than that of serial selection.
- *Basic operations merging.* Metadata graph traversal and query is multi-step convergent iterations. The iteration in each step is based on two basic operations, detecting whether a vertex's property value conforms to some certain values, and gathering all the entities to a frontier queue as the next processing set. With the iteration of multiple steps merging, the performance of GRAM is improved.

Considering the requirements of HPC rich metadata management use cases, we design GRAM as graph traversal and query framework to manage rich metadata. The design and implementation of GRAM focus on managing rich metadata in a more efficient fashion.

3   Evaluation

3.1   Experiment Environment and Datasets

Our experiments are conducted on a NVIDIA Telsa K20m GPU with 6 GB main memory and 2688 CUDA cores. The GPU is installed on a machine with a 2.6 GHz Intel Xeon E5-2670 CPU and 64 GB memory.

To evaluate the metadata management capability of GRAM, we conduct experiments with GRAM on synthetic graphs. Our property graph datasets are generated as power-law metadata graphs by a RMAT graph generator [6], and during the generation, we also refer to Darshan log files [5]. In the graphs, vertices represent three kind of entities, user, job, and data files in Darshan log files, whereas edges reflect the relationships between them. We choose the same parameters as used in Dai's previous work [7] for the RMAT graph generator, that is $a = 0.45, b = 0.15, c = 0.15, d = 0.25$ for distribution parameters, 20 for graph scale and 16 for edge factor. The generated power-law graphs have moderated out-degree skewness, and each contains 2^{20} vertices and $16 * 2^{20}$ edges. Besides the graph topological data, we also generate several sets of uniformly distributed property values for both vertices and edges. When evaluating the 8-step graph traversal query, 8 sets of properties will be generated and used in each step for corresponding vertex and edge property checking.

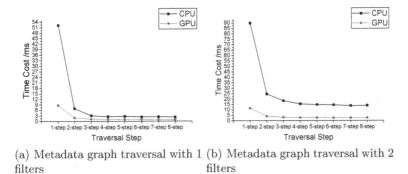

(a) Metadata graph traversal with 1 filters (b) Metadata graph traversal with 2 filters

Fig. 5. The each step time cost of 8-step metadata graph traversal with different filters

3.2   Evaluating on Graph Traversal with Filters

As described before, graph-based rich metadata management can be easily mapped to level-synchronous graph traversal operations, with extra filtering and path selection, which leads to more memory accesses and filtering computations than the traversal of normal graphs. Compared to traditional level-synchronous graph processing, using metadata graph to manage rich metadata requires to improve the performance of rich metadata queries through the high parallelism and high memory bandwidth of GPU. We compare the metadata queries on CPU and the metadata queries on GPU without considering the user scenarios in HPC systems. The metadata graph traversal begins with filtering all entities in this part of experiment. The number of filters determines the number of entities to process in next step. Furthermore, the number of entities is decreasing with the number of filters increasing. As shown in Fig. 5, we change the number of filters in each step in metadata graph traversal. Figure 5a shows each step time cost of 8-step metadata graph traversal with 1 filters. The evaluations on CPU are conducted by 16 threads. As shown in Fig. 5a, the time cost of metadata queries on CPU is 4.44 times lager than the time cost of metadata queries on GPU on average. In addition, with the number of filters increasing to 2, as shown in Fig. 5b, the ratio is 6.43 on average. The efficiency of metadata graph traversal and query on GPU is better with more filters.

While serving metadata queries by property graph traversal, some properties will be filtered. As the evaluation results show, CPU has limitations to manage rich metadata in use cases in HPC fields. GPU's high memory bandwidth helps significantly in reducing the memory access latency and improving the efficiency of memory access. In addition, GPU's parallelism and storage resources can further improve the performance of metadata management.

3.3   Metadata Management Performance

We evaluate the performance of GRAM on the synthetic graph datasets. As we described above, HPC rich metadata management requests are translated into metadata graph traversal and query, the features of which are determined by rich metadata management use cases. Unlike level-synchronous traversal described in Sect. 3.2, rich metadata management use cases begin with a certain vertex, and the number of entities in frontier queue is increasing with the depth of the traversal hierarchy. The level of metadata traversal is not deep depending on the HPC metadata management scenarios, and not less than 3 steps in most cases. Actually, Dai's previous work [7] has found that rich metadata traversal are no more than 8-step graph traversal typically. Therefore, we perform 1 to 8 step metadata graph traversal to audit user in both GRAM-CPU and GRAM-GPU. The filtering probability and the scale of graph dataset in each step, which greatly affect the performance of the metadata management, are determined by the variation of user audit. The performance of GRAM's metadata traversal is shown in Fig. 6a. The x-axis of Fig. 6a illustrates the traversal steps, while the y-axis denotes to the total traversal time. If the traversal level is low, the number of entities to process is relatively small, and the time cost is too small to omit. Overall, we can see that GRAM based on GPU can significantly improve the performance of traversal performance compared to graph traversal based on CPU.

As described in Sect. 2.3, it is an iterative process to manage metadata by operations on arrays. Furthermore, one or more properties need to be filtered according to the criteria. We use multiple detections to realize filtering parallelism. The number of filters influence the traversal performance of GRAM, so

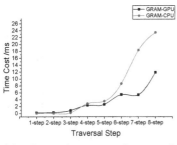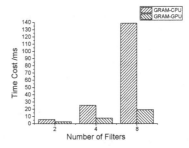

(a) The performance of traversal   (b) The performance of multiple detections

Fig. 6. The performance of rich metadata management

we execute the performance of graph traversal by changing the number of filters. As shown in Fig. 6b, we set the number of filters 2, 4, and 8 respectively, and the corresponding time cost grows with the increment of filter number. The GPU's advantage becomes more obvious when the filter number increases. We do not consider the filter number more than 8 due to usage scenarios.

4 Related Work

Using property graph to manage rich metadata is firstly proposed in Dai's previous work [9], and they have done many researches [7,8] in asynchronous property graph traversal for rich metadata management in HPC systems. Our work also translates rich metadata into one property graph, and uses property graph traversal and query to manage metadata. Dai's previous work [7,8] have focused on an asynchronous property traversal to manage metadata. In fact, the amount of data processed by metadata property graph traversal is large and property graph traversal requires more memory access. Our GPU-based property graph traversal framework for HPC rich metadata management can deal with the problems better.

Diverse property graph databases have been developed to manage property graph in recent years, such as Neo4j [23], DEX [2], G-Store [17], and Titan [4]. These property graph databases have been proposed to conduct property graph traversal and query, but the performance of these property graph databases in rich metadata management is limited. For example, Titan stores property graphs based NoSQL storage systems like HBase [15] or Cassandra [18], in which all vertices are mapped to different rows; edges and properties are mapped to separate columns in the rows of the related vertices. In fact, because of HPC system's requirements of rich metadata management, traversal and query for property graphs need to be more efficiently supported.

There are many distributed graph processing frameworks. The search structure of Pregel [19], PowerGraph [12], GraphX [13] and other distributed graph processing frameworks is level-synchronous, just like breadth first search structure. These distributed graph processing frameworks have focused on different problems, while we focus on rich metadata management in HPC systems.

Harish and Narayanan [14] have given the first CUDA implementations of various graph algorithms. Merrill et al. [20] have implemented a scalable high-performance BFS graph traversal using CUDA. Their concern has been the optimization strategies of the GPU graph traversal, while our focus is the optimization strategies of property graph traversal and query on the GPU. Totem [11] is a CPU-GPU hybrid graph processing engine that overcomes the GPU memory limitations by assigning workloads on CPU cores and GPU cores. MapGraph [10] is a parallel programming framework on GPU, using dynamic scheduling and two-stage decomposition strategy to balance workload thread-divergence problems. CuSha [16] is a user-defined vertex-centric graph processing frameworks that can process large-scale graphs on a GPU. The concern of these graph processing frameworks are not property graph, while HPC metadata property graph processing is more challenging.

5   Conclusions

In this work, we manage rich metadata in property graph traversal and query fashion. Proper graph representation for the metadata graph on GPU is needed. Furthermore, there is lack of optimization techniques specifically for graph traversal to utilize the potentials of GPU. We propose GRAM, a GPU-based property graph traversal framework for HPC rich metadata management. GRAM uses property graph representation on GPU, by which metadata management is transformed to operations on arrays. In addition, we use two optimizations, parallel filtering and basic operations merging, to accelerate graph traversal. The performance comparison of metadata management confirms that GRAM achieves better performance than metadata management on CPU. In addition, our GPU-based graph traversal and query method achieves better performance than the traditional level-synchronous approach.

Acknowledgement. The work is supported by the National Key R&D Program of China (No. 2017YFC0803700), NSFC (No. 61772218, 61433019, U1435217), and the Outstanding Youth Foundation of Hubei Province (No. 2016CFA032).

References

1. Blueprints. https://github.com/tinkerpop/blueprints
2. DEX. http://www.sparsity-technologies.com/
3. Property Graph. http://www.w3.org/community/propertygraphs/
4. Titan. http://thinkaurelius.github.io/titan/
5. Darshan Data (2013). ftp://ftp.mcs.anl.gov/pub/darshan/data/
6. Chakrabarti, D., Zhan, Y., Faloutsos, C.: R-MAT: a recursive model for graph mining. In: SDM (2004)

7. Dai, D., Carns, P., Ross, R.B., Jenkins, J., Blauer, K., Chen, Y.: GraphTrek: asynchronous graph traversal for property graph-based metadata management. In: CLUSTER (2015)

8. Dai, D., Chen, Y., Carns, P., Jenkins, J., Zhang, W., Ross, R.: GraphMeta: a graph-based engine for managing large-scale HPC rich metadata. In: CLUSTER (2016)

9. Dai, D., Ross, R.B., Carns, P., Kimpe, D., Chen, Y.: Using property graphs for rich metadata management in HPC systems. In: PDSW (2014)

10. Fu, Z., Personick, M., Thompson, B.: MapGraph: a high level API for fast development of high performance graph analytics on GPUs. In: GRADES (2014)

11. Gharaibeh, A., Beltrão Costa, L., Santos-Neto, E., Ripeanu, M.: A yoke of oxen and a thousand chickens for heavy lifting graph processing. In: CLUSTER (2012)

12. Gonzalez, J.E., Low, Y., Gu, H., Bickson, D., Guestrin, C.: PowerGraph: distributed graph-parallel computation on natural graphs. In: OSDI (2012)

13. Gonzalez, J.E., Xin, R.S., Dave, A., Crankshaw, D., Franklin, M.J., Stoica, I.: GraphX: graph processing in a distributed dataflow framework. In: OSDI (2014)

14. Harish, P., Narayanan, P.J.: Accelerating large graph algorithms on the GPU using CUDA. In: Aluru, S., Parashar, M., Badrinath, R., Prasanna, V.K. (eds.) HiPC 2007. LNCS, vol. 4873, pp. 197–208. Springer, Heidelberg (2007). https://doi.org/10.1007/978-3-540-77220-0_21

15. Khetrapal, A., Ganesh, V.: HBase and Hypertable for large scale distributed storage systems. Department of Computer Science, Purdue University, pp. 22–28 (2006)

16. Khorasani, F., Vora, K., Gupta, R., Bhuyan, L.N.: CuSha: Vertex-centric graph processing on GPUs. In: HPDC (2014)

17. Kumar, P., Huang, H.H.: G-Store: high-performance graph store for trillion-edge processing. In: SC (2016)

18. Lakshman, A., Malik, P.: Cassandra: a decentralized structured storage system. SIGOPS Oper. Syst. Rev. **44**(2), 35–40 (2010)

19. Malewicz, G., et al.: Pregel: a system for large-scale graph processing. In: SIGMOD (2010)

20. Merrill, D., Garland, M., Grimshaw, A.: Scalable GPU graph traversal. In: PPoPP (2012)

21. Muniswamy-Reddy, K.K., Holland, D.A., Braun, U., Seltzer, M.: Provenance-aware storage systems. In: USENIX ATC, pp. 43–56 (2006)

22. Tanenbaum, A.S., Bos, H.: Modern Operating System, 4th edn. Prentice-Hall, Upper Saddle River (2014)

23. Webber, J.: A programmatic introduction to Neo4j. In: SPLASH (2012)

24. Zhang, Q., Feng, D., Wang, F., Wu, S.: Mlock: building delegable metadata service for the parallel file systems. Sci. China Inf. Sci. **58**, 1–14 (2015)

25. Zhao, D., Shou, C., Maliky, T., Raicu, I.: Distributed data provenance for large-scale data-intensive computing. In: CLUSTER (2013)

GPU-Accelerated Clique Tree Propagation for Pouch Latent Tree Models

Leonard K. M. Poon[✉️] iD

The Education University of Hong Kong, Hong Kong SAR, China
kmpoon@eduhk.hk

Abstract. Pouch latent tree models (PLTMs) are a class of probabilistic graphical models that generalizes the Gaussian mixture models (GMMs). PLTMs produce multiple clusterings simultaneously and have been shown better than GMMs for cluster analysis in previous studies. However, due to the considerably higher number of possible structures, the training of PLTMs is more time-demanding than GMMs. This thus has limited the application of PLTMs on only small data sets. In this paper, we consider using GPUs to exploit two parallelism opportunities, namely data parallelism and element-wise parallelism, for PTLMs. We focus on clique tree propagation, since this exact inference procedure is a strenuous task and is recurrently called for each data sample and each model structure during PLTM training. Our experiments with real-world data sets show that the GPU-accelerated implementation procedure can achieve up to 52x speedup over the sequential implementation running on CPUs. The experiment results signify promising potential for further improvement on the full training of PLTMs with GPUs.

Keywords: GPU acceleration · Clique tree propagation
Pouch latent tree models · Parallel computing
Probabilistic graphical models

1 Introduction

Clustering [7,18] is a fundamental problem in machine learning. For soft clustering, the Gaussian mixture models (GMMs) are often used [23]. However, a GMM contains only one latent variable and can produce only a single clustering. This limitation may make GMMs not suitable for modern clustering applications, especially when the data sets contain many attributes and are multifaceted.

The *pouch latent tree models* (PLTMs) [28,29] have been proposed as a generalization of GMMs to allow multiple latent variables. They can produce clusterings on multiple facets and are more versatile for data of higher dimensions. They have been evaluated on several real-world data sets and have been shown better

© IFIP International Federation for Information Processing 2018
Published by Springer Nature Switzerland AG 2018
F. Zhang et al. (Eds.): NPC 2018, LNCS 11276, pp. 90–102, 2018.
https://doi.org/10.1007/978-3-030-05677-3_8

than GMMs in terms of model quality and clustering performance [27,29]. However, the structure learning of PLTMs can be more time-demanding than GMMs due to the considerably larger number of possible model structures. For GMMs, the structure learning typically involves only the estimation of the number of the mixture components. In contrast, the structure learning of PLTMs involves determining the number of latent variables, the cardinalities of the latent variables, and the connections among the latent variables and the observed variables. The onerous structure training of PLTMs may pose a serious challenge for applying PTLMs on large data sets. Consequently, previous studies considered data with less than 100 attributes and 2000 samples [27,29]. Those sizes of data sets may be regarded as at most moderate in the Big Data Era.

In recent years, graphical processing units (GPUs) have become more prevalent in scientific computing. They have been demonstrated to achieve significant speedup in different artificial intelligence applications that involve high dimensional data, such as those in the fields of computer vision [16,33], constraint satisfaction [5,15], and clustering [1,4,25,31].

In this paper, we consider the possibility of using GPUs to accelerate the training of PLTMs. We focus on the clique tree propagation algorithm for performing exact inference during the training process. The inference task is used for computing the likelihood and marginal probabilities on a data set during training. It is the most strenuous one and needs to be called recurrently for each data sample and each model structure. To evaluate the performance of the GPU-accelerated inference procedure, we use it to compute likelihood of a given PLTM on a given data set. This computation requires running inference on each data sample and exhibits resemblances to the other computationally intensive steps for PLTM training. Our study thus constitutes an important first step for using GPUs to accelerate the whole training process of PLTMs to make it feasible for application on larger data sets.

The rest of the paper is organized as follows. First, we review PLTMs and the inference procedure in Sects. 2 and 3. Then, we describe the GPU-accelerated inference procedure in Sect. 4. Next, we evaluate the performance of the procedure in Sect. 5. After that, we discuss related work in Sect. 6 and conclude the paper in Sect. 7.

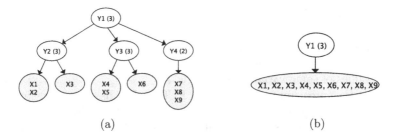

(a)   (b)

Fig. 1. (a) An example of PLTM. The observed variables are shown in shaded nodes. The numbers in parentheses show the cardinalities of the discrete variables. (b) A GMM depicted as a PLTM.

2   Pouch Latent Tree Models

A *pouch latent tree model* [28,29] is a tree-structured probabilistic graphical model. In the model, each internal node represents a latent variable, and each leaf node represents a set of observed variables. All the latent variables are discrete, whereas all the observed variables are continuous. A leaf node, also called *pouch node*, may contain a single observed variable or several of them. An example is shown in Fig. 1a. In the example model, X_1–X_9 are continuous observed variables and Y_1–Y_4 are discrete latent variables. For technical convenience, PLTMs are often treated as Bayesian networks [26].

Consider a PLTM with observed variables $\boldsymbol{X}$ and latent variables $\boldsymbol{Y}$. The dependency of a discrete latent variable Y on its parent $\Pi(Y)$ is characterized by a conditional discrete distribution $P(y|\pi(y))$. Let $\boldsymbol{W} \subseteq \boldsymbol{X}$ be the variables of a pouch node with a parent node $Y = \Pi(\boldsymbol{W})$. The models assume that, given a value y of Y, $\boldsymbol{W}$ follows the conditional Gaussian distribution $P(\boldsymbol{w}|y) = \mathcal{N}(\boldsymbol{w}|\boldsymbol{\mu}_y, \boldsymbol{\Sigma}_y)$, with mean vector $\boldsymbol{\mu}_y$ and covariance matrix $\boldsymbol{\Sigma}_y$. Denote the sets of pouch nodes and latent nodes by $\mathcal{W}$ and $\mathcal{Y}$, respsectively. The whole model defines a joint distribution over all observed variables $\boldsymbol{X}$ and latent variables $\boldsymbol{Y}$

$$P(\boldsymbol{x}, \boldsymbol{y}) = \prod_{W \in \mathcal{W}} P(\boldsymbol{w}|\pi(\boldsymbol{W})) \prod_{Y \in \mathcal{Y}} P(y|\pi(Y)). \qquad (1)$$

Given a model structure m, the parameters can be estimated by the EM-algorithm [13], which is well-known for estimating parameters of models with latent variables. When the model structure is unknown, a greedy search that aims to maximize a model selection score can be used [29].

The GMMs can be considered as a special case of the PLTMs. This is illustrated by the example GMM depicted in Fig. 1b. In the figure, all the observed variables X_1–X_9 in the GMM are drawn as a pouch node, which has a multivariate normal distribution conditional on its parent latent variable Y_1.

Similar to GMMs, PLTMs can be used for clustering. After training PLTMs on a given data set, the data can be partitioned using each of the latent variables Y. Each data point $\boldsymbol{d}$ can be classified to one of the states of Y by computing the posterior probability $P(y|\boldsymbol{d})$ based on the joint distribution defined by Eq. 1.

3   Clique Tree Propagation

Suppose the values of some variables $\boldsymbol{E} \subseteq \boldsymbol{X}$ are observed in a data sample. *Inference* refers to the computation of the posterior probability $P(\boldsymbol{q}|\boldsymbol{e})$, where $\boldsymbol{q}$ are the values of some variables $\boldsymbol{Q} \subseteq \boldsymbol{X} \cup \boldsymbol{Y}$.

Inference is a core computation task for PLTMs. It is used in the E-step of the EM-algorithm to estimate the values of the unobserved variables. It is also used to compute the cluster assignments after training PLTMs for cluster analysis. The inference task is time-demanding. It is a strenuous task and is recurrently called for each data sample and each model structure during PLTM training. Therefore, it is the first target of optimization for streamlining PLTM training.

Inference can be done on PLTMs similarly as the clique tree propagation (also known as belief propagation or junction tree algorithm) on conditional Gaussian Bayesian networks [20]. We describe the main steps of the inference algorithm and the numerical operations below. Readers are referred to [29] for more details on inference on PLTMs and to [11, 12, 20] for the general clique tree algorithm.

Construction of Clique Trees. Clique tree propagation requires converting the original model to a structure called clique tree $\mathcal{T}$ to organize the computation. Construction of clique trees is simple due to the tree structure of PLTMs. To construct $\mathcal{T}$, a clique C is added to $\mathcal{T}$ for each edge in M, such that $C = V \cup \{\Pi(V)\}$ contains the variable(s) V of the child node and variable $\Pi(V)$ of its parent node. A separator node is added for discrete node in the PLTM. It is used to connect the two clique nodes containing the separator variable. The resulting clique tree contains two types of cliques: discrete cliques with at most two discrete variables and mixed cliques with a discrete variable and multiple continuous variables.

Propagation. After a clique tree is constructed, propagation can be carried out on it. The clique tree propagation consists of four main steps: initialization of cliques, incorporation of evidence, message passing, and normalization.

Step 1 initializes the clique tree with the model parameters. The mean vectors and the covariance matrices of a pouch node are copied to its corresponding mixed clique. Similarly, the conditional probability table of a discrete node is copied to the corresponding discrete clique. Note that the root node does not have a corresponding clique. Its marginal probability is multiplied to one of the cliques corresponding to its child variables.

Step 2 incorporates the evidence (observed values) in the potentials. For brevity, here we consider only the case where there is no missing value in the data. Consider a pouch node with variables W and with observed values e. Furthermore, denote its parent variable by Y. This step involves computing the probability values $P(y| W = e) = \mathcal{N}\left(e | \boldsymbol{\mu}_y, \boldsymbol{\Sigma}_y\right)$, where $\mathcal{N}\left(\cdot | \boldsymbol{\mu}_y, \boldsymbol{\Sigma}_y\right)$ denote the normal distribution conditional on the value of Y.

Step 3 performs a series of computations, each on a small part of the clique tree, as represented by the process of message passing. Since the clique tree does not contain any loop, exact inference can be performed by message passing in two phases. In the first phase, messages are passed from the leaf clique nodes to the clique corresponding to the root node of the PLTM. We denote that clique as *pivot*. In the second phase, messages are passed from the pivot along the opposite direction back to the leaf nodes.

For the mixed cliques, the messages to be sent from the mixed cliques have already been computed in step 2. The message passing between discrete cliques requires performing multiplication and division between potential tables of two variable and message of one variable. It also requires marginalizing out a variable to compute the message of one variable from a potential table with two variables.

After message passing is completed, the likelihood for a data sample can be determined from the pivot clique. The likelihood is equal to the sum of the potential entries of the pivot clique.

Step 4 normalizes the clique potentials by multiplying each entry by a particular constant. It converts the potential values to proper probability values. This entails dividing each entry of the potential tables by the likelihood value.

Complexity. Let n be the number of nodes in a PLTM, c be the maximum cardinality of a discrete variable, and p be the maximum number of variables in a pouch node. The time complexity of the inference is dominated by the steps related to message passing and incorporation of evidence on continuous variables. The message passing step requires $O(nc^2)$ time, since each clique has at most two discrete variables due to the tree structure. Incorporation of evidence requires $O(ncp^3)$ time. Although the tree structure of PLTMs allows tractable inference, with time complexity linear to the number of nodes, the inference can still needs much time as it has to be performed many times during PLTM training.

Table 1. Data units for performing inference for each data sample. p denotes the number of variables in a pouch node. c and c' denote the cardinalities of the variables of the node and its parent node, respectively, in the PLTM.

Node type in PLTM	Node type in clique tree	Data type	Number of entries
Continuous node	Mixed clique	Mean vector	$p \times c'$
		Covariance matrix	$p^2 \times c'$
Discrete node	Discrete clique	Potential table	$c \times c'$
All node	Separator	Message to parent	c'
		Message to children	c

4   Implementation for GPUs

In this section, we describe how to adapt the inference of PLTMs for running efficiently on GPUs. We refer to the CPU as host and the GPU as device below.

Data Representation. The original implementation of PLTMs[1] used the object-oriented approach to represent the data units as objects. This poses a challenging for GPU programming. Instead, we represent the data units as arrays for easy access by the GPU kernel functions. The data units required for performing inference are shown in Table 1. Each node in a PLTM has a corresponding clique

---

[1] https://github.com/kmpoon/pltm-east.

node and a separator node in the clique tree.[2] The third column describes the type of data associated with each clique node. The fourth column indicates the number of entries for each type of data.

Device Memory. The data units in Table 1 are used to store interim computation results during inference. Therefore, a clique tree (with cliques and separators) has to be allocated for each data sample. The data units are allocated at the beginning of likelihood computation so that they are available for the inference on multiple data samples in parallel. The memory is allocated in a single batch to minimize the number of API calls. We also allocate an array on the device for storing the likelihood results computed during inference.

Host-Device Memory Transfer. In the first step of inference, the clique tree needs to be initialized by the parameters of the model. We perform initialization on the host and then transfer the array data representing the initialized clique tree to the device. We transfer only the data corresponding to one instance of the clique tree. The data is then copied to the arrays representing the other instances of clique trees for all data samples on the device. This process saves the amount of data needed to be transferred between host and device. It also simplifies the way to transfer the model parameters to the device as the parameter values are now contained in an array rather than in objects. Besides, the data units representing the clique tree, the data matrix is also transferred to device in a single batch at the beginning to minimize the number of transfers.

Parallelism. Most computation of clique tree propagation for PLTMs is done during the two steps for incorporating evidence and message passing. Such computation involves the calculating multiple entries in a target potential or message. Those entries of a potential or message can be calculated in parallel. We refer to this parallelism as element-wise parallelism [36].

However, due to the tree structure of PLTMs, the number of entries of a potential or message is usually small compared to general Bayesian networks. The parallel computation of those entries may not be sufficient to utilize all GPU cores. For example, suppose the latent variables in a PLTM has at most 10 states. Then, the number of entries of a message is at most 10. This is much smaller than the number of cores on a GTX 1080 Ti GPU (3584).

To fully utilize the massive computation power in GPUs, we need to consider other parallelism opportunities. When the likelihood is being computed, the clique tree propagation is performed on each sample independently. Hence, they can be performed in parallel. This form of parallelism is referred to as data parallelism. As a comparison, the number of samples we used in the experiments can be at most 2310. With both data parallelism and element-wise parallelism, the GPU cores can be better utilized.

---

[2] An exception is that the root node sometimes does not have a separate clique node.

Host-Device Coordination. Compared with CPUs, GPUs can perform parallel computation very efficiently. However, they have fewer programming language support and programming on them can be tedious. Therefore, we program on the CPUs to mainly determine the sequence of computation and to delegate the highly parallelizable tasks to GPUs. For example, message passing is conducted one node at a time since the message computation needs to follow the aforementioned scheme of flow. We use the host to determine the sequence of the message passing and then invokes the kernel calls for computing the messages for each node. The kernel call is run with multiple threads on different data samples and different elements of messages in parallel.

Device-Host Memory Transfer. The computed likelihood values of the data samples are stored in an array on the device after the clique tree propagation. The array is transferred to the host and the values are then multiplied together on the host to obtain the final likelihood value on the whole data set.

It is worthwhile to note that the data structure storing the interim results do not need to be transferred back and forth between the host and the device. This reduces the transfer cost. The same situation also applies for the EM-algorithm. Only the final parameter estimates need to be transferred back to the host. The intermediate values can be kept in the device memory during the different iterations of EM steps. This show one resemblance between the inference procedure and the full PLTM training.

Implementation. We implemented the inference method based on the CUDA framework [30]. We used the Scala language for host programming and the JCuda package[3] as Java bindings for CUDA. The Java ecosystem was used to reduce the coding effort since the original implementation was written in Java.

Table 2. Descriptions of real-world data sets from the UCI repository used in the experiments.

Data set	#Attributes	#Classes	#Samples
glass	9	6	214
image	18	7	2310
ionosphere	33	2	351
vehicle	18	4	846
wdbc	30	2	569
wine	13	3	178
yeast	8	10	1484
zernike	47	10	2000

---

[3] http://www.jcuda.org.

5 Experiments

To evaluate the performance of the GPU-accelerated inference method, we use it to compute likelihood of a given PLTM on a given data set. We ran it using real-world data sets in our experiments. We used the same models and data sets in [29] to estimate the actual improvement in practice. Table 2 show the properties of the data sets used. The EAST algorithm [29] were used to train PLTMs on those data sets.

Three different implementations of the clique tree propagation were used in the experiments. The first implementation runs sequentially on CPUs. It serves as a baseline for comparison. The second one performs inference on different data samples in parallel on CPUs. The last one uses the GPUs for acceleration as described previously. The experiments were conducted on a Linux computer with a Xeon E3-1245 v5 CPU and a GeForce GTX 1080 Ti GPU. The CPU has fours cores (eight threads) running at a base frequency of 3.5 GHz. The GPU has 28 streaming multiprocessors with 3584 CUDA cores running with a maximum clock rate of 1.6 GHz.

Table 3. Average elapsed wall time in milliseconds (ms) for computing the likelihood of PLTMs on real-world data sets using different implementations of clique tree propagation, including the sequential version running on CPUs, the parallel version running on CPUs, and the accelerated version running on GPUs. The speedups over the baseline sequential version are shown in parentheses.

	Average running time (ms)		
	CPU-sequential	CPU-parallel	GPU
glass	8.62	3.89 (2x)	1.42 (6x)
ionosphere	48.37	14.67 (3x)	2.76 (18x)
image	1421.30	290.14 (5x)	27.52 (52x)
vehicle	169.90	41.54 (4x)	4.89 (35x)
wdbc	143.04	37.77 (4x)	3.28 (44x)
wine	7.54	2.94 (3x)	1.44 (5x)
yeast	50.74	15.06 (3x)	2.07 (25x)
zernike	2655.91	576.26 (5x)	97.75 (27x)

We measure the performance of the three implementations using the elapsed wall time for likelihood computation. We report the time averaged over 100 repetitions. The experiments first ran 20 repetitions at the beginning to allow the just-in-time compiler of the Java Runtime to come into force. Those repetitions were not included for time reporting.

Table 3 reports the average running time for one likelihood computation in milliseconds. The results show that the GPU acceleration could achieve 5x to 52x speedups over the baseline sequential version. It also attained 2x to 12x speedups over the parallel version running on CPUs. The higher speedups over the sequential version were obtained on data sets with larger number of samples (e.g. image, vehicle, wdbc, yeast, and zernike). This can be explained by the fact that the larger number of samples provide better opportunity for exploiting data parallelism by GPUs.

The considerable speedups shown above has demonstrated that the GPUs can be effective in accelerating the inference task. Since the other computationally intensive tasks in the PLTM training procedure show similar parallelism opportunities as the likelihood computation task, our results signify the promising potential for further improvement on the full training of PLTMs with GPUs.

Table 4. Proportion of GPU activities and overall running time used for the incorporation of evidence routine.

	% of GPU activities	% of Overall time
glass	64.81%	3.02%
ionosphere	82.46%	8.07%
image	98.94%	86.13%
vehicle	97.10%	46.26%
wdbc	84.92%	15.74%
wine	71.70%	3.32%
yeast	32.71%	1.49%
zernike	99.60%	94.25%

To identify possible bottlenecks of the current GPU implementation, we used the tool nvprof provided in the CUDA Toolkits to profile different kernel calls. Table 4 lists the proportion of GPU activities and overall running time spent on the incorporation of evidence routine. We see that this task constituted most of the GPU activities except on the yeast data set. It even accounted for 86% and 94% of the overall running time on image and zernike, respectively. The two data sets happened to take the longest running time.

To understand this phenomenon, recall that the incorporation of evidence routine for a pouch node has a time complexity linear to the cardinality of its parent variable and cubic to the number of the variables in the pouch node. We compare the model properties on four data sets with similar number of attributes in Table 5. We see that the models for image and zernike both have a large pouch node with 10 and 16 variables, respectively. The problem is exacerbated by the high cardinality of the parent variables of those two pouch nodes. The PLTM for wdbc also has a large pouch node with 10 variables. However, that node has a smaller parent cardinality and the model has small pouch size on average. Hence, the incorporation of evidence routine was less significant on wdbc. Future study may consider how to tackle this bottleneck to make PLTMs more efficient on larger data sets.

Table 5. Properties of PLTMs on four data sets. The average and maximum number of variables in a pouch node are listed in the second and third columns, and the cardinality of the parent variable of the pouch node with maximum size in the fourth column.

	Average pouch size	Maximum pouch size	Parent cardinality
ionosphere	4.6	7	3
image	3.6	10	11
wdbc	3.0	10	5
zernike	7.8	16	6

6   Related Work

Several works used GPUs to speed up the EM-algorithm for parameter estimations [3,19,22]. They exploited the innate data parallelism due to the independent computation for different data samples. However, they considered only GMMs. The inference procedure on GMMs is simpler than PLTMs.

Some works used GPUs for belief propagation on Bayesian networks. Element-wise parallelism and arithmetic parallelism was exploited for inference [36] and a statistical model was further proposed for optimizing the GPU parameters [37]. Another work formulated the inference procedure in terms of operations on sparse matrices [6]. Existing matrix packages utilizing GPU computation (e.g. PyTorch) were then used to run the inference. Some studies used better memory layout and better scheduling among memory transfers and works to improve the inference performance on GPUs [5,15]. Some works studied belief propagation on Markov Random Fields used for stereo processing on GPUs [14,17,33]. They considered an approximate inference method that requires passing messages to the same nodes multiple times.

The above methods on inference usually achieve significant speedup only when the potential tables have a large number of entries. However, due to the tree structure in PLTMs, the parallelism exploited by those methods may not be as effective on PLTMs. Besides, our work considered data parallelism that were not available as those methods ran inference on only a single data sample.

PLTMs were proposed as a generalization of the latent tree models (LTMs). The LTMs [34] have discrete observed variables, in contrast to the continuous observed variables in PLTMs. The LTMs have found numerous applications such as density estimation, multidimensional clustering, spectral clustering, and topic modeling [24,35]. Attempts have been made to speed up the training of LTMs. Spectral methods [2] and Progressive EM [9] have been proposed for faster parameter estimation. Heuristics were proposed to guide the structure learning [10,21,32] and Stepwise EM was used to reduce the number of samples involved in computation [8]. Those attempts did not utilize any parallelism for GPUs. On the other hand, their acceleration techniques can possibly be combined with our proposed method to achieve higher speedups.

7   Conclusion

In this paper, we show how to use GPUs to accelerate the clique tree propagation algorithm for PLTMs. We use the likelihood computation task to evaluate the performance of the inference procedure. The experiment results demonstrate that substantial speedups (up to 52x) can be achieved. As the other computationally intensive tasks in the PLTM training procedure show similar parallelism opportunities as the likelihood computation task, our results signify promising potential for further improvement on the full training of PLTMs with GPUs. The GPU acceleration techniques discussed in this paper can be crucial in applying PTLMs on massive data sets.

Acknowledgement. Research on this article was supported by the Education University of Hong Kong under grant RG70/2017-1018R, the Top-up Fund of Dean's Research Fund, and the Small Research Grant of the Department of Mathematics and Information Technology.

References

1. Al-Ayyoub, M., Abu-Dalo, A.M., Jararweh, Y., Jarrah, M., Sa'd, M.A.: A GPU-based implementations of the fuzzy C-means algorithms for medical image segmentation. J. Supercomput. **71**(8), 3149–3162 (2015)
2. Anandkumar, A., Chaudhuri, K., Hsu, D., Kakade, S.M., Song, L., Zhang, T.: Spectral methods for learning multivariate latent tree structure. In: Advances in Neural Information Processing Systems, vol. 24, pp. 2025–2033 (2012)
3. Araújo, G.F., Macedo, H.T., Chella, M.T., Estombelo Montesco, C.A., Medeiros, M.V.O.: Parallel implementation of expectation-maximisation algorithm for the training of Gaussian mixture models. J. Comput. Sci. **10**(10), 2124–2134 (2014)
4. Arefin, A.S., Riveros, C., Berretta, R., Moscato, P.: kNN-MST-agglomerative: a fast and scalable graph-based data clustering approach on GPU. In: 7th International Conference on Computer Science Education, pp. 585–590 (2012)
5. Bistaffa, F., Bombieri, N., Farinelli, A.: An efficient approach for accelerating bucket elimination on GPUs. IEEE Trans. Cybern. **47**(11), 3967–3979 (2017)
6. Bixler, R.M.: Sparse matrix belief propagation. Master's thesis, Virginia Tech (2018)
7. Bouveyrona, C., Brunet-Saumard, C.: Model-based clustering of high-dimensional data: a review. Comput. Stat. Data Anal. **71**, 52–78 (2014)
8. Chen, P., Zhang, N.L., Liu, T., Poon, L.K.M., Chen, Z., Khawar, F.: Latent tree models for hierarchical topic detection. Artif. Intell. **250**, 105–124 (2017)
9. Chen, P., Zhang, N.L., Poon, L.K.M., Chen, Z.: Progressive EM for latent tree models and hierarchical topic detection. In: Proceedings of the Thirtieth AAAI Conference on Artificial Intelligence, pp. 1498–1504 (2016)
10. Choi, M.J., Tan, V.Y.F., Anandkumar, A., Willsky, A.S.: Learning latent tree graphical models. J. Mach. Learn. Res. **12**, 1771–1812 (2011)
11. Cowell, R.G., Dawid, A.P., Lauritzen, S.L., Spiegelhalter, D.J.: Probabilistic Networks and Expert Systems. Springer, New York (1999). https://doi.org/10.1007/b97670

12. Darwiche, A.: Modeling and Reasoning with Bayesian Networks. Cambridge University Press, Cambridge (2009)
13. Dempster, A.P., Laird, N.M., Rubin, D.B.: Maximum likelihood from incomplete data via the EM algorithm. J. R. Stat. Soc. Ser. B (Methodol.) **39**(1), 1–38 (1977)
14. Eslami, H., Kasampalis, T., Kotsifakou, M.: A GPU implementation of tiled belief propagation on markov random fields. In: Eleventh ACM/IEEE International Conference on Formal Methods and Models for Codesign, pp. 143–146 (2013)
15. Fioretto, F., Pontelli, E., Yeoh, W., Dechter, R.: Accelerating exact and approximate inference for (distributed) discrete optimization with GPUs. Constraints **23**(1), 1–43 (2018)
16. Grauer-Gray, S., Kambhamettu, C., Palaniappan, K.: GPU implementation of belief propagation using CUDA for cloud tracking and reconstruction. In: IAPR Workshop on Pattern Recognition in Remote Sensing, pp. 1–4 (2008)
17. Grauer-Gray, S., Cavazos, J.: Optimizing and auto-tuning belief propagation on the GPU. In: Cooper, K., Mellor-Crummey, J., Sarkar, V. (eds.) LCPC 2010. LNCS, vol. 6548, pp. 121–135. Springer, Heidelberg (2011). https://doi.org/10.1007/978-3-642-19595-2_9
18. Jain, A.K., Murty, M.N., Flynn, P.J.: Data clustering: a review. ACM Comput. Surv. **31**(3), 264–323 (1999)
19. Kumar, N.S.L.P., Satoor, S., Buck, I.: Fast parallel expectation maximization for Gaussian mixture models on GPUs using CUDA. In: 11th IEEE International Conference on High Performance Computing and Communications, pp. 103–109 (2009)
20. Lauritzen, S.L., Jensen, F.: Stable local computation with conditional Gaussian distributions. Stat. Comput. **11**, 191–203 (2001)
21. Liu, T.F., Zhang, N.L., Chen, P., Liu, A.H., Poon, L.K.M., Wang, Y.: Greedy learning of latent tree models for multidimensional clustering. Mach. Learn. **98**(1–2), 301–330 (2015)
22. Machlica, L., Vanek, J., Zajic, Z.: Fast estimation of Gaussian mixture model parameters on GPU using CUDA. In: 12th International Conference on Parallel and Distributed Computing, Applications and Technologies, pp. 167–172 (2011)
23. McLachlan, G.J., Peel, D.: Finite Mixture Models. Wiley, New York (2000)
24. Mourad, R., Sinoquet, C., Zhang, N.L., Liu, T., Leray, P.: A survey on latent tree models and applications. J. Artif. Intell. Res. **47**(1), 157–203 (2013)
25. Pangborn, A.D.: Scalable data clustering using GPUs. Ph.D. thesis, Rochester Institute of Technology (2010)
26. Pearl, J.: Probabilistic Reasoning in Intelligent Systems: Networks of Plausible Inference. Morgan Kaufmann Publishers, San Mateo (1988)
27. Poon, L.K.M.: Clustering with multidimensional mixture models: analysis on world development indicators. In: Cong, F., Leung, A., Wei, Q. (eds.) ISNN 2017. LNCS, vol. 10261, pp. 153–160. Springer, Cham (2017). https://doi.org/10.1007/978-3-319-59072-1_19
28. Poon, L.K.M., Zhang, N.L., Chen, T., Wang, Y.: Variable selection in model-based clustering: to do or to facilitate. In: Proceedings of the 27th International Conference on Machine Learning, pp. 887–894 (2010)
29. Poon, L.K.M., Zhang, N.L., Liu, T., Liu, A.H.: Model-based clustering of high-dimensional data: variable selection versus facet determination. Int. J. Approx. Reason. **54**(1), 196–215 (2013)
30. Sanders, J., Kandrot, E.: CUDA by Example: An Introduction to General-Purpose GPU Programming. Addison-Wesley Professional, Boston (2010)

31. Shalom, S.A.A., Dash, M., Tue, M.: Graphics hardware based efficient and scalable fuzzy c-means clustering. In: Proceedings of the 7th Australasian Data Mining Conference, vol. 87, pp. 179–186 (2008)

32. Wang, Y., Zhang, N.L., Chen, T.: Latent tree models and approximate inference in Bayesian networks. J. Artif. Intell. Res. **32**, 879–900 (2008)

33. Xu, Y., Chen, H., Klette, R., Liu, J., Vaudrey, T.: Belief propagation implementation using CUDA on an NVIDIA GTX 280. In: Nicholson, A., Li, X. (eds.) AI 2009. LNCS (LNAI), vol. 5866, pp. 180–189. Springer, Heidelberg (2009). https://doi.org/10.1007/978-3-642-10439-8_19

34. Zhang, N.L.: Hierarchical latent class models for cluster analysis. J. Mach. Learn. Res. **5**, 697–723 (2004)

35. Zhang, N.L., Poon, L.K.M.: Latent tree analysis. In: Proceedings of the Thirty-First AAAI Conference on Artificial Intelligence, pp. 4891–4897 (2017)

36. Zheng, L., Mengshoel, O.: Exploring multiple dimensions of parallelism in junction tree message passing. In: Proceedings of the 2013 UAI Application Workshops: Big Data meet Complex Models and Models for Spatial, Temporal and Network Data (2013)

37. Zheng, L., Mengshoel, O.: Optimizing parallel belief propagation in junction treesusing regression. In: Proceedings of the 19th ACM SIGKDD International Conference on Knowledge Discovery and Data Mining, pp. 757–765 (2013)

HPC-SFI: System-Level Fault Injection for High Performance Computing Systems

Yanqi Wang, Qi Zhang, Yi Liu[(⊠)], and Depei Qian

Sino-German Joint Software Institute,
Beihang University, Beijing 100191, China
wangyanqi0114@outlook.com, liuyi97@263.net

Abstract. Resilience/fault-tolerance has become a key challenge for large-scale parallel systems. To ensure reliability of high performance computing systems, various kinds of techniques have been proposed, such as hardware-level fault-tolerance, checkpointing, replication, algorithm-base fault-tolerance, etc. There are also many software systems to monitor and handle system-failures, e.g. management and job-scheduling system of HPC systems. To evaluate the effectiveness of these systems, it is necessary to provide some kind of tool to inject failures in a HPC system. This paper proposes HPC-SFI, a system-level fault injection tool for HPC systems. Basically, HPC-SFI can generate three kinds of system-failures in a HPC system including in-node faults, failure in the interconnection network and failure of storage/parallel-file system. In addition, HPC-SFI can inject system-faults in pseudo-random model according to pre-defined parameters and probabilities. Preliminary experimental results demonstrate effectiveness of the tool.

1 Introduction

With the scaling up of high performance computers in recent years, resilience, or fault-tolerance, has become a key challenge. Currently, top-ranking supercomputers generally have tens of thousands of processors, e.g. the Summit [1] has 8,712 processors and 26,136 GPUs, while the number of processors in the Sunway TaihuLight [1] is 40,960. Along with the increasing of system scale, hardware/software-failures occur more frequently. Statistics show that the MTBF (mean time between failure) of current most powerful supercomputers has reduced to several hours.

To ensure reliability of high performance computing systems, various kinds of techniques have been proposed, such as hardware-level fault-tolerance, checkpointing, replication, algorithm-base fault-tolerance, etc. There are also many software systems to monitor and handle system-failures, e.g. management and job-scheduling system of HPC systems. To evaluate the effectiveness of these systems, it's necessary to provide some kinds of tools to generate various kinds of failure in HPC systems. However, current fault injection tools either focus on injection of soft-errors and their influences over high-level applications, or inject system-level failure in emulated environments (e.g. virtual machines) to guarantee flexible control over the system.

This paper proposes HPC-SFI, a system-level fault injection tool for HPC systems. Unlike current fault injection tools, our HPC-SFI inject hardware/software-failures in

© IFIP International Federation for Information Processing 2018
Published by Springer Nature Switzerland AG 2018
F. Zhang et al. (Eds.): NPC 2018, LNCS 11276, pp. 103–113, 2018.
https://doi.org/10.1007/978-3-030-05677-3_9

real physical systems. Therefore is more suitable for machine vendors and developers of fault-tolerant-related system software to evaluate the effectiveness of their fault-tolerant mechanisms.

Main characteristics of HPC-SFI include:

(1) HPC-SFI can inject three kinds of failure to a HPC system: in-node faults, failure of the interconnection network and failure in storage/parallel-file-system. Typical in-node faults include processor halt, memory error, network interface/disk failure as well as the system halts.

(2) HPC-SFI cannot only inject deterministic failure in a HPC system, but also generate failure in pseudo-random model according to pre-set parameters and probabilities, which are more approximate to actual systems.

(3) The injected failure can be recovered after a predefined time period.

The rest of this paper is organized as follows. Section 2 discusses our methods of fault-injection; Sect. 3 introduces architecture of the system and implementation detail. Section 4 presents preliminary experimental results; Sect. 5 discusses related work and the paper is concluded in Sect. 6.

2   Approaches

2.1   Types of Failures

Possible hardware/software faults or failure in high performance computer systems are diverse. To make things simple, our HPC-SFI focuses on system-level failure, which means under this kind of failure, part or entirely of the system cannot work correctly. These failure either occur inside computing nodes, or outside the nodes, i.e. in interconnection network or storage system.

Based on the above discussion, our HPC-SFI considers three kinds of failures, described as follows:

(1) **In-node faults/failures**

In-node faults/failures can be further divided into faults/failures in a different component of the node, e.g. processors, memory, network interface card, etc. In addition, crash-down of an entire node should also be considered.

(2) **Failure of interconnection network**

This kind of failure either occurs in network cable or in switches. Obviously it will cause communication errors in multiple nodes.

(3) **Failure of storage or parallel file system**

Current high performance computers generally use dedicated storage systems together with parallel file systems to provide high-throughput I/O and shared storage to parallel applications running in different nodes, while the in-node hard-disk just used as system startup. Failure of storage or parallel file system may occur in various components of the storage system or dedicated I/O nodes, and will influence file-accesses of computing nodes.

2.2   Injection Methods

Different HPC systems have different hardware configurations, and generally come from different vendors. As a software tool, it is difficult for HPC-SFI to obtain controls over dedicated equipment such as interconnection switch or RAID array. In other words, some kinds of failures cannot be generated directly, as a substitution, we generate "effect" of the corresponding failure, e.g. failure of a switch will cause communication interruptions on all the nodes that connected to the switch, failure of storage or parallel file system will cause the corresponding file volume mounted to file systems of each node unable to access.

Table 1 shows phenomenon and injection methods of failure supported by HPC-SFI. As shown in the table, the in-node fault injection acts as the basis of the system, because the other two types of failures, the failure of interconnection network and storage system, are implemented upon the in-node fault injection, that is, inject failures in multiple specific nodes simultaneously.

Table 1. Failure phenomenon and injection methods

Kind of failures	Component	Phenomenon	Injection method
In-node fault/failure	Entire node	System halt	Halt the system by shell commands
	Processor	1-n processor (cores) stop working	Process forcibly consumes processor resources
	Memory	Contents of memory units error	Modify the specified memory content
	Network interface	Communication error	Disable HBA card by shell commands
	In-node fixed-disk	Disk error	Destroy the super block of the disk partition
	File volume access	Volume access error	Destroy the disk file resources
Failure of interconnection network		Communication interruptions in all of the related nodes	Disable HBA cards in all of the related nodes
Failure of storage or parallel file system		File volume access error in all of the related nodes	Destroy parallel file system

As for in-node fault injection, actually most of the in-node faults/failures can be generated using Linux shell commands except memory-fault injection, which is implemented in two forms: i. a kernel module which can access entire memory space; ii. a user-level interface which can be invoked by applications to modify its own data.

Another problem that needs to be solved is the recovery after the failure injection. Considering the system scale of current HPC systems, it is impractical to reboot each node after it is injected faults/failures, instead, the node must be recovered to its original state after a fault injection. Due to that most failures are generated using shell commands, it is easy to recover under the control of the system. The only one failure that need special treatment is the network-related failures, after the HBA card or NIC card is disabled, the node becomes isolated and cannot receive later recovering commands, in this situation, the node must be self-recovered, which is implemented using a shell script working in sequence of "*disable-delay-enable*".

2.3   Deterministic vs. Pseudo-random Fault Injection

To approximate actual failure in HPC systems, the HPC-SFI supports two fault-injection model: the deterministic fault-injection and pseudo-random fault-injection.

(1) Deterministic fault injection

Generate determined failures according to the specified parameters, such as a node, time, and the fault type.

(2) Pseudo-random fault injection

The fault probability is specified by setting the node range and the number of faulty nodes, the time range, and the fault type range. The fault can be generated according to the fault model, so as to simulate the actual running of HPC systems.

In actual HPC systems, the occurrence of faults/failures is non-deterministic and generally unpredictable. We define a four-tuple of fault-injection pseudo-random probability model for HPC systems to describe the probability of fault-injection execution:

$$P_{injec} = \langle T, R, NUM, F \rangle \qquad (1)$$

Where T indicates that within a certain time range, R is the range of the nodes to be tested, NUM is the specified number of injection nodes, and F is the type range of the fault. The above parameters are defined, and a fault injection model is generated by a pseudo-random probability model. Such fault injection is more approximate to the occurrence of faults in real systems and can be used to evaluate the effectiveness of fault-tolerant diagnostics.

HPC-SFI tool failure is generated by the model, and the user can generate a fault parameter configuration by specifying a description file. In the configuration file provided by the tool, the user sets the relevant parameters according to requirements to define the four-tuple of fault injection probability model.

The process is as follows:

```
select NODE[R];
while NUM
  NUM --;
  rand(f);  rand(k);
  while Time
    inject FAULT[f] to NODE[k];
    Time --;
  end
end.
```

This program generates a corresponding fault injection model based on the fault description to implement fault injection control.

3 System Architecture and Implementation

Figure 1 shows the architecture of HPC-SFI. The HPC-SFI tool mainly consists of two parts: the first part is the *master* running in a control node; the second part is the *node-part* running on each node of the target HPC system.

In each node, an application process, named *HPC-SFI broker*, runs in the background waiting for commands from the *master*. On receiving a fault injection command, the *HPC-SFI broker* invokes the *In-node injection module* to generate corresponding faults/failures in the node. The *master* communicates with the *HPC-SFI brokers* via management network of the target HPC system. The *In-node injection module* can also be invoked by other application processes, at this time, the *master* is overridden and fault injection is controlled by the user-defined application.

In the *master*, the *model-generation module* parses the *failure description file* defined by the user, generates the fault parameter profile based on the description file, and uses these fault parameters to determine the type and time of a fault injection. In order to assess the effectiveness of fault injection, we measure reliability parameters such as test coverage and latency when performing the appropriate fault injection.

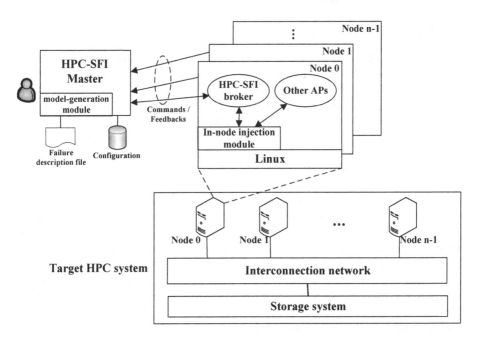

Fig. 1. Architecture of the system.

HPC-SFI realizes three types of failure of HPC system: in-node faults, failure of interconnection network, and failure of storage or parallel file system. Because the failure of the interconnection network and the failure of the storage parallel file system are generated based on the node fault, various faults of the traditional physical machine have been realized: memory faults, processor faults, network communication faults and disk faults.

Memory failure can be injected with a single bit or multiple byte error. The memory-fault injection program requires a scheme to modify the specified memory content, partially or completely setting. The virtual address of the process is converted into a physical address, and the process code segment data are directly modified in the memory according to the physical address, so as to achieve the purpose of fault injection. The Linux kernel module mechanism is introduced to obtain the privilege of modifying any specified memory location.

As mentioned in Sect. 2.2, failure of the interconnection network and storage system are implemented on the basis of in-node fault injection. For instance, when user specifies a switch-failure in the *fault description file*, the *model-generation module* parses the description, looks for the nodes that connects to the failure switch according to the configuration of the target system, then determines the nodes that need to be injected a network interface failure, after that, multiple fault-injection commands are sent to the nodes simultaneously.

4   Experiment Results

4.1   Methodology

We evaluate the HPC-SFI in a cluster environment with four nodes. The experimental target node is an Intel CPU-based computer system running Linux operating system Ubuntu16.04 with 1 GB of memory and 4.13 kernel versions. Unlike current fault injection tools, our HPC-SFI inject hardware/software-failures in real physical systems. So application-level workloads do not affect HPC-SFI fault injection. For the experiment to clearly show the effectiveness of fault injection, we use matrix multiplication as the workload, which consists of multiple loop of the initialization step of input matrix data and the multiplication step.

In our experiments, firstly, we run the workload on the target system and start the HPC-SFI fault injection tool; the user then generates a fault of the specified type by configuring the relevant parameters; after that, the master node sends the message parsing package to the target node, and performs fault injection on the target node. After the fault-injection, the main control node waits for a specific time interval to observe the response of the target system, collect and analyze the fault response records. Specifically, we measure fault injection latency as well as the probabilistic distribution under pseudo-random mode. The fault-injection latency is the elapsed time from the sending of a fault/error injection command in the master to the completion of fault-injection in the specified node.

4.2   Experiment Results

In the experiment, we mainly test the probability of node failure injection and the coverage of the test between nodes. Tables 2 and 3 show the statistical analysis results of fault injection data. Each table provides specific information about the behaviors of the fault injection system. From the system perspective, HPC-SFI can effectively inject the faults to the system node. Further influence of the running state of the application, and diagnose the effectiveness of fault injection through the abnormal behaviors of the application. In the experiment, we realize three types of fault injection. At the same time, we also test the tool from the three directions: fault injection probability, node coverage range and fault delay.

Table 2. Results of injecting memory and processor faults on the single node.

Faulty component	Failure activation probability	Monitoring information	Times of fault node detected	Detected probability	Average fault-injection latency (ms)	Phenomenon
Memory (Injection times T = 20)	100%	System log	20	100%	163.67	The system log shows that the memory contents have been rewritten. The process interrupts an error and sets the SIGNAL
		Processor	19	95%		
	50%	System log	11	55%	226.67	
		Processor	11	55%		
Processor (Injection times T = 20)	100%	System status	20	100%	35.71	The process is forcibly stopped; or the node crashes and needs to be restarted
		Processor				

The date in Table 2 is based on the single-node fault injection, and is capable of verifying the validity of injecting memory and processor faults. To better simulate the random generation of node failure in a cluster. We set the trigger probability in the model-generation module. In the single-node memory fault injection experiment, we set the trigger probability to be 50% and 100% respectively. Through the fault injection of the tool, it can be found that the fault can be injected into the specified position accurately. By observing the system log and processor behavior, and testing the corresponding injection delay, the validity of the tool can be proved. In the process of the memory fault injection, different injection locations and injection time affect different system behaviors. Since the data required to execute the partial loader code has been loaded into the cache, subsequent data does not have to interact with memory, so the fault diagnosis is delayed and the fault is not fully reflected in the application process, but the system log file can reflect the effective injection of the fault.

Table 3. Results of injecting disk faults on the nodes in the cluster.

Faulty component	Number of fault nodes	Node	Selected times	Detected probability	Average fault-injection latency (ms)	Phenomenon
Disk (Injection times T = 50; Node = 4)	2	Node 1	35	48%	41.09	A partition that is not mounted cannot be mounted properly and displays a disk error; the partition being mounted cannot be read or written properly
		Node 2	39	50%	50.67	
		Node 3	41	46%	49.29	
		Node 4	35	56%	45.45	
	3	Node 1	24	70%	46.14	
		Node 2	25	78%	53.17	
		Node 3	23	82%	50.81	
		Node 4r	28	70%	49.17	

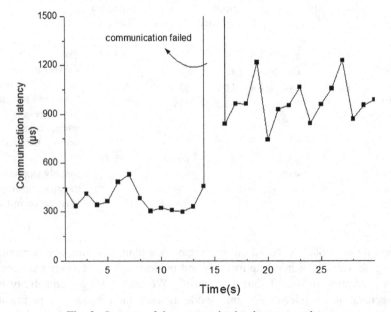

Fig. 2. Latency of the communication between nodes.

The failure model of the fault injection tool is generated by the user through the configuration description file. The tool defines the fault injection probability model by setting relevant parameters according to the specific fault injection requirements. According to the four-tuple of fault injection pseudo-random probability model, we set the test node range R to 4, the specified injection node number NUM is 2 and 3 respectively, and the F fault type is a disk fault. We test the fault injection for parallel file systems with the node coverage, and the results are shown in Table 3. Through the fault injection of the tool, it is proved that the setting of the node parameter can be applied to the fault model, and the fault injection probability conforms to the parameter setting. This kind of fault injection tool based on pseudo-random probability model can be more close to the actual system environment in the choice of fault injection.

We affect normal node communication through the fault injection tool, and the impact of the failure is reflected in the latency of node information interaction. In the HPC system, it is necessary for the fault injection tool to restore part of the fault and maintain communication, and at the same time, tries not to cause permanent failure to nodes to ensure the experiment. As showed in Fig. 2, when the fault is being injected, the message transmission delay between nodes changes dramatically and is much greater than the normal time. After a certain time, the fault will recover itself and normal communication between nodes will resume.

5 Related Work

Fault injection technique provides the capacity of evaluating the risibility of HPC system with synthetic failure occurring in hardware, system, as well as applications. To emulate the effect of failure in HPC, extensive studies have been conducted to explore different fault injection methods. Generally, current work fall into three categories: hardware-implemented fault injection, software implemented fault injection, and simulator and virtual machine based fault injection.

Hardware-implemented fault injection works by triggering errors in hardware with specialized device, such as setups producing electromagnetic interference and radiation [2, 3], or changing the voltage or current of target circuit board [4]. This type of method can mimic failure caused by environmental factors. However, it increases the risk of damage to the target hardware. Furthermore, it is difficult to control the fault location and triggering time.

Software-implemented fault injection method, on the other hand, generates emulated fault effect by inserting instruction into the application or triggering specific system command. Compared with the hardware-implemented counterpart, this type of method provides more flexibility and controllability. Therefore, many existed fault injection tools are implemented in software. For instance, Han et al. [5] proposed DOCTOR, a software implemented fault injection tool that injects hardware and software fault for distributed real-time system. Taking advantage of function available in the operation system, DOCTOR is able to inject architecture-independent hardware errors e.g., memory, CPU and communication fault and their combination, as well as system-level error. What's more, DOCTOR introduces temporal types and probability distribution for fault injection, which empowers the function of injecting realistic errors. Carreira et al. [6]. presented Xception, which injects realistic system and application faults in software by programming the debugging hardware available in modern processors. Based on the hardware feature, faults injected by Xception can affect any process running on the target system. Since software implemented fault injection dependent on the available function in target operation system and hardware, the variety of fault may be limited.

Simulator and virtual machine based fault injection, which emulates fault by revising the instruction of a virtual machine or serves as a module of full-system simulator, e.g., Gem5 [7], is eligible for performing various kinds of synthetic faults to HPC. Since this type of method is independent of hardware architecture and easy to control triggering time and location, there has become an increasing amount of literature focus on virtualization-based fault injection. For example, Guan et al. [8] proposed a fine-grained fault injector on top of QEMU [9] that emulates both software error and hardware failure by intercepting and corrupting instruction issued by an application before they be sent to the host kernel. Levy et al. [10] designed a virtualization based fault injection framework that mimics hardware errors both in individual node and across nodes in HPC system. By integrating error executor running on a virtual machine monitor in each node with error scheduler for dispatching deterministic and stochastic errors across HPC system, their framework is able to mimic more realistic faults in HPC. The main disadvantage of the simulator and virtual based fault injection method is the performance overhead, especially those work in full-system simulator.

6 Conclusion

In this paper, we propose a system level fault injection tool called HPC-SFI for HPC system. It utilizes software implemented fault injection to inject hardware/software failure into actual physical systems, and is intended for validation and evaluation of high-performance computing systems. We implemented a fault injection tool, HPC-SFI, which injected HPC systems with three types of failure: in-node faults, interconnection network failure, and storage/parallel file system failure. It can generate faults according to the parameters and probability, making it closer to the actual system. To avoid some irreversible damage to the node, it can be recovered after a specified time period. HPC-SFI was implemented on a linux cluster system, and extensive experiments were conducted, demonstrating its power and utility. We are also exploring the issues about the specification of fault injection and more extensive fault coverage. After these extensions, we will conduct more practical experiments.

Acknowledgments. The research presented in this paper has been supported by National Key R&D Program of China under grant No. 2016YFB0200100 and Natural Science Foundation of China under Grant No. 91530324.

References

1. The Top500 List, June 2018. http://www.top500.org
2. Karlsson, J., Liden, P., Dahlgren, P., et al.: Using heavy-ion radiation to validate fault-handling mechanisms. IEEE Micro **14**(1), 8–23 (1994)
3. Gunneflo, U., Karlsson, J., Torin, J.: Evaluation of error detection schemes using fault injection by heavy-ion radiation. In: 1989 The Nineteenth International Symposium on Fault-Tolerant Computing. Digest of Papers, pp. 340–347. IEEE (1989)

4. Hsueh, M.C., Tsai, T.K., Iyer, R.K.: Fault injection techniques and tools. Computer **30**(4), 75–82 (1997)
5. Han, S., Shin, K.G., Rosenberg, H.A.: Doctor: an integrated software fault injection environment for distributed real-time systems. In: 1995 Proceedings of International Computer Performance and Dependability Symposium, pp. 204–213. IEEE (1995)
6. Carreira, J., Madeira, H., Silva, J.G., et al.: Xception: software fault injection and monitoring in processor functional units (1995)
7. Binkert, N., et al.: The Gem5 simulator. SIGARCH Comput. Arch. News **39**(2), 1–7 (2011)
8. Guan, Q., Debardeleben, N., Blanchard, S., et al.: F-SEFI: a fine-grained soft error fault injection tool for profiling application vulnerability. In: 2014 IEEE 28th International Parallel and Distributed Processing Symposium, pp. 1245–1254. IEEE (2014)
9. Bellard, F.: QEMU, a fast and portable dynamic translator. In: USENIX Annual Technical Conference, FREENIX Track, vol. 41, p. 46 (2005)
10. Levy, S., Dosanjh, M.G.F., Bridges, P.G., et al.: Using unreliable virtual hardware to inject errors in extreme-scale systems. In: Proceedings of the 3rd Workshop on Fault-tolerance for HPC at Extreme Scale, pp. 21–26. ACM (2013)

Data Fine-Pruning: A Simple Way to Accelerate Neural Network Training

Junyu Li[1], Ligang He[1(✉)], Shenyuan Ren[1], and Rui Mao[2]

[1] The University of Warwick, Coventry, UK
{j.li.9,liganghe,shenyuanren}@warwick.ac.uk
[2] Shenzhen University, Shenzhen, Guangdong, People's Republic of China
mao@szu.edu.cn

Abstract. The training process of a neural network is the most time-consuming procedure before being deployed to applications. In this paper, we investigate the loss trend of the training data during the training process. We find that given a fixed set of hyper-parameters, pruning specific types of training data can reduce the time consumption of the training process while maintaining the accuracy of the neural network. We developed a data fine-pruning approach, which can monitor and analyse the loss trend of training instances at real-time, and based on the analysis results, temporarily pruned specific instances during the training process basing on the analysis. Furthermore, we formulate the time consumption reduced by applying our data fine-pruning approach. Extensive experiments with different neural networks are conducted to verify the effectiveness of our method. The experimental results show that applying the data fine-pruning approach can reduce the training time by around 14.29% while maintaining the accuracy of the neural network.

Keywords: Deep Neural Network · Data pruning · SGD
Acceleration

1 Introduction

Scaling up layers and parameters in modern neural networks improves the performance dramatically and enables the discovery of sophisticated high-level features. However, it also presents enormous challenges such as the training efficiency of Deep Neural Network (DNN).

Many novel training algorithms and deep neural networks have been designed and achieved good performance with benchmark datasets and even in industrial practices. For instance, Constitutional Neural Networks (CNN) demonstrates impressive performance in areas such as image recognition and classification; Very Deep Constitutional Networks (VGG) uses an architecture with tiny convolution filters and shows a significant improvement in network performance; Deep Residual Network (ResNet) is developed to ease the training of the networks that

© IFIP International Federation for Information Processing 2018
Published by Springer Nature Switzerland AG 2018
F. Zhang et al. (Eds.): NPC 2018, LNCS 11276, pp. 114–125, 2018.
https://doi.org/10.1007/978-3-030-05677-3_10

are substantially deeper than those used previously and gain the accuracy from considerably increased depth of the networks; Wide Residual Networks (WRN) that advances from ResNet contains a more complex architecture of network and outperforms regular deep ResNets in accuracy and efficiency.

Different configurations of DNN may lead to different level of accuracy and training efficiency (i.e., time consumption). Therefore, much research has been conducted to find the better configuration of the networks. Many endeavours have also been devoted to accelerating the training process by parallel computing. Our work does not focus on the optimization of the network configuration, but takes another approach. We assume that the configuration of the network has been optimized (or is fixed) with given settings of hyper-parameters such as the learning rate and the number of epochs. We propose to simplify the training process by reducing the training time of each epoch (regardless of the network configuration). In this approach, we dig into the training process, monitor and analyse the loss trend of each training instance. A novel method, named with Data Fine-pruning training, is developed to reduce the time consumption of training a model by sensibly and temporarily pruning a fraction of input training data in each training instance. The experimental results show that comparing to regular training, our approach is effective with majority nets and can reduce the training time by about 14.29% while maintaining the accuracy of the network.

The remainder of this paper is organized as follows. Section 2 introduces research backgrounds and motivations of our work. Section 3 reviews recent remarkable works that are related to our work. Section 4 detailed demonstrates our methods of analysing individual data, the way we run data pruning and formulations of time saved applying our approach. Section 5 illustrates the experiment results we did. Finally, a conclusion is addressed in Sect. 6.

2 Background and Motivation

DNNs have recently led to a series of breakthroughs in many fields such as speech recognition and image classification. Many novel learning algorithms are designed to build an effective model from a set of data and towards a prediction goal, where the model maps each input data to a prediction. Modern DNNs are typically powered by a vital training algorithm: Mini-batch Stochastic Gradient Descent (BSGD). However, there exists a heavy data dependence in the BSGD training which extremely limits the degree of parallelism.

2.1 Mini-batch Stochastic Gradient Descent

BSGD is the most widely used weight updating algorithm in recent notable neural networks. It takes a batch of data instead of using only one example each time as the input data for training. The weights of networks are same for all the instances in a batch during the forward propagation, and the changes in the weights depend on an average loss of a batch data. One core benefit of BSGD is that the changes in weights become much steadier than those in regular Stochastic Gradient Descent (SGD). Moreover, BSGD training can take the advantage of parallel computing by parallelising the calculations within a batch, so that the processing efficiency can further increase.

$$\omega_{t+1} = \omega_t - \gamma \frac{1}{b} \sum_{i=1}^{b} \nabla_{\omega_t} \ell(f_{\omega_t}(x_i), y_i) \tag{1}$$

where b is the size of a batch data, ω is a weight vector, γ is a learning rate, and $\ell(f_\omega(x), y)$ is a loss function measuring how wrong the model is in terms of its ability to estimate the relationship between data x and corresponding label y.

2.2 Problem Setting

Figure 1 shows the loss trends when training a commonly used network – ResNet with the depth of 18 layers. The sub-figure on the top describes the trend of the values of the loss function over the testing data, which demonstrates that there are four main periods. Such different performance levels are closely related to the changes in the learning rate, where the changing points are at 60, 120, 160. The loss falls sharply from 1.5 to 0.67 in the first interval. However, from the second stage onwards, the decreasing rate slows down in each part. It can be observed from the figure that there exists a plateau in each training period with the corresponding learning rate. Such plateau always occurs in training no matter which network is used. On the contrary, the sub-figure at the bottom reflects the accuracy of the network with the test data. It can be seen that the accuracy increases as the loss decreases and the accuracy curve also contains the plateaus during the training.

In this paper, we aim to reduce the time spent on such training plateaus while achieving similar training results.

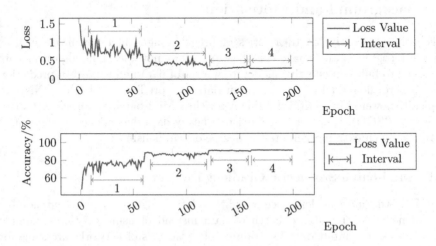

Fig. 1. A motivation example

3   Related Work

DNNs can produce much better results than most of other techniques in many fields [3,5,12,19,23] such as human face recognition. However, training the nets usually take quite a long time and the cost has a significant upward trend [11]. An outstanding amount of effort has been put into extending deep learning models, improving prediction performance and reducing training time consumption [8,10, 20–22]. Regarding to the various latest acceleration mechanism for deep learning system, the technique of those could be sorted into two main cases: (i) utilize a set of GPUs to work for deep models and large training sets to take benefits from huge computing capacity facility so as to deal with large scale of models and data, (ii) optimize the training algorithms to enhance training efficiency so that directly reduce the time consumption of training.

3.1   Hardware Accelerating

GPUs are quite suitable for the computations in training a network since SGD and its variants carry high arithmetic density. It is known to all that GPU has advantages in computation capacity, thus applying a set of GPUs to train nets can deliver considerably efficient training of modestly sized Deep Neural Network practical [1,2,4,6]. A common limitation of such strategies is the size of GPU onboard memory. It restricts network model and training data to be small so that the model and data can be fitted into the GPU memory. As a result, the parameters of the network and the number of data used each time are usually reduced in order to utilise the GPU(s) computation. Apart from that, there exists a mismatch in speed between GPU compute and interconnects, which leads the system extremely hard to do data parallelism in real time via a parameter server.

3.2   Algorithm Accelerating

There are a number of works on optimising training algorithm have been done up to now. Momentum [17] and Nesterov Accelerated Gradient [16] are the methods that help accelerate SGD in the relevant direction and dampens oscillations that always happen around local optima. The momentum term increases for dimensions whose gradients point in the same directions and reduces updates for dimensions whose gradients change directions. As a result, nets gain faster convergence and reduced oscillation. Adagrad [7] and its extension (Adadelta) [24] are the algorithms for gradient-based optimisation that mainly do: adapt the learning rate to the parameters, performing smaller updates for parameters associated with frequently occurring features, and more significant updates for parameters associated with infrequent features. Adam [9] is another method that computes adaptive learning rates for each parameter. It considers the decaying averages of past and past squared gradients, and update the parameters in a similar way used in Adadelta. Besides, Asynchronous Stochastic Gradient Descent (ASGD) algorithms [13–15,25] represented by Hogwild [18] purposes to update the parameter by many workers where they are sharing a parameter server.

3.3 Data Accelerating

According to the studies on previous works on accelerating the training process, we find that there is no method that prunes the training data in a reasonable way so as to train the network with significant data that is a subset of original one. In this way, the time cost of training will be reduced by the number of data that is pruned. Our work is the first to propose an algorithm powered by such an idea. The method does not require making any changes to the original training settings, but real-time analyses performance on each data to make a choice on keeping or ignore. Please note that the decisions are not intended to be permanent, as such decisions are made based on a period of performances.

4 The Data Fine-Pruning Approach

Our data fine-pruning approach reduces the training time of some specific epoch and therefore reduce the overall training time. We first investigate the loss trends of individual data in Sect. 4.1. Second, we analyse the type of input data that should be selected for temporary pruing. Next, we introduce the data selection process and present the data fine-pruning approach in detail in Subsects. 4.2 and 4.3. Finally, Sect. 4.4 formulates the time consumption reduced by our approach.

4.1 Loss Trends of Individual Data

Figure 2 presents the changes in the value of the loss function over two representative data in two separate training. The two trainings are carried out with the same network. The loss of data 1 manifests a trend of continuous dropping from the beginning to the end in the first training. In contrast, an increasing trend has been observed with data 2. However, things change in the second run, where both data 1 and data 2 experience the decrease in loss. These two data have similar trends as that of overall network performance in the second run. The results indicate that the individual input data may produce varied performance in different runs of training even on the same network.

At the end of the training, data 2 cannot be correctly allocated to the category that it is supposed to be due to the high loss produced in the first run. However, it still costs the time and computing power to make the model adjustments using data 2 in each epoch. Our approach makes use of the fact that some data consistently produce bad results but still cost the time and resources during the training process.

Based on the above analysis, we proposed a pruning method for the training data. It temporarily prunes some data that have poor performance evaluated at real-time during training. Our experiments show that temporarily pruning the data that performed poorly in recent training rounds makes little changes to the final model.

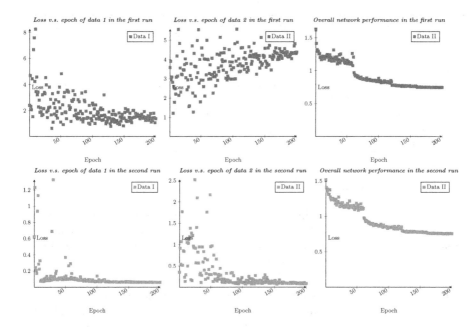

Fig. 2. Performance of same data in same network but different runs

4.2   Loss Monitoring and Pruning Selection

Algorithm 1 outlines the loss monitoring procedure and the selection method for data pruning. The loss of each data is monitored during the training process. The $DroppingCount$ is defined for each data to measure its training performance and used to decide which data should be selected to prune. A larger $DroppingCount$ of data x, denoted by $DroppingCount[x]$ indicates a higher probability for this data item to be to pruned. At the end of training in each epoch, the algorithm examines each loss of the data, denoted by $l(f_{\omega_t}(x), y)$ (where y is the label of data x), within the current batch (line 4). Note that f_{ω_t} denotes the network with parameters of ω at the moment of t. Then the algorithm compares the loss of each data with the loss of the current batch, denoted by $l(f_{\omega_t}(Batch_n))$. The loss value of a batch is the average of all losses in the batch. The algorithm selects the data that perform poorly in this batch and increase their $DroppingCount$ values (lines 5–7).

Considering that a data item shows the varied behavior through the training stages, the $DroppingCount$ of data is held for a window (i.e., a preset number of epochs) and reset at the end of the window (lines 1–3). The algorithm judges the behavior of a data item according to the $DroppingCount$ value of this data item in the latest window. The size of the window is initialized at the beginning and can be dynamically adjusted during the training. Note that e in the algorithm is the number of current epoch.

Algorithm 1. Loss Monitoring and Pruning Selection

1: **if** e mod $Window == 0$ **then**
2:      $DroppingCount = EmptyDictionary$
3: **end if**
4: **for all** (x, y) such that $(x, y) \in BatchData$ **do**
5:      **if** $\ell(f_{\omega_t}(x), y) >= \ell(f_{\omega_t}(Batch_n)) * (1 + tolerance)$ **then**
6:          $DroppingCount[x]+ = 1$
7:      **end if**
8: **end for**

4.3   Data Fine-Pruning

In each window, the algorithm records the data losses and count their corresponding *DroppingCount*. The window size is set according to the changes in learning rate. The windows size is set to a factor of the duration (number of epochs) of the learning rate (e.g., if the duration of the learning rate is 60, the window size is set to be 60 or 30). The analysis is performed for the entire window. However, the data pruning is only performed for the later portion of the window starting from an epoch defined by *StartingPoint*. A fluctuation of the accuracy caused by the adjustment of the learning rate typically lasts for a period and the period becomes shorter as the training progresses. Thus we start to reduce the *StartingPoint* by *Attenuation* after the first window (lines 2–4). This measure leads to more pruning rounds so as to further reduce time consumption.

Algorithm 2. Data Fine-pruning during Training

1: **for** $e = 1; e <= Epoch; e + +$ **do**
2:      **if** $e > PruningWindow$ **then**
3:          $StartingPoint = int(StartingPoint/Attenuation)$
4:      **end if**
5:      **if** e mod $PruningWindow >= StartingPoint$ **then**
6:          **if** e mod $PruningBlock < PruningCount$ **then**
7:              $KeepList = min_{NumData-PruningNum}(DroppingCount)$
8:              $(x, y) = (x, y)[KeepList]$
9:          **end if**
10:     **end if**
11:     $\omega_{t+1} = \omega_t - \gamma \frac{1}{b} \sum_{i=1}^{b} \nabla_{\omega_t} \ell(f_{\omega_t}(x_i), y_i)$
12: **end for**

In the later part of each window (line 5), we select some of the epochs to train with the pruned data (line 6), while the original data is still used in other epochs. We only prune the data temporarily because the behaviour of a data varies in different stages of the training process. In the algorithm, *PruningBlock* defines the block of epochs in which the pruned data are used; *PruningCount* is the number of the epochs that performs the data pruning. In each data pruning epoch, the data are ranked in the decreasing order of *DroppingCount* and the first *PruningNum* number of data in the rank list are pruned in the current epoch (lines 7–8). In another word, the data with higher *DroppingCount* values will has more chances to be pruned. *KeepList* stores the indexes of the data that are kept in the training; x is the data index while y is the label of the data. Then the weights of the network are adjusted by BSGD (line 11) at the end of each epoch.

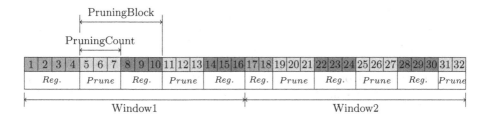

Fig. 3. An example of network training with data fine-pruning method

An exemplar training process using our data fine-pruning method is illustrated in Fig. 3. The numbers in the figure is the index of the training epoch. The rounds with gray colour are those running with the regular data before the *StartingPoint*. The two parameters, *PruningBlock* and *PruningCount*, jointly determine the allocation of pruning training and regular training.

4.4 Analysis of Performance Improvement

The time consumption of the regular training for a network can be formulated by Formula 2. The time of regular running is denoted by $t_{regular}$, the number of epochs by n, the time of forward and backward propagation a batch of data by T, and the number of batches by b. The total time equals to all time consumed over a set of epochs.

$$t_{regular} = \sum_{i=1}^{n} T * b \tag{2}$$

The number of rounds that are trained with the pruned data is denoted by n_{prune}, the size of pruning window by w, the pruning count by c, starting point of pruning by a, the number of iterations using the pruned data by r. According to Algorithm 2, the value of n_{prune} can be obtained by either Formula 3 in the case where the total number of epochs can be divided by the size of the pruning window, or Formula 4 otherwise.

$$n_{prune} = (\left\lfloor \frac{w - a}{r} \right\rfloor * c + (w - a) \bmod r) * \left\lfloor \frac{n}{w} \right\rfloor \tag{3}$$

$$n_{prune} = (\left\lfloor \frac{w-a}{r} \right\rfloor * c + (w-a) \bmod r) * \left\lfloor \frac{n}{w} \right\rfloor$$

$$+ \left\lfloor \frac{n \bmod w - a}{r} \right\rfloor * c + (n \bmod w - a) \bmod r \quad (4)$$

As the number of batches processed in each epoch changes after applying the data-pruning, the average batches over the entire training can be calculated basing on Formula 5.

$$b_{prune} = \frac{1}{n}(\sum_{i=1}^{n_{prune}} T + \sum_{i=1}^{n-n_{prune}} T) \quad (5)$$

t_{prune} denotes the training time with the data pruning approach, t_0 is the computing overhead of the approach, t_{save} is the saved time, which can be obtained by Formula 6 and further by Formula 7.

$$t_{prune} = \sum_{i=1}^{n}(T * b_{prune}) + \sum_{i=1}^{n_{prune}} (t_0) \quad (6)$$

$$t_{save} = t_{regular} - t_{prune} \quad (7)$$

5   Experiments

Our data pruning approach is deployed on several modern neural networks including LeCun network (LeNet), residual network (ResNet), wide residual network (WRN) as well as Vgg network (Vgg). Performance of our method is evaluated with different hyper-parameters and architectures of such networks. Table 1 presents the average value of the best three accuracies of both regular training and data-pruning training as well as the percentage of saved time (*Speedup* in the table). Our experiments are conducted on a workstation with a CPU Intel i7-7700K, a GPU Nvidia GTX 1080 Ti, a hard disk Samsung SSD 970 Pro, four 16GB DDR4 2400 Hz memory, Ubuntu 18.04, Cuda 9.0 and cuDNN 7.0.

Table 1 presents the average time consumption of regular training, data fine-pruned training and the percentage of save time (*Speedup*) on four networks: LeNet, VggNet, ResNet and WRN. The data we used in the experiments is a popular benchmark dataset Cifar-10. It can be seen from the table that our data pruning approach can effectively save the training time. Further, higher percentage of time can typically be saved with a larger network. In the best case when WRN-22 is used for training, 14.29% of time is saved. Besides, According to our experiments, the overhead of data pruning approach is very lightweight. It only adds around averaged 4.2 seconds over 200 epochs of the training.

The aim of our data pruning approach is to reduce the training time while maintaining the accuracy. Table 2 compares the accuracy between our approach and regular training. It can be seen from the table that the difference in accuracy is typically less than 0.4% except LeNet with a difference of 0.43%. The reason why LeNet shows the worse accuracy is because of the limitation of the net

Table 1. Time consumption of pruning data training and regular training

	LeNet	VggNet-13	VggNet-16	VggNet-19	ResNet-18
Regular	1220 s	2028 s	2554 s	3110 s	1277 s
Pruned	1071.73 s	1873.67 s	2356.74 s	2867.7 s	1109.92 s
Overhead	4.27 s	4.33 s	4.26 s	4.30 s	4.08 s
Speedup	11.80%	7.40%	7.56%	7.65%	12.76%
	ResNet-34	ResNet-50	WRN-10	WRN-16	WRN-22
Regular	2047 s	3931 s	3 h 24 min	5 h 8 min	6 h 53 min
Pruned	1767.79 s	3379.82 s	2 h 56 min	4 h 26 min	5 h 54 min
Overhead	4.21 s	4.18 s	4.12 s	4.25 s	4.32 s
Speedup	13.43%	13.92%	13.73%	13.81%	14.29%

Table 2. Accuracy comparison between pruning data training and regular training

	LeNet	VggNet-13	VggNet-16	VggNet-19	ResNet-18
Regular	75.15%	93.92%	93.79%	93.35%	91.25%
Pruned	74.72%	93.56%	93.44%	93.30%	91.16%
	ResNet-34	ResNet-50	WRN-10	WRN-16	WRN-22
Regular	92.86%	93.75%	92.13%	94.22%	95.08%
Pruned	92.85%	93.46%	91.78%	94.20%	94.71%

itself. Comparing LeNet to others, LeNet has a quite small number of layers and parameters, which makes the network more uncertain and unstable. The smallest difference in accuracy observed in our experiments is 0.01% (with ResNet-34).

6 Conclusions and Future Works

Training a deep neural network can be a very time-consuming process. In this paper, we present a data fine-pruning technique, which analyzes the loss of each data at real time and prunes a set of data that performs poorly in recent training epochs. It achieves the noticeable saving of training time while maintaining the accuracy of the results.

There is more work to be done in future. First, our experiments show that some data are commonly identified as *bad* data and are repeatedly selected for pruning. We would like to investigate whether the *bad* data contain the common features. If such common features do exist and can be identified, we can probably make use of the finding and further reduce the training time.

Second, the data that perform poorly may relate to the type of the networks. We would like to conduct more in-depth research regarding the relation between the *bad* data and the type of networks. If this could be established, we expect to further improve the performance in practice.

Acknowledgement. This work is partially supported by the National Key R&D Program of China 2018YFB1003201 and Guangdong Pre-national Project 2014GKXM054.

References

1. Bottou, L.: Large-scale machine learning with stochastic gradient descent. In: Lechevallier, Y., Saporta, G. (eds.) COMPSTAT 2010, pp. 177–186. Springer, Heidelberg (2010). https://doi.org/10.1007/978-3-7908-2604-3_16
2. Chilimbi, T.M., Suzue, Y., Apacible, J., Kalyanaraman, K.: Project adam: building an efficient and scalable deep learning training system. In: OSDI, vol. 14, pp. 571–582 (2014)
3. Cireşan, D., Meier, U., Schmidhuber, J.: Multi-column deep neural networks for image classification. arXiv preprint arXiv:1202.2745 (2012)
4. Cui, H., Zhang, H., Ganger, G.R., Gibbons, P.B., Xing, E.P.: GeePS: scalable deep learning on distributed GPUs with a GPU-specialized parameter server. In: Proceedings of the Eleventh European Conference on Computer Systems, p. 4. ACM (2016)
5. Dahl, G.E., Yu, D., Deng, L., Acero, A.: Context-dependent pre-trained deep neural networks for large-vocabulary speech recognition. IEEE Trans. Audio Speech Lang. Process. **20**(1), 30–42 (2012)
6. Dean, J., et al.: Large scale distributed deep networks. In: Advances in Neural Information Processing Systems, pp. 1223–1231 (2012)
7. Duchi, J., Hazan, E., Singer, Y.: Adaptive subgradient methods for online learning and stochastic optimization. J. Mach. Learn. Res. **12**(Jul), 2121–2159 (2011)
8. He, K., Zhang, X., Ren, S., Sun, J.: Deep residual learning for image recognition. In: Proceedings of the IEEE Conference on Computer Vision and Pattern Recognition, pp. 770–778 (2016)
9. Kingma, D.P., Ba, J.: Adam: a method for stochastic optimization. arXiv preprint arXiv:1412.6980 (2014)
10. Krizhevsky, A., Sutskever, I., Hinton, G.E.: ImageNet classification with deep convolutional neural networks. In: Advances in Neural Information Processing Systems, pp. 1097–1105 (2012)
11. LeCun, Y., Bengio, Y., Hinton, G.: Deep learning. Nature **521**(7553), 436 (2015)
12. Lei, Y., Scheffer, N., Ferrer, L., McLaren, M.: A novel scheme for speaker recognition using a phonetically-aware deep neural network. In: 2014 IEEE International Conference on Acoustics, Speech and Signal Processing (ICASSP), pp. 1695–1699. IEEE (2014)
13. Li, M., et al.: Scaling distributed machine learning with the parameter server. In: OSDI, vol. 14, pp. 583–598 (2014)
14. Liu, J., Wright, S.J., Ré, C., Bittorf, V., Sridhar, S.: An asynchronous parallel stochastic coordinate descent algorithm. J. Mach. Learn. Res. **16**(1), 285–322 (2015)
15. Mnih, V., et al.: Asynchronous methods for deep reinforcementlearning. In: International Conference on Machine Learning, pp. 1928–1937(2016)
16. Nesterov, Y.: A method for unconstrained convex minimization problem with the rate of convergence $o(1/k^2)$. In: Doklady AN USSR, vol. 269, pp. 543–547 (1983)
17. Qian, N.: On the momentum term in gradient descent learning algorithms. Neural Netw. **12**(1), 145–151 (1999)

18. Recht, B., Re, C., Wright, S., Niu, F.: HOGWILD: a lock-free approach to parallelizing stochastic gradient descent. In: Advances in Neural Information Processing Systems, pp. 693–701 (2011)
19. Richardson, F., Reynolds, D., Dehak, N.: Deep neural network approaches to speaker and language recognition. IEEE Sig. Process. Lett. **22**(10), 1671–1675 (2015)
20. Simonyan, K., Zisserman, A.: Very deep convolutional networks for large-scale image recognition. arXiv preprint arXiv:1409.1556 (2014)
21. Srivastava, N., Hinton, G., Krizhevsky, A., Sutskever, I., Salakhutdinov, R.: Dropout: a simple way to prevent neural networks from overfitting. J. Mach. Learn. Res. **15**(1), 1929–1958 (2014)
22. Szegedy, C., et al.: Going deeper with convolutions. In: Proceedings of the IEEE Conference on Computer Vision and Pattern Recognition, pp. 1–9 (2015)
23. Taigman, Y., Yang, M., Ranzato, M., Wolf, L.: DeepFace: closing the gap to human-level performance in face verification. In: Proceedings of the IEEE Conference on Computer Vision and Pattern Recognition, pp. 1701–1708 (2014)
24. Zeiler, M.D.: ADADELTA: an adaptive learning rate method. arXiv preprint arXiv:1212.5701 (2012)
25. Zheng, S., et al.: Asynchronous stochastic gradient descent with delay compensation. In: International Conference on Machine Learning (2017)

Balancing the QOS and Security in Dijkstra Algorithm by SDN Technology

Zhao JinJing[1(✉)], Ling Pang[1], Xiaohui Kuang[1], and Rong Jin[2]

[1] National Key Laboratory of Science and Technology on Information System Security, Beijing 100101, China
misszhaojinjing@hotmail.com, lingpang313@yahoo.com
[2] Beijing Space Information Relay and Transmission on Technology Centre, Beijing 100094, China

Abstract. Dijkstra algorithm is widely used in a lot of common network routing protocols. We consider the problem of quality of service (QoS) and the Security features of the network routing area using software defined networks (SDN). The SDN framework enables an efficient decoupled implementation of dynamic routing protocols which could aware the communication network status. In this work we consider the varying delay status of the communication network along with other network security parameters. The routing problem is formulated as a multi-constrained shortest path problem. A new improved Dijkstra algorithm is presented named as QS-Dijkstra. The implement and experiment show that QS-Dijkstra algorithm is able to minimize traffic routing through vulnerable links while satisfying the QoS constraints of the network.

1 Introduction

Dijkstra algorithm is widely used in a lot of common network routing protocols, like OSPF and IS-IS. The main idea of Dijkstra algorithm is how to find a shortest path from a source node to a destination node in a network. So each network link has a cost value to present its status, and this cost is used to calculate the shortest path. In the practice, the link cost is defined as a static cost value in OSPF protocol, as the reference bandwidth divided by interface bandwidth or simply as 1 to reduce the shortest path weight to a hop count. The reason is that it's a very easy way in practice. But as the value of the link cost, it could not cover the feathers and status of the link.

In this work we present a practical way to calculate a more reasonable link cost in Dijkstra algorithm and consider the problem of QoS and the security features of the network routing procedure using SDN technology [1–3]. The SDN framework provides an approach to calculate the shortest path between source and destination based on dynamic link statuses through SDN's high network monitoring capability. A lot of useful link information, like link type, link ownership, interface bandwidth, transition delay and historical record, can be collected and computed by the SDN controller to enable more safe, reliable and efficient paths. In this way, we can consider the varying delay status of the communication network along with other network security parameters and get a presence of a passive/active adversary in the network routing area.

© IFIP International Federation for Information Processing 2018
Published by Springer Nature Switzerland AG 2018
F. Zhang et al. (Eds.): NPC 2018, LNCS 11276, pp. 126–131, 2018.
https://doi.org/10.1007/978-3-030-05677-3_11

The remainder of this paper is organized as follows: double constrained shortest path problem is discussed and the derivation of QoS constraints and related cost metrics are presented in Sect. 2, the implementation details are provided in Sect. 3, Sect. 4 investigates the performance of the proposed framework. Conclusions and final remarks are discussed in Sect. 5.

2 System Model

Consider a graph representation of the communication network. $G(V, E, \omega)$ is a weighted undirected graph model and describes an N nodes and E links network. The node set is $V = \{v_1, \ldots, v_N\}$, and the edge set is $E = \{e_{ij}|i,j = 1, 2, \ldots, N\}$. The weight ω_{ij} on the edge e_{ij} is defined as the cost of the link. In this article, the interplaying between QOS and security features is concerned in the network routing process. The security metrics of the link between nodes i and j could include these features as:

(1) History $L_{ij}H$: a link that was previously targeted by an attacker in a particular time could be more likely to be attacked again.
(2) Security installed measures $L_{ij}S$: a link with high encryption is typically hard to be listened or hijacked. So $L_{ij}S$ values are dependent on the pre-installed and pre-configured security measures of nodes of the link.
(3) Bandwidth $L_{ij}B$: A link with high bandwidth is more difficult to be congested by data flow.
(4) Ownership $L_{ij}O$: a self-owned or in the same domain channel is more secure than a shared or leased channel by other domains.

The vulnerability metric $L_{ij}M$ should reflect the attributes that make a link more security.

$$L_{ij}M = L_{ij}H * \left(\alpha L_{ij}S + \beta L_{ij}B + \gamma L_{ij}O\right) \tag{2}$$

Where α, β, and γ are the weights of $L_{ij}S$, $L_{ij}B$ and $L_{ij}O$ depending on the impact importance of the considered security parameters.

Assume every link $e_{ij} \in E$ has two weights $c_{ij} > 0$ and $d_{ij} > 0$ (c_{ij} is cost and d_{ij} means delay). For source and destination nodes (s, t), let P_{st} denote the set of paths from s to t. Further, for any path p define

$$c(p) = \sum_{(i,j)\in p} L_{ij}M \tag{3}$$

$$d(p) = \sum_{(i,j)\in p} d_{ij} \tag{4}$$

The routing problem seeks to find the paths between s and t nodes with minimum link cost c (p_{st}), which satisfies $d(p_{st}) \leq T_{max}$. This is a typical NP problem named constrained shortest path (CSP) [4, 5], which can be solved by the Lagrangian Relaxation Based Aggregated Cost (LARAC) algorithm [6].

3 Implementation

The architecture of SDN network comprised of Floodlight controller and Mininet switches. In the floodlight controller, applications can be written in Java and can interact with the built-in controller modules via a JAVA API. Other applications can be written in different languages and interact with the controller modules via the REST API. And the controller allows the implementation of built-in modules that can communicate with their implementation of the OpenFlow controller (i.e. OpenFlow Services). The controller, on the other hand, can communicate with the switches via the OpenFlow protocol through the abstraction layer present at the forwarding hardware.

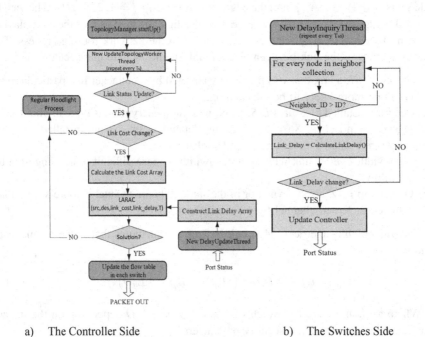

a)   The Controller Side   b)   The Switches Side

Fig. 1. QS-Dijkstra algorithm implementation. The algorithm is separated into two parts; a controller function which is implemented in Floodlight using Java, and a switch function implemented in Mininet using Python.

We propose a Vulnerable-Link Avoidance Dijkstra (QS-Dijkstra) algorithm to capture the problem of best-effort avoiding vulnerable links while maintaining the delay constraint. QS-Dijkstra algorithm uses the previously-defined vulnerability metric in Eq. (2) to arrive at a set of feasible paths between source node s and destination node t.

The flowchart of the QS-Dijkstra algorithm that is implemented is shown in Fig. 1. The algorithm is separated into two parts, the switch side and the controller side. The algorithm of the controller side performs the following tasks:

(1) Listening to messages from switches and calculating *link-delay* value of each link, and then constructing the *link-delay* cost matrix.

(2) Calculating the *link-vulnerability* cost matrix according to the metric developed in formula (2); this matrix can be modified and calibrated by network operators or managers.

(3) Running a *topology-update* thread, and checking the *link-vulnerability* cost matrix updates every T_s; if a change is detected, the controller recalculates the routing paths.

(4) Calculating the routing paths based on the link cost metrics of interest, and updating the flow table of each switch by advertise a PACKET OUT message to switches.

The main function of the algorithm in the switches side is to collect the values of *link-delays* for the directly connected switches. This is done through an independent thread responsible for periodically testing the link between that switch and all connected switches with higher ID. The sampling time is parametric and is tuneable by the network managers; in our simulation environment, *Tsd* is set to 60 s. Link delay testing is done 3 times every *Tsd* and the average value is then compared with the last known value. If the new delay is significantly different from the previous value, the switch updates the controller accordingly.

4   Simulation and Results

We build two large scale network environment with the same topology and route information. One is running the Dijkstra routing protocol, the other is for QS-Dijkstra. In order to reach a high performance, in each environment, we use the high-performance workstation with 10 Intel Xeon Westmere EP six-core processors. Whose maximum process speed could reach 11.251Tflops. Thus, the whole network includes 260 routers and a controller. For every node, we pick a random number from [1, 10] for its connection number. And the commercial network flow generator Spirent TestCentre is chosen to generate some popular network application data, like http, IP, TCP, UDP. And it sends the same packets to the two networks synchronously.

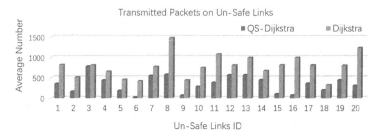

Fig. 2. The number of transmitted packets on un-safe links. There are 20 links which have very high vulnerable level.

In this test case, the link cost and link delay is randomized in the [0–100]. The maximum path delay constraint T still set as 1000 s. After calculating the link vulnerability metric, there are 20 links which have very high vulnerable level. We sampled the packets number transmitted through these links every 200 s and calculate the average value on each links. The result is shown in Fig. 2, which shows that the packets transmitted on these un-safe links in QS-Dijkstra are much less than in Dijkstra.

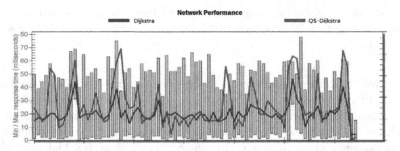

Fig. 3. The average response time of routers. In order to evaluate the network performance in the two networks, the average response times are recorded every 15 s.

From the results shown in Fig. 3, the conclusion could be proved that the network performance in QS-Dijkstra does not lost much except for a few short intervals, and the maximum responds time in these intervals is still could be acceptable.

5   Conclusion

In this paper, we consider the varying delay status of the communication network along with other network security parameters. Our approach capitalizes on the SDN framework and technology. The implement and experiment show that QS-Dijkstra algorithm is able to minimize traffic routing through vulnerable links while satisfying the QoS constraints of the network.

In the future work, the algorithm could consider more security and performance features of links and routing nodes, to make a more effective routing protocol.

References

1. Nunes, B., Mendonca, M., Nguyen, X.-N., Obraczka, K., Turletti, T.: A survey of software-defined networking: past, present, and future of programmable networks. IEEE Commun. Surv. Tutor. **16**, 1617–1634. https://doi.org/10.1109/surv.2014.012214.00180.pdf
2. Software-Defined Networking. http://en.wikipedia.org/wiki/Software-defined_networking
3. Open Networking Foundation: Software-defined networking: the new norm for networks. ONF White paper (2012)

4. Xiao, Y., Thulasiraman, K., Xue, G., Juttner, A.: The constrained shortest path problem: algorithmic approaches and an algebraic study with generalization. AKCE Int. J. Graphs Comb. **2**, 63–86 (2005)
5. Kuipers, F., Van Mieghem, P., Korkmaz, T., Krunz, M.: An overview of constraint-based path selection algorithms for QOS routing. IEEE Commun. Mag. **40**, 50–55 (2002)
6. Jüttner, A., Szviatovski, B., Mécs, I., Rajkó, Z.: Lagrange relaxation based method for the QOS routing problem. In: Twentieth Annual Joint Conference of the IEEE Computer and Communications Societies, vol. 2, pp. 859–868 (2001)

Labeled Network Stack: A Co-designed Stack for Low Tail-Latency and High Concurrency in Datacenter Services

Wenli Zhang[1(✉)], Ke Liu[1], Hui Song[1], Lan Yu[1], and Mingyu Chen[1,2]

[1] Institute of Computing Technology, Chinese Academy of Sciences, Kexueyuan South Road 6, Haidian District, Beijing, People's Republic of China
{zhangwl,liuke,songhui,yulan,cmy}@ict.ac.cn
[2] University of Chinese Academy of Sciences, Yuquan Road 19(A), Shijingshan District, Beijing, People's Republic of China
http://acs.ict.ac.cn/network/index-eng.html

Abstract. Many Internet, mobile Internet, and IoT services require both low tail-latency and high concurrency in datacenters. The current protocol stack design pays more attention to throughput and average performance, considering little on tail latency and priority. We address this question by proposing a hardware-software co-designed Labeled Network Stack (LNS) for future datacenters. The key innovation is a payload labeling mechanism that distinguishes data packets in a TCP link across the full network stack, including the application, the TCP/IP and the Ethernet layer. This design enables prioritized data packets processing and forwarding along the full data path, to reduce the tail latency of critical requests. We built a prototype datacenter server to evaluate the LNS design against a standard Linux kernel stack and the mTCP research, using IoT kernel benchmark MCC. Experiment results show that the LNS design can provide an order of magnitude improvement on tail latency and concurrency.

Keywords: Tail latency · High concurrent server · Priority · Label Network stack

1 Introduction

For the new generation of cloud computing server applications such as mobile Internet and IoT, with characteristics of high concurrency and low latency constraints, the behavior, motivation and access time of concurrent clients are all uncertain [1], so the unconscious resource competition from massive concurrent requests will lead to fluctuations in service latency. Google put forward the data center "Tail Latency" issue [2], usually measured with the 99th percentile latency.

© IFIP International Federation for Information Processing 2018
Published by Springer Nature Switzerland AG 2018
F. Zhang et al. (Eds.): NPC 2018, LNCS 11276, pp. 132–136, 2018.
https://doi.org/10.1007/978-3-030-05677-3_12

UC Berkeley also highlighted the long tail problem in web applications [3]. One main goal of their FireBox project [4] is to cope with tail latency for 2020 cloud computing systems.

Long tail latency will seriously affect Quality of Service (QoS). So, to guarantee the tail latency not exaggerated too much, the utilization rate of data center resources for online services is usually not very high, i.e., the CPU utilization rate is generally <30%. Besides, the long TCP connection has become the mainstream for cloud client/server communication now, i.e. MQTT. Long connection is used to support many mobile clients, for the server to locate the client (i.e. many IoT devices only have internal IPs) and to reduce the overhead of multiple authentications, however, it would bring about high concurrency problem, and make the tail latency more serious, because of long-term resource occupation.

How to control tail latency has become an important direction for cloud computing and big data research in recent years. User-mode TCP/IP and NIC offload are mainly involved recently. While Li et al. [7] found that application, hardware and operating system may all cause tail-delayed response. However, many studies overlook one important factor. Different requests have different delay requirements, while the current works improve delay commonly without differentiate the requests. Traditional layered network stacks only provide priority in the flow granularity coarsely at some layers, and lack of finer grained priority control mechanisms.

Therefore, we proposed a label-based network stack, using payload labeling and codesign across layers to support full-path data-sensing and prioritization. Then, we design and implement a prototype. Test results showed that the LNS got an order of magnitude improvement on tail latency and concurrency over the mainstream systems. Our two main contributions are as follows.

(1) **Labeled Network Stack (LNS)** to achieve full-data-path QoS guarantee. The LNS is to support distinguishing, isolation and prioritizing in packet granularity across the full data path through payload labeling. It is different from the traditional flow level control method that only based on predefined protocol header. So, the LNS can do more efficiently to get both high concurrency and low tail latency.

(2) **Prototype of LNS** to show an order of magnitude improvement on tail latency and concurrency over the mainstream. Based on LNS idea and standard X86 Linux server, we did hardware-software co-design on NIC, TCP/IP stack, server framework layers and formed the first testbed for LNS. Tests show that significant improvement. Besides IoT and mobile Microservices, our server fits into application with features on long connection, high concurrency and user experience requirement widely.

2 Labeled Network Stack

We first discuss the motivation on LNS, then address our design.

2.1 Why LNS?

Some requests in the data flow are naturally of priority requirement for many cloud services. For example, order operation should be more sensitive on latency than browsing in electronic commerce. However, traditional method lacks distinguishing, isolation and prioritizing abilities for packets. This inevitably causes delay for critical services, especially in the case of resource reuse contention.

Without a doubt, there are many labels in traditional networks, such as ECN congestion label and DSCP differentiated service field, but no label works through the whole packet processing after the header peeled off. So, when without priority policy, data packet processing would use system resources in unordered state, which inevitably leads to high entropy [5]. While the current mainstream NICs, TCP/IP stacks, and server frameworks all do not support priority for the full data path.

Then, we put forward the idea to prioritize some requests in network flow according to application features and do hardware-software co-design optimization in full stack, which finally form the LNS.

2.2 LNS Idea

The main idea is that (1) **payload labeling mechanism**. When to send a packet, the sever framework will attach a label in front of the payload according to application requirement. For example, to control overhead 1 bit is added as priority in our experiment, where 0×1 stands for high priority and 0×0 stands for the low. When the encrypted packet arrives at the receiver, it should be decrypted before protocol analysis, and put to the right priority queue by label identifying. Finally, it accesses database with labeled RPC. For simplicity, the priority in this work is randomly labeled by programmers in flow generator, while later the label can be attached based on application characteristics automatically; (2) **multi-path priority in packet**, including queue partition in the intelligent NIC, multi-queue zero-copy driver, custom user-mode TCP/IP stack and other layers. It provides a mechanism to avoid frequent blockages caused by a single queue and prioritize in packet granularity. (3) **tail latency QoS scheduling**. As shown in Fig. 1, through payload labeling and priority scheduling in all layers, it can reduce the latency of critical operations more accurately and improve both overall service efficiency and user experience. In LNS we coordinate well with the design idea on distinguishing, isolate and prioritizing. To focus, we only research tail latency in single node in this paper.

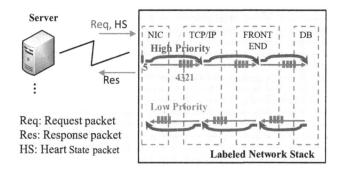

Fig. 1. Main idea of LNS. Its features include full-path payload labeling priority in packet granularity and high priority taking precedence. Assumed the 5th arriving packet is of high priority, it can be served first before the other four in queue

3   Implementation

Based on the LNS idea, we developed a prototype to achieve label identification and scheduling across process stages, including customized NIC Sando, mTCP-based user-mode protocol stack and epoll-based event driven server framework with priority enhancement.

4   Evaluation

We answer a question in this section that: can we have order of magnitude improvement on tail latency and concurrency over the mainstream? In Sect. 4.2, experiment results show that the LNS design can provide that high performance.

4.1   Experiment Setup

We used mainstream X86 servers to build a test system. It uses MCC [8] to simulate long connections of massive IoT devices with sever, and the load balancer distributes the data to 4 servers for related processing (limited by the amount of Sando card). The monitor [8] adopts the full-traffic accurate measurement to get server-side latency in nanosecond (once timing itself costs about 2.7 ns by executing clock_gettime). To facilitate the distinction, when the LNS is running on the process node, it is briefly as LNS with Sando for short. A target system is abbreviated as e1000-Linux, which runs the X86 standard hardware and software, then alternative the kernel stack as the user-level protocol stack mTCP [6] to form the second target system shortly as e1000-mTCP.

4.2   High Concurrency and Low Tail Latency

As shown in Fig. 2, while ranging the 99th percentile latency from 1 to 60 ms, the LNS with Sando system can reach up 10 million connections, which increases an order of magnitude compared with e1000-Linux system, and at least 1 times more than e1000-mTCP, with 4 nodes in the test system.

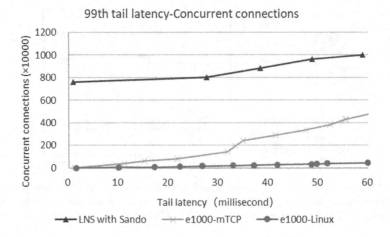

Fig. 2. 99-percentile tail latency - Concurrent connection

5 Conclusion

This paper proposes a Labeled Network Stack (LNS) technique for future datacenters, to provide order of magnitude improvement on tail latency and concurrency. Its main innovation is a labeling mechanism that labels the payload (packet body) rather than the packet header. Such payload labeling enables distinguishing different payload requests in the same flow across the full network stack to schedule along the full data path, including NIC hardware, driver, protocol stack and service software. Evaluation results on a prototype system show that the hardware-software co-designed LNS technique with label-driven prioritization has advantages of both Low tail latency and High concurrency.

Acknowledgment. This work is supported by National Key Research and Development Plan of China under Grant No. 2017YFB1001602.

References

1. Zhang, Y., et al.: Treadmill: attributing the source of tail latency through precise load testing and statistical inference. ISCA-43 (2016)
2. Dean, J., et al.: The tail at scale. Commun. ACM **56**(2), 74–80 (2013)
3. Zats, D., et al.: DeTail: reducing the flow completion time tail in datacenter networks. ACM SIGCOMM Comput. Commun. Rev. **42**, 139–150 (2012)
4. Asanovi'c, K.: FireBox: a Hardware Building Block for 2020 Warehouse-Scale Computers. In: FAST (2014)
5. Xu, Z., et al.: Low-entropy cloud computing systems. ASCIENTIA SINICA Informationis. https://doi.org/10.1360/N112017-00069
6. Jeong, E., et al.: mTCP: A highly scalable user-level TCP stack for multicore systems. In: Proceedings of NSDI 2014 (2014)
7. Li, J., et al.: Tales of the tail: hardware, OS, and application-level sources of tail latency. In: Symposium on Cloud Computing, pp. 1–14 (2014)
8. http://acs.ict.ac.cn/network/MCC.html or http://acs.ict.ac.cn/network/HCMonitor.html

A Deep Learning Approach for Network Anomaly Detection Based on AMF-LSTM

Mingyi Zhu, Kejiang Ye[(✉)], Yang Wang, and Cheng-Zhong Xu

Shenzhen Institutes of Advanced Technology, Chinese Academy of Sciences,
Shenzhen, China
{my.zhu,kj.ye,yang.wang1,cz.xu}@siat.ac.cn

Abstract. The Internet and computer networks are currently suffering from different security threats. This paper presents a new method called AMF-LSTM for abnormal traffic detection by using deep learning model. We use the statistical features of multi-flows rather than a single flow or the features extracted from log as the input to obtain temporal correlation between flows, and add an attention mechanism to the original LSTM to help the model learn which traffic flow has more contributions to the final results. Experiments show AMF-LSTM method has high accuracy and recall in anomaly type identification.

1 Introduction

The Internet and computer networks are currently suffering from different security threats [1]. The Global State of Information Security Survey 2015 [2] found there is a great increase in security incidents during the last several years. Network anomalies stand for a large fraction of the Internet traffic and compromise the performance of the network resources [1,3]. With the growing network scale, the traditional methods face two problems: (i) the processing speed is too slow, unable to cope with the massive network traffic data in today's Internet environments; (ii) it may invade the user's privacy. This situation can be alleviated by using machine learning methods, which are successfully used in many other areas. However, most of the traditional machine learning methods always focus on the traffic itself and extract their own characteristics to detect the potential anomalies.

As we know the data transmitted in network is in the form of *flows*. There is always a temporal correlation between flows, which is also true for abnormal traffic in the network. In previous work, researchers focus on the characteristics of traffic itself, but ignore that many network anomalies have potential temporal correlation. RNN (Recurrent Neural Networks) is widely used in the fields that are time series related. Recently, there are some works using RNN and LSTM (Long-Short Term Memory) to detect abnormal traffic [4,5], but they only use

© IFIP International Federation for Information Processing 2018
Published by Springer Nature Switzerland AG 2018
F. Zhang et al. (Eds.): NPC 2018, LNCS 11276, pp. 137–141, 2018.
https://doi.org/10.1007/978-3-030-05677-3_13

a single flow to repeat multiple times, which can only learn the relationship between themselves and cannot learn the relationship between different flows.

This paper presents an anomaly detection method using deep learning model based on AMF-LSTM. The proposed method has three important features: (i) use the previous traffic flows as auxiliary features of the traffic to be detected; (ii) use LSTM to find the hidden temporal correlation between these flows, and (iii) use the attention mechanism to make model focus on the traffic and features that are useful for the results.

2   AMF-LSTM Model

We proposed an AMF-LSTM (Attention-base Multi-Flow LSTM) model for network anomaly detection. *Attention* means that our model is based on the attention mechanism [6]. *Multi-Flow* means that we not only use the characteristics of the current flow itself to detect the anomalies, but also use the previous traffic flows with temporal correlation to assist in detecting abnormal traffic. *LSTM* means the main body of our network is based on the long short-term memory networks [7]. Figure 1 shows the structure of AMF-LSTM model.

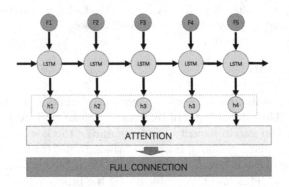

Fig. 1. Structure of AMF-LSTM

3   Experiment

We use CICIDS2017 [8] as the experimental dataset. The dataset contains benign and the most up-to-date common attacks, which resembles the true real-world data. The implemented attacks includes the most common attacks based on the 2016 McAfee report [9].

Our experiment mainly has the following hyperparameters: n, the number of flows are selected to detect the traffic; the *learning rate*, which is the step size of neural network for each learning; and the number of LSTM *hidden nodes*, which is the number of nodes that LSTM uses to learn.

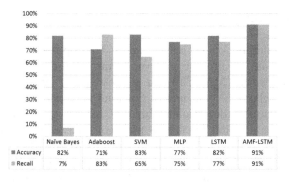

Fig. 2. Accuracy and recall of 8-category classification

We first study the effect of learning rate and hidden nodes on the model accuracy, and find the best value of hidden nodes is 256, and the optimal learning rate is 0.0001. Then, we perform two sets of experiments with n = 10 and n = 20. The experimental results are similar, probably because the attention can focus on where it is needed. We compare the performance of our model with several classic machine learning algorithms, such as Naive Bayes, SVM, AdaBoost, MLP, and the original LSTM. The results of accuracy and recall comparison are shown in the Fig. 2. We can see that our model is significantly better than other machine learning algorithms, both in accuracy or recall.

We further conduct a deeper study on model with n = 10, lr = 0.0001, node_num = 256, which achieves the best performance. The evaluation metrics are shown in the Table 1. As we know, it is far more harmful for a system to judge abnormal traffic as normal traffic than to judge normal traffic as abnormal traffic. Therefore, we pay more attention to the value of recall. According to the table, our model can identify most of the anomalies correctly.

Table 1. The results of different evaluation metrics

	Precision	Recall	F1-score	Flows
Normal	0.98	0.91	0.94	348631
DDoS	0.83	0.98	0.90	25606
PortScan	0.82	0.99	0.90	31786
BOT	0.05	0.75	0.10	394
Infiltration	0.00	0.75	0.01	8
Web attack	0.04	0.81	0.07	436
Patator	0.38	0.53	0.44	2767
DoS	0.87	0.88	0.87	50532

4   Related Work

In prior studies, a number of approaches have been proposed for network anomaly detection. Sun et al. [10] present a survey of intrusion detection techniques for mobile ad-hoc networks (MANET) and wireless sensor networks (WSN). Sperotto et al. [11] explain the concepts of flow and classified attacks, and provide a detailed discussion of detection techniques. Abbes et al. [12] introduce an approach that uses decision trees with protocol analysis for effective intrusion detection. Khan et al. [13] use genetic algorithms to develop rules for network intrusion detection. Tthere are also large number of methods using Neural Network. An example of ANN-based IDS is RT-UNNID [14]. Thilina et al. [15] propose a novel framework to perform intruder detection and analysis using deep learning nets and association rule mining. Yuan et al. [16] use the LSTM-CNN framework to find user's anomalous behavior. Most recently, Zhu et al. [4] use CNN model for network anomaly detection and identification and achieve better performance than traditional machine learning algorithms. Although RNN [5] and LSTM [17] have been used to detect abnormal traffic before, they only use a single flow as the input of RNN and recurrent itself multiple times. In our opinion, they can only learn the relation in the traffic itself, and can not fully utilize the characteristics of RNN, which can learn the potential relations between different traffic.

5   Conclusion

This paper presents a method for abnormal traffic detection in the Internet by using deep learning model based on AMF-LSTM. We use the statistical features of multi-flows rather than a single flow as the input to obtain temporal correlation between flows, and add an attention mechanism to the original LSTM to help the model learn which traffic flow has more contributions to the result. Compared with other classic machine learning algorithms, our model achieves about 10% improvement in accuracy and recall on the multi-classification problems.

Acknowledgment. This work is supported by the National Key R&D Program of China (No. 2018YFB1004804), National Natural Science Foundation of China (No. 61702492, U1401258), and Shenzhen Basic Research Program (No. JCYJ20170818153016513, JCYJ20170307164747920).

References

1. Garcia-Teodoro, P., Diaz-Verdejo, J., Maciá-Fernández, G., Vázquez, E.: Anomaly-based network intrusion detection: techniques, systems and challenges. Comput. Secur. **28**(1–2), 18–28 (2009)
2. Ahmed, M., Mahmood, A.N., Hu, J.: A survey of network anomaly detection techniques. J. Netw. Comput. Appl. **60**, 19–31 (2016)

3. Benson, T., Akella, A., Maltz, D.A.: Network traffic characteristics of data centers in the wild. In: Proceedings of the 10th ACM SIGCOMM Conference on Internet Measurement, pp. 267–280 (2010)
4. Zhu, M., Ye, K., Xu, C.-Z.: Network anomaly detection and identification based on deep learning methods. In: Luo, M., Zhang, L.-J. (eds.) CLOUD 2018. LNCS, vol. 10967, pp. 219–234. Springer, Cham (2018). https://doi.org/10.1007/978-3-319-94295-7_15
5. Yin, C., Zhu, Y., Fei, J., He, X.: A deep learning approach for intrusion detection using recurrent neural networks. IEEE Access **5**, 21954–21961 (2017)
6. Chorowski, J.K., Bahdanau, D., Serdyuk, D., Cho, K., Bengio, Y.: Attention-based models for speech recognition. In: Advances in Neural Information Processing Systems, pp. 577–585 (2015)
7. Hochreiter, S., Schmidhuber, J.: Long short-term memory. Neural Comput. **9**(8), 1735–1780 (1997)
8. Intrusion detection evaluation dataset (cicids2017) (2018). http://www.unb.ca/cic/datasets/ids-2017.html
9. Mcafee labs threats report (2018). https://www.mcafee.com/cn/security-awareness/articles/mcafee-labs-threats-report-mar-2016.aspx
10. Sun, B., Osborne, L., Xiao, Y., Guizani, S.: Intrusion detection techniques in mobile ad hoc and wireless sensor networks. IEEE Wirel. Commun. **14**(5), 56–63 (2007)
11. Sperotto, A., Schaffrath, G., Sadre, R., Morariu, C., Pras, A., Stiller, B.: An overview of IP flow-based intrusion detection. IEEE Commun. Surv. Tutor. **12**(3), 343–356 (2010)
12. Abbes, T., Bouhoula, A., Rusinowitch, M.: Efficient decision tree for protocol analysis in intrusion detection. Int. J. Secur. Netw. **5**(4), 220–235 (2010)
13. Khan, M.S.A.: Rule based network intrusion detection using genetic algorithm. Int. J. Comput. Appl. **18**(8), 26–29 (2011)
14. Amini, M., Jalili, R., Shahriari, H.R.: RT-UNNID: a practical solution to real-time network-based intrusion detection using unsupervised neural networks. Comput. Secur. **25**(6), 459–468 (2006)
15. Thilina, A., et al.: Intruder detection using deep learning and association rule mining. In: IEEE International Conference on Computer and Information Technology (CIT), pp. 615–620 (2016)
16. Yuan, F., Cao, Y., Shang, Y., Liu, Y., Tan, J., Fang, B.: Insider threat detection with deep neural network. In: Shi, Y., et al. (eds.) ICCS 2018. LNCS, vol. 10860, pp. 43–54. Springer, Cham (2018). https://doi.org/10.1007/978-3-319-93698-7_4
17. Kim, J., Kim, J., Thu, H.L.T., Kim, H.: Long short term memory recurrent neural network classifier for intrusion detection. In: International Conference on Platform Technology and Service (PlatCon), pp. 1–5 (2016)

FSObserver: A Performance Measurement and Monitoring Tool for Distributed Storage Systems

Xiao Zhang[1,2]($\boxtimes$), Lanxin Kong[1], Shunyi Zhu[1], Zhanhuai Li[1,2],
and Xiaonan Zhao[1,2]

[1] School of Computer Science, Northwestern Polytechnical University, Xi'an, China
zhangxiao@nwpu.edu.cn
[2] MIIT Key Laboratory of Big Data Storage and Management, Xi'an, China

Abstract. It is a big challenge to measure and monitor the performance of a large-scale distributed storage system accurately. We present a flexible approach based on the message analysis, named FSObserver, which can accurately and fine-grained trace individual request or response by observing network traffic. Experiments results show that our approach can get accurate performance with slight performance degradation.

1 Introduction

Over the past few years, there are tremendous efforts to evaluate and debug the performance problems of large-scale distributed storage systems. Some practitioners concentrate on monitoring individual devices and machines independently. Some researchers focus on detailed analysis of all messages by inserting some unique IDs into messages during instrumenting the system. Some others are immersed in the study of the storage system log [1]. System evaluation based on inner messages analysis has been intensively studied in [2,3]. When designing a monitoring and evaluation system, we should consider the independence, accuracy, high performance, and broad-applicability.

In this paper, we propose FSObserver, an out-of-band approach to capture performance related messages between clients and servers. It extracts performance characteristics from the messages. The core idea of FSObserver is to capture the request and reply messages between clients and servers. It extracts the time, size and operations information from messages. The size of this information is very small compared with the size of the messages. By analyzing each individual message, we can accurately evaluate the performance characteristics such as IOPS, throughput, and latency.

In the following sections, we discuss how to monitor and evaluate the Ceph distributed file system, and show the experiment results.

© IFIP International Federation for Information Processing 2018
Published by Springer Nature Switzerland AG 2018
F. Zhang et al. (Eds.): NPC 2018, LNCS 11276, pp. 142–147, 2018.
https://doi.org/10.1007/978-3-030-05677-3_14

The remainder of the paper is organized as follows. In Sect. 2 we present the related work that evaluates Ceph and other distributed storage systems. Section 3 describes the architecture of FSObserver, and explains how it works on the Ceph distributed file system. Section 4 illustrates the performance evaluation results of FSObserver and other widely used tools fio[1] respectively. Finally, we conclude this paper and present the future work of this study.

2   Related Work

Performance of a distributed storage system is very important in data centers. Past studies proposed various methods to debug and diagnose the systems. They concentrated on the in-band and out-of-band monitoring systems, black box and white box, intrusive, and log analysis and so on. There are several tools developed to monitor the performance of Ceph clusters[2]. Many black-box diagnosis techniques have been devised for performance evaluation in distributed systems. Dianna et al. used 5 tools to evaluate the performance and scalability of the Ceph distributed storage system [4]. Wang et al. evaluated the file and block I/O performance and scalability of Ceph, using a commercial high-end storage system [5]. Computer-system logs provide a glimpse into the states of a running system, and system diagnostics research around logs never stopped [6].

3   Design and Implement

3.1   Architecture of FSObserver

The FSObserver are designed to measure different aspects of performance in a large-scale distributed file system by packets analysis. We designed a flexible packet analyzer, which can capture related packets and save a little information from the payload. The analyzers can be turned on/off by a controller. These designs can get performance data without too much impact on the system. Figure 1(a) shows the architecture of FSObserver. There are 3 kinds of components in the FSObserver. The recorder processes can be turned on/off dynamically.

– Recorder
  It captures related packets using libpcap[3], which is a portable C++ library for network traffic capture. When a recorder process captures a read request packet, it analyzes the header of payload and outputs key information, such as time, transaction id, data length. We measure the impact of the recorder in several read/write scenarios. The performance impact is less than 5%.
– Controller
  It can start/stop some observers according to the administrator's input. The FSObserver can be used flexibly for various purposes.

---

[1] http://freshmeat.net/projects/fio/.

[2] http://www.ceph.com/performance/.

[3] http://www.tcpdump.org/.

– Observer

This is a python program for analyzing the output of observers. It gets IOPS by counting how many finished IO requests in a given period in the results. In our prototype, we output the performance information into a text file inside the nodes under test. Meanwhile, we run the observer on the same nodes. The performance characteristic of the nodes including IOPS, throughput, and latency can be calculated through one sequential scan of the text file. In a large-scale system, we can use the mechanism similar to ganglia. As shown in Fig. 1(b), we divide nodes into different monitor group. The nodes in one group save the raw performance data in a database like MySQL or RRDtool.

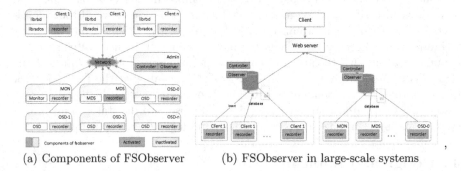

(a) Components of FSObserver   (b) FSObserver in large-scale systems

Fig. 1. Architecture of FSObserver

3.2 Implement of FSObserver for Ceph

After capturing a related packet using libpcap, it extracts the necessary information for performance measurement. Our main purpose is to get performance data, so we only need to analyze the messages with tag equals to 0x07. Further, we can only capture and analyze messages from a specific client.

The observer program analyzes the results from recorders. It can get IOPS, throughput and latency data from the results. For example, IOPS is calculated by counting the number of transactions finished in a given period. To analyze the performance of a certain client, we only need to deploy a recorder on the client. We can also get the same metric from records from all related OSD nodes with the client. We put the implementation on the GitHub[4].

4   Evaluation

We evaluate the accuracy and application of our tools. First, we compare the test results of FSObserver and widely used benchmarks to show the accuracy

---

[4] https://github.com/zhangxiao2000/fsobserver.

of our tools. Then, we measure the performance of a real user application to demonstrate how to use FSObserver in a real environment. The test environment comprised 10 commodity servers. 6 nodes work as Ceph servers, 4 nodes act as Ceph clients. The release version of Ceph is 12.2.4 Luminous.

4.1 Block Storage Interface

We use fio to test the performance of block storage interface. In our environments, we first test the performance use fio, then we lunch FSObserver and test the performance with fio again. We get two performance data from fio, and one performance data from FSObserver.

There are 6 different workloads used in our test, including sequence read, write, and mixed workloads and random read, write, and mixed workloads. For each workload, we test performance with different block sizes from 4k to 128k. Due to the page limitations, we only show the results of read and write. From these figures, the results of fio are almost the same, while one is taken without a recorder, the other was taken with FSObserver is working. The CPU and memory used by FSObserver are also very small. According to our experiments, it only used less than 0.3% CPU during the whole test (Figs. 2, 3 and 4).

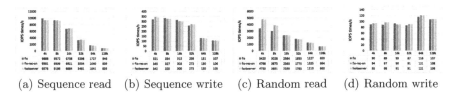

(a) Sequence read   (b) Sequence write   (c) Random read   (d) Random write

Fig. 2. The IOPS measured by fio and FSObserver

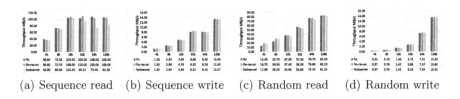

(a) Sequence read   (b) Sequence write   (c) Random read   (d) Random write

Fig. 3. The throughput measured by fio and FSObserver

4.2 Capture Real Workloads

In this part, we demonstrate how to get the I/O sequence of a real application. The process of compiling a Linux kernel is a complex task. There are 67 thousand

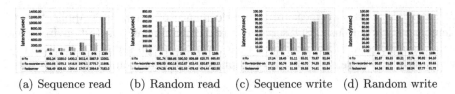

(a) Sequence read   (b) Random read   (c) Sequence write   (d) Random write

Fig. 4. The latency measured by fio and FSObserver

files in the Linux kernel 4.16.4. During the compiling process, several compilers read thousands of files and generate about 71 thousand new files. Figure 5 shows the IO throughput per minutes during the compiling process. We can find that during the compiling process, the write throughput is kept at a high level.

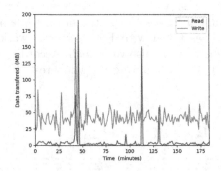

Fig. 5. Real workloads of compiling a Linux kernel

5   Conclusion

In this paper, we present a flexible performance monitoring tool for large-scale distributed storage systems. We have implemented it for Ceph. The experiments show that it can get coincident performance data with other widely used tools. We compared the accuracy with wide adapted benchmarks and measure a performance for a real application.

Acknowledgment. This work is supported by the NFS of China under Grant No. 61472323 and No. 61502392 and the Ministry of Science and Technology of China, National Key Research and Development Program (No. 2018YFB1004401).

References

1. Yuan, D., Zheng, J., Park, S., Zhou, Y., Savage, S.: Improving software diagnosability via log enhancement. ACM Trans. Comput. Syst. (TOCS) **30**(1), 4 (2012)
2. Zhao, Y., Cao, Y., Chen, Y., Zhang, M., Goyal, A.: Rake: semantics assisted network-based tracing framework. IEEE Trans. Netw. Serv. Manage. **10**(1), 3–14 (2013)
3. Määttä, M., Räty, T.: Automatic model creation to support network monitoring. IEEE Access **2**, 142–152 (2014)
4. Gudu, D., Hardt, M., Streit, A.: Evaluating the performance and scalability of the Ceph distributed storage system. In: 2014 IEEE International Conference on Big Data (Big Data), pp. 177–182. IEEE (2014)
5. Wang, F., Nelson, M., Oral, S., Atchley, S.: Performance and scalability evaluation of the Ceph parallel file system. In: Proceedings of the 8th Parallel Data Storage Workshop, pp. 14–19. ACM (2013)
6. Oliner, A., Ganapathi, A., Xu, W.: Advances and challenges in log analysis. Commun. ACM **55**(2), 55–61 (2012)

vGrouper: Optimizing the Performance of Parallel Jobs in Xen by Increasing Synchronous Execution of Virtual Machines

Peng Jiang[1], Ligang He[1(✉)], Shenyuan Ren[1], Junyu Li[1], and Yuhua Cui[2]

[1] Department of Computer Science, University of Warwick, Coventry CV4 7ES, UK
Ligang.He@warwick.ac.uk
[2] Shandong Worldwide Byte Security Co.Ltd., Jinan, China
cuiyh@jzxtsec.com

Abstract. Xen is one of the most popular virtualization platforms nowadays, which has been broadly used by the industry. Credit scheduler, the default scheduler of Xen, was initially designed for serial jobs, which achieves good performance overall for serial jobs. Unfortunately, the parallel jobs are likely to co-exist with serial jobs in the same host in practice, the resource contention between virtual machines results in severe performance degradation of the parallel jobs. In this paper, we propose vGrouper, a progressive solution to enhance the performance of the parallel jobs. The vGrouper focuses on synchronizing the execution time of the parallel nodes in order to achieve the best performance of the parallel job. Moreover, the vGrouper guarantees that the parallel job nodes are able to run concurrently on pCPUs for the entire time slice, which maximizes the efficiency of communication between parallel nodes. A prototype of vGrouper is implemented, the experimental results demonstrate that the performance of the parallel job and resource utilization in Xen have been significantly improved.

Keywords: Xen · Virtual machine · Virtualization · Parallel jobs
Scheduling

1 Introduction

The Xen virtualization platform has been embraced by industry nowadays due to its impressive scalability and outstanding performance. However, the credit scheduler, which is the default scheduling strategy of Xen, has been identified to be less capable of scheduling parallel jobs. A parallel job usually relies on communication between nodes, which is a completely different working fashion from the serial job. Due to the lack of knowledge of the parallel job, the credit

© IFIP International Federation for Information Processing 2018
Published by Springer Nature Switzerland AG 2018
F. Zhang et al. (Eds.): NPC 2018, LNCS 11276, pp. 148–152, 2018.
https://doi.org/10.1007/978-3-030-05677-3_15

scheduler treats the nodes of each parallel job node as a normal serial job, where the particularity of the parallel job is completely disregarded. The shortcoming of credit scheduler has been discussed in several studies [2–5].

In this paper, we propose vGrouper, a progressive solution to further enhance the performance of the parallel job to a new level. The vGrouper focuses on synchronizing the execution time of the parallel nodes in order to improve the performance of the parallel job. Moreover, the vGrouper guarantees that the parallel job nodes are able to run concurrently on pCPUs for the entire time slice, which maximizes the efficiency of communication between parallel nodes.

2   Background and Related Work

2.1   Credit Scheduler

The credit scheduler, which is a proportionally sharing scheduling strategy based on fair allocation of resource, was initially designed for scheduling serial jobs. Each VM will be given credits to consume during execution, which indicates that how many physical resources a VM can have. There two parameters *weight* and *cap* can be used for customizing the bias of resource allocation according to user's need, where the *weight* indicates the relative proportion of execution time and *cap* stands for the maximum amount time of execution time of a VM. In credit scheduler, two priorities are used to indicate the status of a VM. $UNDER$ priority is given to those VMs which are remaining credits, while a VM running out of credits is given $OVER$ priority. Each vCPU of the VM is allowed to executed for a certain time, and the VMs with $UNDER$ priority will be scheduled one by one.

2.2   Related Work

Several optimizations have been made to improve the performance of the parallel job in Xen. Chen and et al. found that overcommitted vCPUs brings performance degradations to concurrent jobs in [1], they mitigate the negative impact by adjusting the time length of execution of VMs according to the type of the workload. Shao and et al. also reveal the problem of overcommitted vCPUs in their research and indicate there is potential penalty on the performance of the parallel job in Xen [3], they choose to expose the workload types of VMs to Xen hypervisor to alleviate the decrease of the performance of the parallel job.

3   Problem Analysis

In the virtualized environment, a pCPU is proportionally shared among several vCPUs, and each vCPU in the local job queue is scheduled for a certain length of time periodically. We first make some assumptions on the environment of the virtual system based on the policies of credit scheduler and common experience of configuration. Firstly, the size of each parallel job is smaller than the number of pCPUs. Secondly, VMs of serial workloads are assumed to be in busy status. Thirdly, the VMs of the parallel job are Uniprocessor systems and only committed to execute the parallel jobs. Forthly, the total number of the VMs in system is much bigger than the number of the pCPUs of the host.

Let p be the number of pCPUs, s be the size of a parallel job and j be the total number of VMs. As the credit scheduler targets for global workload balanced, the VMs will be evenly and randomly allocated to the pCPUs. Therefore, we know the probability of the parallel nodes being allocated to different pCPUs is:

$$P_A = \frac{\prod_{i=0}^{i<s} p - i}{p^s} \tag{1}$$

Moreover, the nodes of the parallel job should be placed at the same positions of their run queues so that they can be scheduled simultaneously. We know the size of each run queue is:

$$q = j/p \tag{2}$$

Thus, the probability of all parallel nodes being placed at the head of the run queues is:

$$P_B = \frac{1}{q^{s-1}} \tag{3}$$

Therefore, the probability of a parallel job being simultaneously placed on the head of run queues by the credit scheduler is:

$$P_C = \frac{\prod_{i=0}^{i<s} p - i}{p^s} \cdot \frac{1}{q_{min}^{s-1}} \tag{4}$$

We introduce execution efficiency E_s to indicate the percentage of the parallel sub-tasks being simultaneous executed in a time slice. Additionally, as $dom0$ processes the I/O request in Xen, it is compulsory to schedule $dom0$ along with the parallel nodes. Thus, overall evaluation on the efficiency of scheduling a parallel job in Xens:

$$E_{overall} = \frac{\prod_{i=0}^{i<s+1} p - i}{p^{s+1}} \cdot \frac{1}{q_{min}^s} \cdot E_s \tag{5}$$

As can be seen, the probability of a parallel job being properly scheduled by credit scheduler is extremely low. Therefore, a co-scheduler is required to assist the credit scheduler to make the appropriate decision on scheduling the parallel job. The problem can be illustrated by Fig. 1.

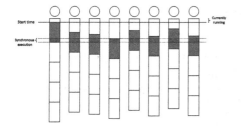

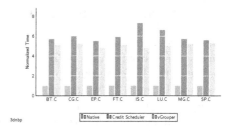

Fig. 1. Problem of parallel job in Xen

Fig. 2. NPB performance of a parallel job with size of four

4   Co-scheduling Solution

The co-scheduling solution solve the problem using three steps. Firstly, it identifies the parallel job in Xen, which requires the VMs of parallel job to be labeled by the users so that co-scheduler is able to identify parallel workload. Secondly, the co-scheduler relocates the VMs of the parallel jobs to avoid overcommitted pCPUs. All VMs of the parallel jobs will be examined in this step, if multiple VMs of a parallel lie on the same job queue of pCPU, the vGrouper is expected to redistribute then to different job queues by migrating. Notably, this step is only taken one time when a parallel job is created. Thirdly, for each parallel job, we choose a flag VM which indicates the parallel job is encountered. When the flag VM is about to be scheduled online, the vGrouper schedule all related VMs of the same parallel job together with the flag VM as a group by boosting the parallel nodes. The boost mechanism of credit scheduler allows current running vCPUs to be preempted by others to accelerate the responding time, which can be used by vGrouper to simultaneously scheduled the VMs of a parallel job together.

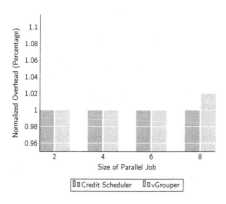

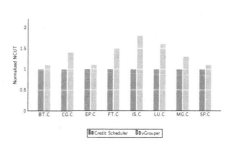

Fig. 3. The overhead of co-scheduling process

Fig. 4. Number of Communications per Uni Time (NCUT)

5   Experiments and Evaluation

We conduct several experiments to evaluate the performance of vGrouper. Firstly, we test the vGrouper with NPB benchmark suite. As Fig. 2 illustrates, the performance of the benchmarking program is significantly increase as expected, especially on IS and LU, which contains lots of communications between the VMs of the parallel job. Secondly, we observe the overhead of the vGrouper. Figure 3 shows that overhead incurred by the vGrouper is negligible, even though that there is a slight increase as the size of the parallel job increases. Finally, we evaluate the improvement of the utilization. We introduce Number of Communications Per Uni Time (NCUT) as a metric to assess utilization of the system. As can be seen from Fig. 4, the frequency of communications in unit time is dramatically increased as the receiving VMs of communications are guaranteed to be online.

6   Conclusion

In this paper, we investigate the reasons for performance degradation of the parallel job in Xen and analyze the importance of simultaneous scheduling to the execution of the parallel job in Xen. We present vGrouper to assist the credit scheduler in handling the parallel application by increasing the length of synchronous execution of a parallel job. The experiments show that vGrouper effectively optimizes the performance of the parallel job in Xen and increases the utilization of the system.

References

1. Chen, H., Jin, H., Hu, K., Huang, J.: Scheduling overcommitted VM: behavior monitoring and dynamic switching-frequency scaling. Future Gener. Comput. Syst. **29**(1), 341–351 (2013). https://doi.org/10.1016/j.future.2011.08.006. Including Special section: AIRCC-NetCoM 2009 and Special section: Clouds and Service-Oriented Architectures
2. Huang, W., Liu, J., Abali, B., Panda, D.K.: A case for high performance computing with virtual machines. In: Proceedings of the 20th Annual International Conference on Supercomputing, ICS 2006, pp. 125–134. ACM, New York (2006). https://doi.org/10.1145/1183401.1183421
3. Shao, Z., Wang, Q., Xie, X., Jin, H., He, L.: Analyzing and improving MPI communication performance in overcommitted virtualized systems. In: 2011 IEEE 19th Annual International Symposium on Modelling, Analysis, and Simulation of Computer and Telecommunication Systems, pp. 381–389, July 2011. https://doi.org/10.1109/MASCOTS.2011.27
4. Weng, C., Wang, Z., Li, M., Lu, X.: The hybrid scheduling framework for virtual machine systems. In: Proceedings of the 2009 ACM SIGPLAN/SIGOPS International Conference on Virtual Execution Environments, VEE 2009, pp. 111–120. ACM, New York (2009). https://doi.org/10.1145/1508293.1508309
5. Ye, K., Jiang, X., Chen, S., Huang, D., Wang, B.: Analyzing and modeling the performance in Xen-based virtual cluster environment. In: 2010 IEEE 12th International Conference on High Performance Computing and Communications, HPCC, pp. 273–280, September 2010. https://doi.org/10.1109/HPCC.2010.79

Systolic Array Based Accelerator and Algorithm Mapping for Deep Learning Algorithms

Zhijie Yang, Lei Wang$^{(\boxtimes)}$, Dong Ding, Xiangyu Zhang, Yu Deng, Shiming Li, and Qiang Dou

College of Computer, National University of Defense Technology,
Changsha, China
Leiwang@nudt.edu.cn

Abstract. As the depth of DNN increases, the need for DNN calculations for the storage and computing power of the underlying computing platform is increasing. In this work, we implement an accelerator on FPGA for deep learning algorithms (CNN and RNN). The core computing module of the accelerator is a 32 * 32 systolic array of PEs. A mapping method for variable size of CNN and RNN algorithms is proposed. The experiment result shows that the maximum power consumption of the accelerator is 7.5W@100Mhz, the peak performance is 0.2Tops/s, and the real performance is 7.6Mops@100Mhz when running the 1st layer of LeNet-5.

Keywords: Accelerator · Systolic array · DNN · Data mapping

1 Introduction

At present, almost all large companies are developing their own artificial intelligence chips. Facebook's hardware is optimized for its Caffe2 framework [1]. Amazon is building an ecosystem of cloud infrastructure by AWS [2]. The most notable example of deep learning algorithm accelerators is Google's TPU [3]. Google Data Center has been using TPU to accelerate AI services such as image recognition and language translation.

Compared with CPUs and GPUs, TPU can provide high performance and high energy efficiency. For example, TPU1 can provide 92Top/s with 8-bit integer [3]. Google's TPU brings systolic design, which is an old hardware architecture [4], back to the face of architecture designers. The core computing unit of the TPU is a 256 * 256 systolic array of MACs. The systolic array structure can effectively support the memory intensive and computing intensive features

© IFIP International Federation for Information Processing 2018
Published by Springer Nature Switzerland AG 2018
F. Zhang et al. (Eds.): NPC 2018, LNCS 11276, pp. 153–158, 2018.
https://doi.org/10.1007/978-3-030-05677-3_16

of deep learning algorithms. Google introduced some details of TPU1 in a paper published at ISCA 2017 [3]. However, Google did not disclose much detail about TPU2 and TPU3 until now.

Therefore, in order to design deep learning accelerators based on the systolic array, we need to solve the following problems: How to implement a deep learning accelerator using a systolic array and map different deep learning algorithms to it? The main contributions of this paper are:

(1) An RTL design of the accelerator architecture whose core computing unit is a 32 * 32 systolic array and necessary peripheral modules.
(2) We propose a method for mapping arbitrary size convolution and matrix multiplication operations to the fixed-sized systolic array to accelerate CNN and RNN computation.

We synthesis the accelerator to Xilinx's FPGA V7 690T, and perform detailed functional verification and performance, power and area analysis. The experiment results show that the inference process of the CNN model and RNN model can be run correctly on this accelerator and be accelerated. The real performance is 7.6Mops@100Mhz when running the first layer of LeNet-5.

2   Related Work

In addition to google [3] and microsoft work [6], the Cambricon designed a new generation of edge intelligent processor Cambricon 1M. Farabet et al. proposed an extensible data flow hardware architecture for running the generic vision algorithm neuFlow on Xilinx V6 FPGA platform [5]. Chen et al. made a custom multi-chip machine-learning architecture [7]. Alwani et al. constructed a fused-layer CNN accelerator for the first five convolutional layers of the VGGNet-E network [8]. Li et al. designed an 8-Bit fixed-point CNN hardware inference engine [9].

3   Systolic Array Design

Figure 1 shows the overall architecture of the proposed accelerator design. It contains the systolic array, input memory, output memory, weight memory, controller, and an AXI interface for data exchange with the host computer.

3.1   Processing Element Design

Figure 2 shows the module diagram of the processing element (PE). The PE contains input registers, part sum registers, weight registers, and the counter.

The input register is used for receiving an incoming data at each cycle from the upper computing unit or input memory for MAC and transferring input data to lower PE. The weight register is used for storing weights and forward weights to the right PE. The part sum register is responsible for keeping the temporary result and continuously accumulate with the new result. The counter is used for counting the cycles, because, for some algorithm, it will take several cycles to propagate the result to the adjacent PEs. When the counter reaches the specified threshold, the final result is transmitted to the upper unit or the output memory.

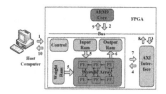 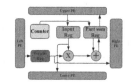 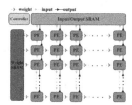

Fig. 1. Overall design of the accelerator.   **Fig. 2.** Systolic array PE.   **Fig. 3.** Two-dimensional systolic array's data flow. (Color figure online)

3.2   Array Structure and Data Flow

As shown in Fig. 3, the structure of a two-dimensional systolic array has the following data flow. In the systolic array, the input data flow, represented by the green dotted solid arrow, is input into the systolic array from the top and propagates to the bottom until the bottommost PE discards it after use. The weight data flow, represented by the blue dot-shaped hollow arrow, is similar to the input data flow but it propagates from the left to the right. The output data flow, represented by the black solid black arrow, is output from each PE and it propagates from the bottom to the top.

3.3   Controller Design

The controller module has the following functions. It controls the data to be read into the memory from the buffer, starts the computation, controls the data to flow into the array, and controls the results to flow out of the array and to write back to memory. Finally, it controls the results to be returned to the buffer to be taken by the host computer.

4   Data Mapping Method

4.1   Mapping of CNN Algorithm

We only discussed the computation of convolution layer at this section. FC layers mapping to the systolic array is similar to RNN algorithm's mapping.

The convolutional layer receives N feature maps as input. Each input feature map is convolved by a $K*K$ size kernel to generate one pixel in one output feature map. The stride is S. M output feature maps will be the set of input feature maps for the next conv layer. Figure 4 shows the mapping to an ideal systolic array, assuming that the size of the systolic array is $M \times (C \times R)$ and the stride is 1. The horizontal axis input is the kernel, the first row is $weight[0][t_i][*][*]$, t_i is from 0 to $N-1$. The second row is $weight[1][t_i][*][*]$ and so on. The data in the second row is provided one cycle later than the element of the same position in the first row, and so on. The vertical axis input is the data block corresponding to the input feature map, as shown in Fig. 4. The input feature map's data flows as similar as the kernel's data flow.

The last point of the first row of the systolic array is completed in $K \times N + R \times C - 1$ cycles. Each PE in the first row saves the output feature map of output channel 0. Assuming that the 1st PE of the 1st row can read the first $point[0, 0]$ of the output channel 0 of output feature map and in $K \times N$ and at $K \times N + 1$, it can read the second $point[0, 1]$. In this way, the last $point[C - 1, R - 1]$ is read at $K \times N + R \times C - 1$ cycles. And so forth, the point in time at which each PE completes the operation is represented as an anti-diagonal line as shown in the Fig. 4. After completing the operation, all results are transmitted vertically.

Assume that the size of the systolic array is $A \times B$. The ideal systolic size of the algorithm is $M \times C \times R$. It can be seen as a box with the size of $A \times B$, overlaid on the ideal systolic array layout, and filled with zeros where there is no data at the boundary.

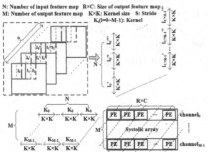

Fig. 4. A CNN ideal mapping algorithm.

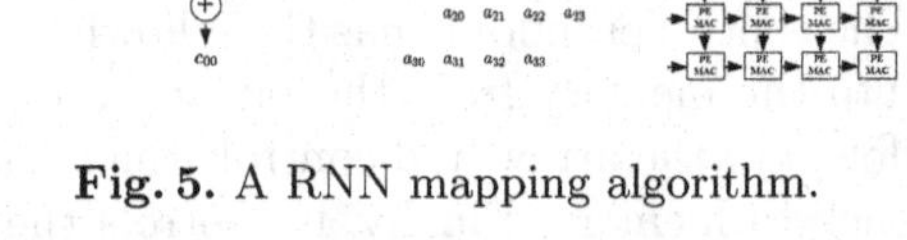

Fig. 5. A RNN mapping algorithm.

4.2   Mapping of RNN Algorithm

The core operation of RNN is matrix multiplication used by forwarding propagation. And matrix multiplication's operation method is very suitable for the systolic array. Both of them use a row to multiple a column.

Thus, as shown in Fig. 5, the left matrix is input in rows of the systolic array and the right matrix in the columns of the systolic array. Then the matrix product from the corresponding position of the systolic array can be got. Consider a matrix multiplication $A \times B = C$ and a systolic array of size $M \times N$. The size of A is $r \times s$, the size of B is $s \times t$ and size of C is $r \times t$. When $r <= M$, $t <= N$, the matrix multiplication can be operated by the systolic array in one pass. While if $r > M$ or $t > N$, it is necessary to split r or t. Separate the rows of matrix A into parts and divide the columns of matrix B into parts. When the result is not an integer, PEs not used in the array are filled with zeros.

5 Experimental Result

5.1 Implementation

The accelerator is implemented in Verilog RTL. Vivado 2017.04 is used for synthesis and implementation. The implementation platform is Xilinx's FPGA V7 690T. This paper implements a one-dimensional $1 * 24$ systolic array, $2 * 2$, $4 * 4$, $8 * 8$, $16 * 16$ and $32 * 32$ systolic arrays, and compares the results. The clock frequency is set to 100 MHz. Its power consumption is about 7.5 W. The comparison of power consumption of different size systolic array is shown in Fig. 6(a). As shown in the Fig. 6(b), the on-chip resource consumption ratios of the various size of systolic arrays are compared.

5.2 Performance Evaluation

In the design, the operand of each PE unit is 32-bit fixed-point, and the clock frequency is set to be 100MHz. Because the performance metrics are limited by the size of the specific problem, our metrics in subsequent performance evaluations are subject to the above conditions. *Peak Performance:* The peak performance is 0.2Tops@100Mhz when the data is completely filled with the array. *Throughput:* The peak throughput of the $32 * 32$ systolic array is 1600 Mresults/s. The real throughput rate calculated is 60.3 Mresults/s when running the 1st layer of LeNet-5. *Performance/Area Ratio:* As shown in Fig. 6(c), as the array grows, the performance/area ratio decreases. This also shows that as the number of computing units increases, the performance (throughput) revenue per PE tends to decrease.

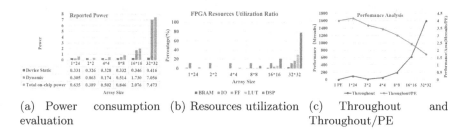

(a) Power   consumption   (b) Resources utilization   (c)   Throughout   and
evaluation   Throughout/PE

Fig. 6. Comparison of high level synthesis results of the systolic array of different sizes.

6 Conclusion and Future Work

This work proposes the implementation of a DNN accelerator based on a 32 *
32 systolic array. Then the data mapping method for mapping variable sizes
of CNNs and RNNs to the systolic array is proposed. In the future, we will
enlarge the systolic array and design an instruction set in order to satisfy the
requirements of the controller so that the accelerator can achieve more complex
functions.

Acknowledgment. This project is supported by HGJ2017ZX01028103.

References

1. Hazelwood, K., Kalro, A., Law, J., Lee, K., Lu, J., Noordhuis, P., et al.: Applied machine learning at Facebook: a datacenter infrastructure perspective. In: IEEE International Symposium on High Performance Computer Architecture, pp. 620–629. IEEE Computer Society (2018)
2. Tang, B., S.O. Information, Y.N. University: Case study of the application of field programmable gate array FPGA in the smart skill. Application of IC (2018)
3. Jouppi, N.P., Young, C., Patil, N., Patterson, D., Agrawal, G., Bajwa, R., et al.: In-datacenter performance analysis of a tensor processing unit, pp. 1–12 (2017)
4. Kung, H.T., Leiserson, C.E.: Systolic arrays (for VLSI). In: Proceedings of Sparse Matrix Conference, pp. 256–282 (1978)
5. Farabet, C., Martini, B., Corda, B., Akselrod, P.: NeuFlow: a runtime reconfigurable dataflow processor for vision. In: Computer Vision and Pattern Recognition Workshops, vol. 9, pp. 109–116. IEEE (2011)
6. Chung, E., Fowers, J., Ovtcharov, K., Papamichael, M., Caulfield, A., Massengill, T., et al.: Serving DNNs in real time at datacenter scale with project brainwave. IEEE Micro **38**(2), 8–20 (2018)
7. Chen, Y., Sun, N., Temam, O., Luo, T., Liu, S., Zhang, S., et al.: DaDianNao: a machine-learning supercomputer. In: IEEE/ACM International Symposium on Microarchitecture, vol. 5, pp. 609–622. IEEE (2014)
8. Alwani, M., Chen, H., Ferdman, M., Milder, P.: Fused-layer CNN accelerators. In: IEEE/ACM International Symposium on Microarchitecture, pp. 1–12. IEEE (2016)
9. Li, Z., et al.: Laius: an 8-bit fixed-point CNN hardware inference engine. In: 2017 IEEE International Symposium on Parallel and Distributed Processing with Applications and 2017 IEEE International Conference on Ubiquitous Computing and Communications (ISPA/IUCC). IEEE (2017)

A Fine-Grained Performance Bottleneck Analysis Method for HDFS

Yi Liu[1], Yunchun Li[1], Honggang Zhou[1], Jingyi Zhang[2], Hailong Yang[1(✉)], and Wei Li[1]

[1] School of Computer Science and Engineering, Beihang University, Beijing 100191, China
{luice,lych,zhg,hailong.yang,liw}@buaa.edu.cn
[2] School of Instrumentation Science and Opto-electronics Engineering, Beihang University, Beijing 100191, China
16171093@buaa.edu.cn

Abstract. The performance issue of HDFS has always been a great concern due to its widely adoption in both production and research environments. However, a fine-grained performance analysis tool is missing to effectively identify the bottlenecks as well as to provide useful guidance for performance optimization. In this paper, we propose a fine-grained performance bottleneck analysis tool, which extends HTrace with fine-grained instrumentation points that are missing in Hadoop official distribution. In addition, we propose an effective trace merging method that improves the understandability of our analysis. We analyze the performance of HDFS under different kinds of workloads and get undiscovered insights.

Keywords: HDFS · Instrumentation · Bottleneck analysis
Performance optimization

1 Introduction

Distributed file systems are widely used in various computing domains such as supercomputing and big data analytics. However, diagnosing performance issues of distributed file systems is still a challenging task, because the performance bottleneck of a distributed file system may come from various components of the system, and even interaction between different components. Therefore, effective performance analysis tools for distributed file systems such as Hadoop are of vital importance. Currently, many researches focus on end-to-end performance analysis frameworks, which capture the information flow of each request of the distributed file system and then obtain the performance information of each component of the system and the interaction between the components such as Dapper [5], Magpie, Stardust [6], Xtrace [1], HTrace [2], etc.

© IFIP International Federation for Information Processing 2018
Published by Springer Nature Switzerland AG 2018
F. Zhang et al. (Eds.): NPC 2018, LNCS 11276, pp. 159–163, 2018.
https://doi.org/10.1007/978-3-030-05677-3_17

Among the above performance analysis tools, HTrace has been merged into Hadoop release to provide useful performance data. However, the default HTrace instrumentation within Hadoop has the following limitations for fine-grained performance analysis. Firstly, the default Hadoop provides very limited instrumentation points without detailed information captured. For example, the major components of HDFS [4] such as *Namenode*, *Datanode* and their interactions are not instrumented. For example, we can not conclude whether *Namenode* bookkeeping is the bottleneck because Hadoop's official implementation haven't instrumented *Namenode*. Secondly, the default instrumentation in Hadoop cannot obtain the detailed parameter information for the function calls instrumented. For better analyzing the performance of a distributed file system, not only the time series of each function call but also the size of bytes processed by each function need to be known in order to identify the potential performance bottlenecks. Lastly, instrumentation information provided in default Hadoop is difficult to retrieve and visualize. For example, in just a few minutes, hundreds of megabytes of trace files are generated, making it hard to locate and diagnose the performance issues.

Therefore, this paper focuses on the performance analysis of HDFS by extending HTrace to provide fine-grained instrumentation. In addition to solve the trace explosion problem, we propose a trace compression method that merges the traces of repeated function calls and only maintains the representative statistics during instrumentation. Finally, through experiments on representative big data workloads, we obtain some useful insights.

2   Methodology

2.1   Fine-Grained Instrumentation

The instrumentation of Hadoop's official distribution mainly instrument client sensed delay or *Datanode* sensed delay. HDFS contains more complex interaction beyond *Datanodes* and the client node. What's more, we can not distinguish network delay from the local file I/O delay. Due to this reason, we instrument some new performance-related blocks. They mainly reside in *Namenode*, *Datanodes*. Our purpose is to get fine-grained *Namenode* performance, *Datanode* local I/O performance, *Datanode* network performance, *Datanode* and *Datanode* data exchange performance. Except for simply obtaining function call duration, our instrumentation also encodes important function arguments into traces such as data size processed, block id and filename so we can monitor data process rate, I/O error occurrence. One of the biggest challenges of our instrumentation is that Java has many polymorphous functions. In the case, we will instrument every function and merge them in the trace processing procedure.

2.2   Trace Compression

The running of HDFS will generate a huge volume of traces. In our experiments, after several minutes of Spark execution, a trace larger than 1 GB will generate.

Traditional HDFS performance analysis tools neglect this fact and rely on human labor to find the bottleneck in a large amount of data.

We present an effective method for compressing traces. We observe that before compressing, there are many repeated function call. For example, the *receiveBlock* function usually contains hundreds of *receivePacket* functions. We merge repeated function call receivePacket in this circumstance and only extract several representative statistics from these merged function calls. The number of call trees will reduce by more than 90% after trace compression. Formally, we do a breadth-first traversal from bottom to top inside a call tree and merge the subtrees with the same structure. After compression inside every call tree, we compress these trees with the same structure.

3 Evaluation

3.1 Experiment Setup

Our experiments are conducted with a cluster with seven nodes with one master node (which is *Namenode* in HDFS), five slave nodes (which are *Datanode* in HDFS) and one client Node. The master node and slave nodes are equipped with Xeon E5-5620, 16 GB memory. To achieve higher throughput, we use Intel Xeon Phi (Knights Landing) for workload generating. The many-core and high volume of memory enable Phi to start many HDFS clients simultaneously. The implementation is shown in Fig. 1. The trace is generated into local files that are collected and stored in database. The *Workload Generator* component generates HDFS I/O requests. The *Recover Call Tree* component reads from user configuration to decide the function calls to keep. The *Trace Compress* component traverses call trees and performs compression. Finally, the *Bottleneck Visualization* component displays the compressed call tree.

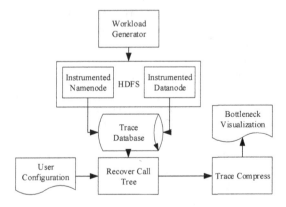

Fig. 1. The implementation overview of our HDFS performance analysis tool.

3.2   Performance Bottleneck Analysis

Across Workloads. We choose the tiny sized workload input from *Hibench*. For machine learning workloads, data will be iterated for many times generating large traces thus we use sampling (sample rate is 0.05) to reduce trace size. For *Wordcount* workload, the largest delay is caused by *FileSystem#createFileSystem* which spends total 90.21 s. The second largest delay is caused by *DFSOutput-Stream#close* which spends total 10.54 s. Local I/O plays an ignorable role here. The delay of *Datanode* flushing buffer into local file system is too small to measure. And also we can conclude that using faster storage medium won't speed up application greatly. We can see the bottleneck is in the client node. The process for initiating *FileSystem* object has a large potential to optimize. We have a similar conclusion for *Sort*, *Terasort*, *Pagerank*, *LogisticRegression* and *Nweight* workloads. *Bayes* workload is different from the above workloads. The largest delay is caused by *BlockSender#*sendBlock. Reading from local file system causes 3.10 s delay and reading from remote *Datanode* causes 0.49 s delay.

Impact of File Size. We use *Wordcount* workload to explore the impact of file size on HDFS performance. We use tiny, small, large, huge sized workloads which contains 32000, 320000000, 3200000000, 32000000000 respectively. Due to the trace size explosion, we use a sample rate of 1, 0.01, 0.001, 0.0001 respectively. With the increase of data size, the impact of *FileSystem#createFileSystem* is becoming weaker. In tiny sized workload, this operation causes total 91.92 s delay compared with application time 28 s (we add up delay from different *Datanodes*). In small-sized workload, it takes 1.55 s compared with application time 32 s. And in larger sized workloads, it hasn't been sampled. So in small-sized workloads, the file system creation process is an import bottleneck.

Impact of Request Frequency. In [3], the authors directly model real request patterns from the AliCloud on IOPS, Inter-arrival time, session size and read request size. However, Alicloud is a very large cluster contains tens of thousands of nodes. For our small cluster, we multiply IOPS with different factors α but retains the distribution the model. With request frequency increasing, we can explore which part of HDFS facing the request pressure as shown in Table 1.

The delay of request mainly caused by *sendBlock* operation. However, the average delay of this operation is decreasing. Although *FileSystem#createFileSystem* plays an important role in request delay, its duration has little to do with request frequency. We can find out that the delay of *sendBlock* first increase but then decrease with request frequency increasing. In small frequency, HDFS is in cold start state thus the delay is relatively large. And when request frequency is very large, the resource contention is more severe. The *BlockSender#sendPacket*, *FSNamesystem#getBlockLocations* (*Namenode* searching for block locations for a given file) operation has the same conclusion. Contrary to common sense, the bottleneck under frequent request is neither in *Namenode* nor in *Datanode*. Thus optimization for the concurrent request in client node is more important.

Table 1. The average delay (second) of some major functions under different request frequencies.

Function	$\alpha = 0.001$	$\alpha = 0.005$	$\alpha = 0.01$	$\alpha = 0.05$	$\alpha = 0.1$	$\alpha = 0.5$
FileSystem# createFileSystem	0.1567	0.1842	0.1827	0.2060	0.1887	0.1992
sendBlock	0.0054	0.0026	0.0020	0.0012	0.0009	0.0015
BlockSender# sendPacket	0.0005	0.0004	0.0002	0.0001	0.0001	0.0002
FSNamesystem# getBlockLocations	0.0088	0.0006	0.0005	0.0003	0.0007	0.0014
Total	0.0423	0.0439	0.0426	0.0648	0.0801	0.0674

4 Conclusion

In this paper, we propose an extension to HTrace in order to support fine-grained performance bottleneck analysis for HDFS. In addition, we propose a trace compression method to merge the repeated function calls for efficient performance analysis. We've also done a series of experiments to explore the bottleneck under different workloads and get useful insights.

Acknowledgment. The authors would like to thank all anonymous reviewers for their insightful comments and suggestions. This work is supported by National Key Research and Development Program of China (Grant No. 2016YFB1000304) and National Natural Science Foundation of China (Grant No. 61502019).

References

1. Fonseca, R., Porter, G., Katz, R.H., Shenker, S., Stoica, I.: X-trace: a pervasive network tracing framework. In: Proceedings of the 4th USENIX Conference on Networked Systems Design and Implementation, p. 20. USENIX Association (2007)
2. Apache HTrace: htrace (2015). https://htrace.incubator.apache.org/
3. Ren, Z., Shi, W., Wan, J., Cao, F., Lin, J.: Realistic and scalable benchmarking cloud file systems: practices and lessons from alicloud. IEEE Trans. Parallel Distrib. Syst. **PP**(99), 1 (2017)
4. Shvachko, K., Kuang, H., Radia, S., Chansler, R.: The Hadoop distributed file system. In: 2010 IEEE 26th Symposium on Mass Storage Systems And Technologies (MSST), pp. 1–10. IEEE (2010)
5. Sigelman, B.H., et al.: Dapper, a large-scale distributed systems tracing infrastructure. Technical report, Google, Inc (2010)
6. Thereska, E., et al.: Stardust: tracking activity in a distributed storage system. In: ACM SIGMETRICS Performance Evaluation Review, vol. 34, pp. 3–14. ACM (2006)

Mimir+: An Optimized Framework of MapReduce on Heterogeneous High-Performance Computing System

Nan Hu, Zhiguang Chen, Yunfei Du, and Yutong Lu[✉]

School of Data and Computer Science, Sun Yat-sen University,
Guangzhou, China
yutong.lu@nscc-gz.cn

Abstract. In this paper, we present an optimized data processing framework: Mimir+. Mimir+ is an implementation of MapReduce over MPI. In order to take full advantage of heterogeneous computing system, we propose the concept of Pre-acceleration to reconstruct a heterogeneous workflow and implement the interfaces of GPU so that Mimir+ can facilitate data processing through reasonable tasks and data scheduling between CPU and GPU. We evaluate Mimir+ via two benchmarks (i.e. the WordCount and large-scale matrix multiplication) on the Tianhe-2 supercomputing system. Experimental results demonstrate that Mimir+ achieves excellent acceleration effect compared with original Mimir.

Keywords: High-performance computing · MapReduce
Heterogeneous

1 Introduction

With the continuous development of information technology, the data generated in daily life, industrial productions and scientific researches are exploding. The convergence of high-performance computing and big data processing is becoming a promising solution to efficiently tackle with the massive data.

MapReduce is a programming paradigm popularized by Google [1] which presents a parallel computing model and method for large-scale data processing. Implementations of MR-MPI [5] have given practical and feasible solutions to transplant MapReduce to high-performance computing system. However, MR-MPI suffers from a severe shortcoming which is its simple memory management. In our previous work, we presented Mimir [2] which is an optimized framework based on MR-MPI. Mimir redesigns the execution model to incorporate a number of sophisticated optimization techniques that achieve similar or better performance with significant reduction in the amount of memory used. Nevertheless, we can see that MR-MPI and Mimir mainly perform their calculation in CPUs.

© IFIP International Federation for Information Processing 2018
Published by Springer Nature Switzerland AG 2018
F. Zhang et al. (Eds.): NPC 2018, LNCS 11276, pp. 164–168, 2018.
https://doi.org/10.1007/978-3-030-05677-3_18

Among the latest TOP500 list published in June 2018, Summit captured the number one spot with a performance of 122.3 petaflops on High Performance Linpack. Each node of Summit is equipped with two 22-core Power9 CPUs, and six NVIDIA Tesla V100 GPUs. Summit's championship demonstrated the capabilities and potentiality of heterogeneous high-performance computing system. Although MapReduce-MPI and Mimir can implement the MapReduce model well on high-performance computing system, their lack of heterogeneous architecture will cause a problem that the heterogeneous resources cannot be fully utilized.

We continued the work of Mimir and present Mimir+ in this paper. This work targets to promote the calculation speed of Mimir and support heterogeneous GPU acceleration on high-performance computing system.

The remainder of the paper is organized as follows. Section 2 introduces the optimizations of Mimir+. Section 3 describes the experimental environment and results. Other research related to our paper is presented in Sect. 4. We conclude this paper in Sect. 5.

2   Design of Mimir+

In this section, we introduce the main optimizations and designs in Mimir+.

2.1   Heterogeneous Workflow

The original Mimir designs two special objects called KV containers and KMV containers to help manage the intermediate data $<key, value>$ pairs between map phase and reduce phase. Similar to Mimir and MR-MPI, Mimir+ still adopts the KV containers and four basic phases: map, aggregate, convert and reduce. However, in order to further improve the computation speed, we reconstruct a heterogeneous workflow for Mimir+. Specifically, Mimir+ integrates the map phase and the aggregate phase into one process called MAP, and the convert phase and the reduce phase are integrated into another process called REDUCE.

Figure 1 shows the reconstructed workflow of Mimir+. The first thing to do in MAP is to process the input data according to a user-defined callback function. Here, we implement a new interface for GPU to perform the map jobs and users can select whether to perform the calculation on the GPU or on CPU by using the corresponding interfaces. Then, Mimir+ performs the MPI_Alltoallv function to exchange the KVs and stored them in KVCs through an interleaved execution model. When the MAP process ends, the REDUCE process starts and Mimir+ converts $<key, value>$ in KVC to $<key, <value1, value2, value3...>>$ into the KMVC. Mimir+ also has two types of interfaces in reduce phase for users to determine whether they will use GPU to calculate the reduce jobs or not. A user-defined reduce_GPU function implemented in CUDA is needed to start the data processing in GPU and the final output data will be transferred back from GPU memory.

2.2   Design of GPU Acceleration Modules

When we implement the heterogeneous workflow of Mimir+, we can't simply load the map/reduce tasks and data into GPU because GPU is not suitable for receiving fragmented data. Here we propose a concept of Pre-acceleration. Pre-acceleration actually refers to the operations we perform before we use GPU to calculate data. Specifically, operations like data partitioning, data communication and data transmission required before GPU acceleration can all be regarded as a part of Pre-acceleration. In combining the concept of Pre-acceleration, we divide the GPU acceleration process into four modules to achieve an efficient and convenient management. Figure 2 shows a brief architecture of Pre-processing Module, Transmission Module, Calculation Module and Feedback Module.

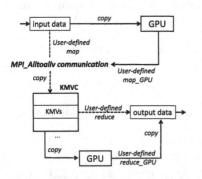

Fig. 1. Workflow of Mimir+

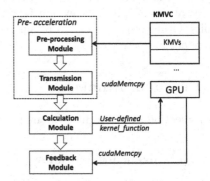

Fig. 2. GPU acceleration modules

3   Evaluation

In this section, we evaluate the acceleration effect of Mimir+ and compare it with the original Mimir.

3.1   Performance Comparison

We perform WordCount (WC) and matrix multiplication on 4 nodes of heterogeneous computing system: Tianhe-2. Each node in Tianhe-2 is equipped with a 2-way 8-cores Intel Xeon CPU E5-4640, 128 GB memory, running at 2.40 GHz. The GPU equipped on the node is NVIDIA Tesla K80 GPU with two sets of 12 GB GDDR5 memory (24 GB in total), 4992 stream processors, the memory bandwidth is 240 GB/s. Each node installs a 64-bit Linux 3.10.0 operating system, and we use mvapich2-2.2, gcc-4.8.5 and CUDA 8.0 to conduct the tests on Mimir+.

The results of WC are shown in Fig. 3(a). As we can notice, Mimir+ obtains a comparatively good acceleration effect on WC. With the increase of test data,

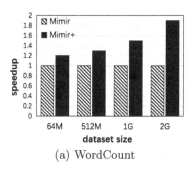

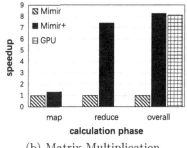

(a) WordCount   (b) Matrix Multiplication

Fig. 3. Performance comparison on WordCount and matrix multiplication

the acceleration effect achieved by Mimir+ is becoming more and more obvious. Because the tasks of WordCount in MapReduce do not require intensive computing, the effect of acceleration in Mimir+ is not fully reflected.

Since the tasks of matrix multiplication vary from the map phase and the reduce phase, we tested and compared the two phases separately in the other experiment. Moreover, in order to compare the difference between the calculation of heterogeneous systems and pure parallel GPU computing, we performed the matrix multiplication in GPU alone using CUDA with the same input data and put the result into comparison. The results are shown in Fig. 3(b). In the map phase, because of the little calculation, the effect of acceleration is not good. However, in the reduce phase which contains a huge amount of calculation, Mimir+ achieves a considerable speedup of about 7.4 compared with Mimir. After comparing Mimir+ and Mimir in map and reduce phase, we performed an overall test and the whole framework can achieve a speedup of about 8.1 to 8.3. Nevertheless, the calculations performed in GPU alone achieved a speedup of about 8.5 which is close to Mimir+.

4   Related Work

MapReduce is an extremely popular model and many researches intend to improve the performance of MapReduce jobs on heterogeneous system.

Phoenix [6,8] proposed by Colby Ranger et al. from Stanford University is a MapReduce implementation on shared memory system targeting thread-based parallel programming. Shared memory minimizes indirect costs caused by parallel task spawning and data communication. Mrphi [4] is also a MapReduce implementation optimized for the Intel Xeon phi. Different from these systems, Mimir+ works on large-scale distributed-memory systems.

Mars [3] is a MapReduce implementation totally deployed on GPUs. In Mars, there are a large number of threads running in parallel on the GPUs. Each thread computes a KV pair at a time. To avoid multi-threaded write conflicts, Mars uses a lock-free strategy to ensure that parallel programs are correct, with minimal synchronization costs.

On high performance computing system, Tsoi et al. developed a heterogeneous computing system, Axel [7], which consist of FPGAs and GPUs, and they implemented a MapReduce framework on Axel which significantly promoted the speed of calculation.

5 Conclusion

In this paper, we propose an optimized MapReduce framework on heterogeneous high-performance computing system: Mimir+. This framework inherits the core idea of MR-MPI, reconstructs a heterogeneous workflow and implements the GPU acceleration interfaces so that we can accelerate the data processing of MapReduce jobs and make full use of resources on heterogeneous high-performance computing system. Our results on the Tianhe-2 supercomputer prove that Mimir+, compared to the original Mimir, significantly improves the speed of data processing during the computing phase for data-intensive applications.

Acknowledgments. We are grateful to the anonymous reviewers for their valuable suggestions that will be used to improve this paper. This work is partially supported by National Key R&D Program of China 2017YFB0202201, National Natural Science Foundation of China under U1611261, 61433019, U1435217, 61872392 and the Program for Guangdong Introducing Innovative and Entrepreneurial Teams under Grant NO. 2016ZT06D211.

References

1. Dean, J., Ghemawat, S.: MapReduce: simplified data processing on large clusters. ACM (2008)
2. Gao, T., et al.: Mimir: memory-efficient and scalable mapreduce for large supercomputing systems. In: Parallel and Distributed Processing Symposium, pp. 1098–1108 (2017)
3. He, B., Fang, W., Luo, Q., Govindaraju, N.K., Wang, T.: Mars: a mapreduce framework on graphics processors. In: International Conference on Parallel Architectures and Compilation Techniques, pp. 260–269 (2008)
4. Lu, M., Liang, Y., Huynh, H.P., Ong, Z., He, B., Goh, R.S.M.: MrPhi: an optimized mapreduce framework on Intel Xeon Phi coprocessors. IEEE Trans. Parallel Distrib. Syst. **26**(11), 3066–3078 (2015)
5. Plimpton, S.J., Devine, K.D.: Mapreduce in MPI for large-scale graph algorithms. Parallel Comput. **37**(9), 610–632 (2011)
6. Talbot, J., Yoo, R.M., Kozyrakis, C.: Phoenix++: modular MapReduce for shared-memory systems. In: International Workshop on Mapreduce and ITS Applications, pp. 9–16 (2011)
7. Tsoi, K.H., Luk, W.: Axel: a heterogeneous cluster with FPGAS and GPUS. In: International Symposium on Field-Programmable Gate Arrays, pp. 115–124 (2010)
8. Yoo, R.M., Romano, A., Kozyrakis, C.: Phoenix rebirth: scalable MapReduce on a large-scale shared-memory system. In: IEEE International Symposium on Workload Characterization, pp. 198–207 (2011)

DLIR: An Intermediate Representation for Deep Learning Processors

Huiying Lan[1,2,3(✉)] and Zidong Du[1,3]

[1] Intelligent Processor Research Center, Institute of Computing Technology (ICT),
CAS, Beijing, China
lanhuiying@ict.ac.cn
[2] University of Chinese Academy of Sciences (UCAS), Huairou, China
[3] Cambricon Tech. Ltd., Beijing, China

Abstract. The Deep learning processor (DLP), especially ASIC-based accelerators, have been proved to be a promising device for accelerating the computation of deep learning algorithms. However, the learning cost of mastering these DLPs is high as they use different programming interfaces. On the other hand, many deep learning frameworks are proposed to ease the burden of developing deep learning algorithms, but few of them support DLPs. Due to the special features in DLPs, it is hard to integrate a DLP into existed frameworks.

In this paper, we propose an intermediate representation (called DLIR) to bridge the gap between DL frameworks and DLPs. DLIR is a tensor-based language with built-in tensor intrinsics that can be directly mapped to hardware primitives. We show that DLIR allows better developing efficiency and is able to generate efficient code.

Keywords: Deep learning processor · Intermediate representation
Deep learning framework · Deep learning

1 Introduction

Deep learning processors (DLPs) have become powerful devices for processing large scale neural networks, especially ASIC-based DLPs [1–6]. However, DLPs are still not fully accepted by DL participants due to the lack of programming supports. On the other hand, many DL programming frameworks [7–10] have been proposed to ease the burden of developing DL algorithms but often only on traditional devices (e.g., CPUs and GPUs). Primitives on such devices are basically scalar computations and they use cache in their system. Therefore, frameworks designed for such devices are often lower operators to fine-grained operations and completely ignore the management of on-chip memories. For example, TVM [11] is a software stack for deep learning, which leverages Halide IR to present computation loops and extracts several useful scheduling primitives

© IFIP International Federation for Information Processing 2018
Published by Springer Nature Switzerland AG 2018
F. Zhang et al. (Eds.): NPC 2018, LNCS 11276, pp. 169–173, 2018.
https://doi.org/10.1007/978-3-030-05677-3_19

to allow users to manually optimize the computation. However, TVM require the user to describe the computation through scalar operations and use *tensor_intrinsics* scheduling primitive to map the tensor operation to instructions in the backend DLP (which is VTA in the case of TVM). This complicates the programming of the DLP as the code describing the computation of the tensor intrinsics is completely unnecessary. XLA is a recent proposed backend embedded in TensorFlow to provide subgraph optimizations. It proposes an High-level optimizer (HLO) and also with an IR to represent the computation graph received from the TensorFlow frontend. Although XLA provides tensor semantics that in a way match DLP primitives, operators in XLA is very high-level and does not provide hardware-specific operations such as memory copying between main memory and on-chip scratchpad memory which is extensively used in DLPs. Such frameworks lack necessary components to seamlessly support a DLP. Therefore, an indirection layer that is specifically designed for DLPs is on demand to bridge the gap between frameworks and DLPs.

Our solution is an indirection layer composed of an intermediate representation (called DLIR), a compiler and runtime. DLIR is a tensor-based IR, inherently support tensor types (neurons and synapses) and tensor intrinsics (e.g., convolution, pooling, matmul) that can be directly mapped to hardware primitives. By leveraging such structures, DLIR compiler is able to generate highly efficient code that is comparable to hand-optimized instructions.

2   Intermediate Representation Language

In this section, we introduce the intermediate representation language, i.e., DLIR, which can be interpreted into operations supported by DLPs. In order to reduce the learning costs, DLIR is designed to be embedded in C++ as a library. It can be directly called by front-ends functions and generate instructions for backend.

2.1   Data Structure

DVIR defines two N-dimensional (N-D) tensor data types, *Neuron* and *Synapse* to encapsulate data and be used as operands of HLIR operators (see Sect. 2.2). Both types are defined using a built-in data structure, *Dimension*, which helps specify the tiling of a dimension. Due to the limited on-chip resources, an N-D array often needs to be partitioned into several segments to fit into on-chip buffers. Computation partitioning on DLPs is complicated as there are multiple dimensions for a N-D tensor. A dimension with size d can be tiled as $d = n \times s + r$, which requires at least three variables to describe the partitioning. *Dimension* is introduced to encapsulate these variables. By iterating through combinations of segments of different dimentions of a tensor, we are able to traverse all possible segments in the tiled tensor. In addition, to enbale explicit memory copy between the main memory and on-chip buffers, we provide two data structures, i.e., *NeuronBuffer* and *SynapseBuffer*, to represent allocated data on on-chip buffers. A segment in *Neuron* will be transferred to a corresponding *NeuronBuffer*.

2.2   Operators

We classify the programming supports of current DLPs according to whether they require programmers to manually write tiling and computation partitioning within a layer, i.e., the ability to process arbitrary scale of computation. We call the code generator (CG) provided by DLPs as high-level code generator (HLCG) and low-level code generator (LLCG). HLCG refers to CGs that can process arbitrary scale of computation, e.g., CG of DianNao and ShiDianNao. LLCG refers to CG that can compile programs at the level of assembly or ISA, e.g., Cambricon ISA. Accordingly, we provides two levels of operator that can map to these two CGs, i.e., high-level operators (HLOP) and low-level operators (LLOP). Therefore, both types of CG can be integrated into DLIR.

These two levels of OP are also corresponding to the data structures. HLOP takes *Neuron* or *Synapse* as input and output parameters, and LLOP takes segments in a *Neuron* or *Synapse* as input and output parameters. Both HLOP and LLOP can be translated directly into hardware-specific assembly languages or instructions by invoking HLCG and LLCG.

In addition to directly invoke vendor-provided CG to generate code, HLOPs can also be first interpreted to LLOPs, and then translated to instructions. With such transformation, DLPs with LLCGs can also use HLOPs as the official programming interface which is typical for DL frameworks.

3   Compilation

The compilation process is shown in Fig. 1. Operations in the computational graph can be mapped to HLOPs. For DLPs using HLCGs, DLIR passes the parameters to HLCGs to generate executable code. For those using LLCGs, DLIR will invoke the HLOP defined with LLOPs and memory operations to generate LLOP sequences, which will then be compiled by the LLCGs. In the function that defines HLOPs by LLOPs, users need to specify loop tiling, data segmentations and the use of on-chip buffers in such functions. In addition, as DLPs have strict restriction on data layout, the compiler will rearrange a tensor according to the dimension informations so that the required data can be sequentially fetched.

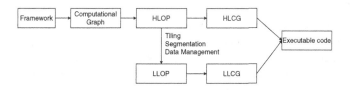

Fig. 1. Compilation process of DLIR

4   Evaluation

We use Caffe as the front-end as it is a commonly used DL framework. We reimplement *Setup*, *Forward* and *Backward* functions in the layers in Caffe. Each call of these functions will invoke the DLIR compiler to generate an instruction sequence that will be transferred to our backend and executed. We use Cambricon as the backend, as it is a state-of-the-art ISA and architecture proposed for NN algorithms, and it involves many representative features of DLPs.

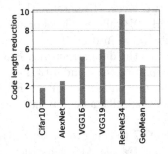

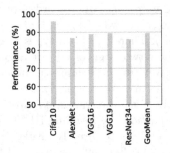

Fig. 2. Code length reduction of using DLIR compared to hand-written code.

Fig. 3. Performance of DLIR compared to hand-optimized code.

4.1   Developing Efficiency

We evaluate the developing efficiency of DLVM on five large realistic networks, i.e., Cifar10, AlexNet, VGG16, VGG19 and ResNet34, covering five representative algorithms (convolution, pooling, fully-connected, batch normalization, and local respond normalization) used in popular deep learning networks. Figure 2 shows that by using DLIR, we can reduce the source code by 4.19× on average. The highest reduction comes from ResNet34 (i.e., 9.72×), and the lowest reduction comes from Cifar10 (i.e., 1.75×). The more layers a network composed of, the higher the reduction ratio is. Because the code reduction is primarily gained from eliminating redundant implementations of the same algorithm with different scales.

4.2   Performance

We evaluate the performance of DLVM on the mentioned networks to show that DLIR is able to generate efficient code. The performance is demonstrated in Fig. 3. DLIR achieves 89.37% performance compared to that of hand-optimized code on average. The performance loss primarily comes from the missing overlapping between computations and memory accesses especially between layers and the memory accesses saved by layer fusion. However, the hand-optimized code could takes seasoned programmers days to maximize the optimize. In DLIR, we mostly concern about usability instead of performance, therefore this performance loss is acceptable for us.

5 Conclusion

In this paper, we propose an intermediate representation (DLIR) to bridge the gap between high-level DL frameworks and DLPs. DLIR is composed of an intermediate representation language with special designed data structures (i.e., *Dimension, Neuron* and *Synapse*), hierarchic operators and memory operations. By leveraging DLIR, we are able to shorten the code by 4.19× on five large networks on average. In addition, the compiler is able to generate code with up to 89.37% performance compared to hand-optimized code using Cambricon as the backend.

Acknowledgement. This work is partially supported by the National Key Research and Development Program of China (under Grant 2017YFA0700902, 2017YFB1003101), the NSF of China (under Grants 61472396,61432016, 61473275, 61522211, 61532016, 61521092, 61502446, 61672491, 61602441, 61602446, 61732002, and 61702478), the 973 Program of China (under Grant 2015CB358800), National Science and Technology Major Project (2018ZX01031102) and Strategic Priority Research Program of Chinese Academy of Sciences (XDBS01050200).

References

1. Chen, T., Du, Z., Sun, N., Wang, J., Wu, C.: DianNao: a small-footprint high-throughput accelerator for ubiquitous machine-learning. In: Proceedings of the 19th International Conference on Architectural Support for Programming Languages and Operating Systems (ASPLOS), Salt Lake City, UT, USA, pp. 269–284 (2014)
2. Chen, Y., et al.: DaDianNao: a machine-learning supercomputer. In: Proceedings of the 47th Annual IEEE/ACM International Symposium on Microarchitecture (MICRO-47), pp. 609–622 (2015)
3. Zhang, S., et al.: Cambricon-X: an accelerator for sparse neural networks. In: Proceedings of the 49th Annual IEEE/ACM International Symposium on Microarchitecture (MICRO-49) (2016)
4. Liu, D., et al.: Pudiannao: a polyvalent machine learning accelerator. In: Proceedings of the Twentieth International Conference on Architectural Support for Programming Languages and Operating Systems, ASPLOS 2015, Istanbul, Turkey, 14–18 March 2015, pp. 369–381 (2015)
5. Du, Z., et al.: ShiDianNao: shifting vision processing closer to the sensor. In: Proceedings of the 42nd Annual International Symposium on Computer Architecture, Portland, OR, USA, 13–17 June 2015, pp. 92–104 (2015)
6. Liu, S., et al.: Cambricon: an instruction set architecture for neural networks. In: 43rd ACM/IEEE Annual International Symposium on Computer Architecture, ISCA 2016, Seoul, South Korea, 18–22 June 2016, pp. 393–405 (2016)
7. Abadi, M., et al.: TensorFlow: a system for large-scale machine learning, p. 18 (2016)
8. Collobert, R., Kavukcuoglu, K., Farabet, C.: Torch7: a matlab-like environment for machine learning
9. Nervana Systems (2016). github.com/nervanasystems/neon
10. Jia, Y., et al.: Caffe: convolutional architecture for fast feature embedding. arXiv preprint arXiv:1408.5093 (2014)
11. Chen, T., et al.: TVM: end-to-end optimization stack for deep learning. CoRR abs/1802.04799 (2018)

GPU Memory Management Solution Supporting Incomplete Pages

Li Shen[✉], Shiqing Zhang, Yaohua Yang, and Zhiying Wang

National University of Defense Technology, Changsha, China
zhangshiqing12@nudt.edu.cn

Abstract. Despite the increasing investment in integrated GPUs and next-generation interconnect research, discrete GPUs connected by PCI Express still account for the dominant position of the market, the management of data communication between CPU and GPU continues to evolve. This paper analyze the address translation overhead and migration latency introduced by this paged memory management solution in CPU-GPU heterogeneous systems. Based on the analysis, a new memory management scheme is proposed: paged memory management solution supporting incomplete pages, which can limit both address translation overhead and migration delay. "Incomplete" refers to a page that has only been partially migrated. This new memory management solution modifies the address translation and data migration process with only minor changes in hardware.

1 Introduction

The current GPU paged memory management solution is designed and implemented based on the unified memory [1–3]. When the requested page is missing on the device side, the system transfers the page to the local memory automatically. Paged memory management solution introduces two major overheads: address translation overhead and migration latency [4]. Due to the large GPU memory capacity and limited number of TLB entries, large pages can reduce address translation overhead. On the other hand, the migration delay is positively related to the page size.

In order to limit the address translation overhead and migration delay at the same time, this paper proposes a new GPU memory management scheme: paged memory management solution supporting incomplete pages. "Incomplete" refers to a page that has only been partially migrated. We implemented it on the gpgpu-sim simulator. Experimental results show that, compared to page memory management, it can reduce address translation overhead and migration latency at the same time.

© IFIP International Federation for Information Processing 2018
Published by Springer Nature Switzerland AG 2018
F. Zhang et al. (Eds.): NPC 2018, LNCS 11276, pp. 174–178, 2018.
https://doi.org/10.1007/978-3-030-05677-3_20

This paper has the following three contributions:

1. We analyzed the address translation overhead and migration latency introduced by paged memory management solution. Based on this, a new memory management scheme is proposed: paged memory management solution supporting incomplete pages, which can limit both address translation overhead and migration delay.
2. We defined the "incomplete" page status, added records of the migrated range in the TLB and page table entries, modified the address translation operation, and divided it into two steps: check hit/miss and check whether it has been migrated, to support our new memory management scheme.
3. We modified the page migration operation and adjusted the functionality of GPU memory management unit (GMMU), so that it can specifies migration scope and merge requests when generating migration requests, to support our new memory management scheme and increase bandwidth utilization.

2   Related Work

Lustig and Martonosi [5] designed a fine-grained data dependency tracking mechanism to reduce migration delays. However, the system does not migrate data automatically, and introduces the overhead of tracking full/empty bits. Zheng et al. used the idle bandwidth to pre-migrate unrequested page based on the observation that PCI-E bandwidth utilization is low [4]. Agarwal et al. [6] use memory system information about the characteristics of heterogeneous memory systems to set the conditions for page migration. However, subsequent experiments have shown that the overhead exceeds the performance gains compared to the simple "migrate at the first request" strategy. Vesely et al. [7] analyzed address translation in heterogeneous systems and found that the cost in the GPU was an order of magnitude higher than the CPU. Ausavarungnirun et al. [8] designed and implemented Mosaic to provide application transparency support for multiple page sizes. In Mosaic, TLB and page tables need to support both large pages and small pages. The complex design introduces a lot of additional hardware modifications and overhead.

3   Paged Memory Management Solution Supporting Incomplete Pages

3.1   Overall Design

Compared with paged memory management solution, this new scheme has the following two differences. In the address translation process, in addition to determining whether the request is hit or miss, it is also checked whether the data in the requested address range has been migrated to the GPU memory. During the migration process, the system does not transfer the entire page. The generated migration request needs to specify the scope of the transfer. The architectural view of GPU MMU and TLBs in paged memory management solution supporting incomplete pages is shown in Fig. 1.

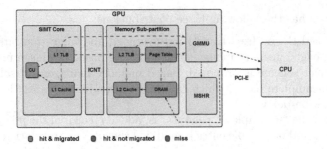

Fig. 1. Architectural view of GPU MMU and TLBs in paged memory management solution supporting incomplete pages

3.2 Address Translation

When querying each level of the TLB or the page table, the first step is to check whether the page is recorded. If it is missing, the request is passed to the next level TLB or page table. If it is hit, then check if the request address range has been migrated to the GPU. If it has been migrated, the address is translated and returned for cache access; if not, the GMMU informs the corresponding L1 TLB to suspend the request processing, generates a migration request and sends it to the CPU. When determining whether the request address has been migrated to the GPU, the page status and the migrated range are queried sequentially.

3.3 Migration Process

Since only the partial pages corresponding to the request are migrated, the migration request needs to inform the migration scope. It improves the ratio of calculation and memory access, reduces the unnecessary data transmission overhead, and significantly reduces the migration delay. In order not to waste CPU-GPU bandwidth, the scope of the migration request sets the minimum length based on the bandwidth value. The GMMU views the migration request waiting to be processed when generating a new migration request, and merges the requests whose migration range is less than the default threshold.

3.4 Data Access

When the requested data is migrated to the GPU local memory, the page table and the TLB are updated, then the request address is re-queried from the L1 TLB, and the cached and dram are accessed step by step with the converted address until the required data is obtained. Since the address translation and migration phases have already handled possible data misses, data can be obtained locally on the GPU.

Table 1. Simulator configuration

Simulator	GPGPU-Sim 3.x
GPU Arch	NVIDIA GTX-480 Fermi-like, 15 CUs @ 1.4 GHz
Caches	16 KB/CU L1, Mem Side 128 kB/Channel L2
TLBs	128-entry Per CU L1, 512-entry Shared L2
Clock Freqs	Core:IC:L2:DRAM 700:700:700:1024 (MHz)
GPU GDDR5	12-channels, 384 GB/sec aggregate
MSHR	128Entries/Memory Partition

4 Evaluation

4.1 Simulator and Benchmarks

We implemented our solution on gpgpu-sim [9,10]. The system configuration we use is shown in Table 1, including the key parameters of the GPU core and memory partition. It is assumed that the GPU memory is large enough so that no over-subscription will occur. We test under both 16 GB/sec and 32 GB/sec as representative of the current and future bandwidth [11]. The 10 benchmarks tested in our experimental are from ispass2009-benchmarks in gpgpu-sim. They come from different benchmark suites and are applied in various fields. BFS, MUM and NN are included in Rodinia, which is a general benchmark suite in GPGPU research.

4.2 Performance Comparison

We use 1 KB migration unit size as an example of multiple valid ranges migration, and the page size is 2 MB. Figure 2 shows that, when the bandwidth is 16 GB/sec, the performance of our new solution ("Incomplete") is much better than paged memory management solution ("Complete", which is called baseline in the following part). On average, our scheme improves from baseline's 82.43× deceleration to 1.36× acceleration compared with programmers controlled transfer.

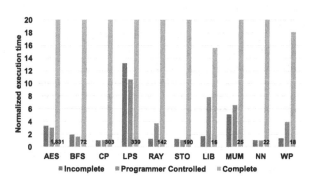

Fig. 2. Performance comparison under 16 GB/sec bandwidth. Workload execution time (lower is better) is normalized to ideal copy + execute overlap execution time.

5 Conclusion and Future Work

We defined the "incomplete" page status, added records of the migrated range in the TLB and page table entries, and divided the address translation operation into two steps: check hit/miss and check whether it has been migrated, to support our new memory management scheme. We modified the page migration operation and adjusted the functionality of GMMU, to support our new memory management scheme and increase bandwidth utilization.

But our experimental part is not perfect enough. There are many aspects to be tested and analyzed, including the performance comparison with Mosaic. We will complete the follow-up experiments in the next period of time, and analyze the experimental results to further improve our scheme. In addition, our scheme wastes part of memory capacity while reducing address translation overhead and migration delay, and this part of the cost needs to be further solved.

References

1. Harris, M.: Unified memory in CUDA 6. GTC On-Demand, NVIDIA (2013)
2. Lindholm, E., Nickolls, J., Oberman, S., Montrym, J.: NVIDIA Tesla: a unified graphics and computing architecture. Proc. IEEE Micro **28**(2), 39–55 (2008)
3. Landaverde, R., Zhang, T., Coskun, A.K., Herbordt, M.: An investigation of unified memory access performance in CUDA. In: Proceedings of IEEE High Performance Extreme Computing Conference, pp. 1–6 (2014)
4. Zheng, T., Nellans, D., Zulfiqar, A., Stephenson, M., Keckler, S.W.: Towards high performance paged memory for GPUs. In: Proceedings of IEEE International Symposium on High Performance Computer Architecture, pp. 345–357 (2016)
5. Lustig, D., Martonosi, M.: Reducing GPU offload latency via fine-grained CPU-GPU synchronization. In: Proceedings of IEEE International Symposium on High Performance Computer Architecture, pp. 354–365 (2013)
6. Agarwal, N., Nellans, D., Stephenson, M., O'Connor, M., Keckler, S.W.: Page placement strategies for GPUs within heterogeneous memory systems. ACM SIGPLAN Not. **50**, 607–618 (2015)
7. Vesely, J., Basu, A., Oskin, M., Loh, G.H., Bhattacharjee, A.: Observations and opportunities in architecting shared virtual memory for heterogeneous systems. In: Proceedings of IEEE International Symposium on Performance Analysis of Systems and Software, pp. 161–171 (2016)
8. Ausavarungnirun, R., et al.: Mosaic: a GPU memory manager with application-transparent support for multiple page sizes. Carnegie Mellon University, SAFARI Research Group, Technical report TR-2017-003 (2017)
9. Bakhoda, A., Yuan, G.L., Fung, W.W.L., Wong, H., Aamodt, T.M.: Analyzing CUDA workloads using a detailed GPU simulator. In: Proceedings of IEEE International Symposium on Performance Analysis of Systems and Software, pp. 163–174 (2009)
10. Aamodt, T.M., et al.: GPGPU-Sim 3.x manual (2012)
11. Ajanovic, J.: PCI express 3.0 overview. In: Proceedings of Hot Chips: A Symposium on High Performance Chips (2009)

Leveraging Subgraph Extraction for Performance Portable Programming Frameworks on DL Accelerators

Xiao Zhang[1,2,3(✉)], Huiying Lan[1], and Tian Zhi[1]

[1] Intelligent Processor Research Center, Institute of Computing Technology (ICT), CAS, Beijing, China
zhangxiao@ict.ac.cn
[2] University of Chinese Academy of Sciences (UCAS), Beijing, China
[3] Cambricon Tech. Ltd., Beijing, China

Abstract. Deep learning framework plays an important role in connecting hardware platform and algorithm. In recent years, some domain-specific deep learning accelerators with better performance and energy efficiency were proposed by researchers. However, current frameworks lack enough considerations about how to better support the possible new features brought by accelerators. In this paper, we propose to build a performance portable programming framework with subgraph extraction. The intuition is that increasing ratio of optimizations are taken from the top-level framework to the low-level software stack of accelerator. In response to this development trend, framework needs to pay more attention to the splitting strategy of computation graph for the heterogeneous computation.

1 Introduction

In recent years, we have witnessed many significant breakthroughs of deep learning algorithm in a multitude of domains. This superior accuracy, however, comes at the cost of high computational complexity. Researchers try to design more efficient architectures based on the features of deep learning algorithm and get some promising results [3–5, 7–10]. These results show that domain-specific accelerators outstand in both speed and energy efficiency compared to traditional solutions.

On the other hand, in order to explore and deploy deep learning algorithm conveniently, both academia and industry have developed several deep learning frameworks, such as MXNet [2], TensorFlow [1] and Caffe [6]. Those frameworks automatically optimize the computation flow, generate high-performance kernels and schedule kernels in parallel if possible.

However, there is a gap between emerging DL accelerators and existing programming frameworks. In order to run deep learning algorithm with the highest performance, some accelerators and its software stacks have tried to break the wall and search optimal solution in a large space. Unfortunately, current deep learning frameworks only provide limited adaptions for this new feature.

© IFIP International Federation for Information Processing 2018
Published by Springer Nature Switzerland AG 2018
F. Zhang et al. (Eds.): NPC 2018, LNCS 11276, pp. 179–184, 2018.
https://doi.org/10.1007/978-3-030-05677-3_21

2 Motivation

2.1 DLA and Graph Fusion

We designed and implemented a deep learning accelerator and its software stack, and we call the accelerator DLA in following sections. The design of DLA is concluded from multiple deep learning accelerators, including NVidia DLA, DaDianNao [4] and TPU. There are multiple cores in DLA. Each core in DLA can complete a computation task independently, which makes it actually a parallel model with shared global memory.

Compared to traditional limited method that fusing some specific sequence composed of element-wise operators issued by framework, software stack of DLA offers a more radical solution. It optimizes and fuses the total graph (see the Fig. 1). This strategy has several benefits. First, the experts developed lower stack can give better solution because they know more about hardware architecture. Also, fusing a large graph into a single node greatly saves the kernel launch cost, which is important for inference task.

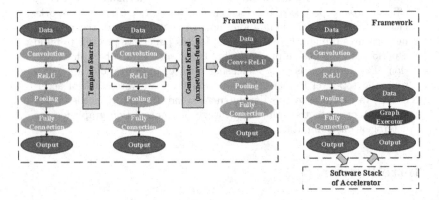

Fig. 1. In left part, the framework searches limited templates and generates new kernels to replace them. In right part, optimization stack of accelerator receives the whole graph, optimizes and generates a new executor back to framework.

2.2 Heterogeneous Computation

Heterogeneous computation is unavoidable for DLA and other accelerators. Some operators in new algorithms are hard to parallelize or to abstract to the tensor operators offered by accelerators, and the frequency of embedding accelerator in mobile device might be reduced to save energy. As a result, assigning some parts on CPU might bring better total performance. Thus, before we use lower software stack to optimize graph, we need to extract a subgraph composed by operators assigned on DLA. In other words, framework should have a clever split strategy and method to extract appropriate subgraph from the original deep networks.

3   Subgraph Extraction

When we try to extract a subgraph based on whether each operator is well-supported by accelerator, the direct intuition is to make it a maximum connected convex subgraph. Connectivity guarantees data relation between operators which is necessary for most optimizing methods. Maximum grants the largest searching space and reduces kernel launch overheads. Convexity is used as a constraint to avoid circle which leads to dead lock when scheduling. A subgraph **S** of a directed acyclic graph **G** is convex if and only if there is no directed path between two vertices of **S** which contains an arch not in **S** (see the Fig. 2).

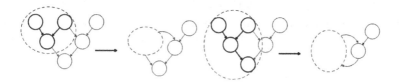

Fig. 2. Example of convex and non-convex subgraph.

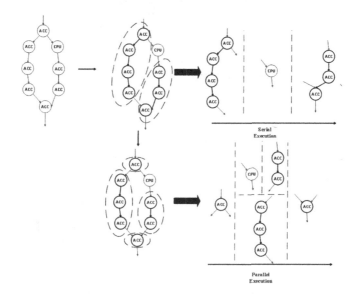

Fig. 3. Post-prune strategy. The ACC node represents operator assigned on accelerator, and the CPU node represents operator assigned on CPU.

Merging a large subgraph into a single node helps the corresponding computation to run faster, however, it may hinder scheduler to get maximum parallelism in some case. As Fig. 3 shows, the fused graph must wait for all its input to be ready even though some inputs are not necessary at the early stage of its computation. Similarly, although not all the outputs of a subgraph are generated at the final stage, all descendants must keep waiting until computation of total subgraph finishes. So, we append a post-prune process to split each subgraph into smaller parts, each of which has only one input and output operator.

4   Evaluation

The experiment platform is DLA, a multi-core deep learning accelerator as we mentioned before. We first evaluate the performance before and after the graph fusion to demonstrate the validation of graph fusion. As shown in Fig. 4, performance of all six entire-network benchmarks are improved, which achieves a speedup of 1.18× on average compared with the baseline, which we do not implement the graph fusion. Specifically, the improvement of ResNet34 and ResNet50 is clearly higher than other four networks.

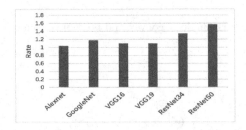

Fig. 4. Relative speedup of graph.

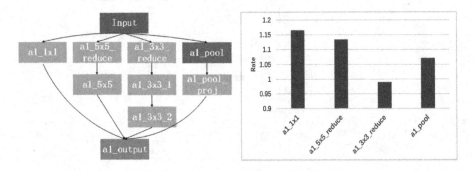

Fig. 5. Left figure shows the structure of the inception-v3 block. Right figure shows speedup after the post-prune strategy. Horizontal axis label represents part of the block assigned to CPU

Then we evaluate the speedup of the post prune process. We use the intuitive maximum connected convex subgraph extraction strategy as the baseline.

In order to accurately evaluate the prune strategy, we choose a basic block of operators with multiple branches from inception-v3 networks for its enough braches. To trigger subgraph extraction, we separately assign operators on different branch to CPU and evaluate the speedup. As the result shown in the Fig. 5, except for assigning operator on the critical path to CPU, performance of the other three heterogeneous computation get a speedup of 1.1× on average, which is an obvious improvement.

5   Conclusion

In this paper, we propose a performance portable programming framework. The key motivation is that framework needs a subgraph extraction strategy to better balance schedule parallelism and fusion efficiency. We implement such a framework by migrating MXNet. This strategy is designed to cooperate framework with lower software stack in heterogeneous computation task, because none of them can complete the whole task independently. This strategy can be used in a wider field if accelerators choose to take over framework to optimize the computation graph by themselves.

Acknowledgment. This work is partially supported by the National Key Research and Development Program of China (under Grant 2017YFA0700902, 2017YFB1003101), the NSF of China (under Grants 6147239, 61432016, 61473275, 61522211, 61532016, 61521092, 61502446, 61672491, 61602441, 61602446, 61732002, 61702478), the 973 Program of China (under Grant 2015CB358800), National Science and Technology Major Project (2018ZX01031102) and Strategic Priority Research Program of Chinese Academy of Sciences (XDBS01050200).

References

1. Abadi, M., et al.: Tensorflow: a system for large-scale machine learning (2016)
2. Chen, T., et al.: MXNet: a flexible and efficient machine learning library for heterogeneous distributed systems. Statistics (2015)
3. Chen, T., et al.: DianNao: a small-footprint high-throughput accelerator for ubiquitous machine-learning. In: Proceedings of the 19th International Conference on Architectural Support for Programming Languages and Operating Systems, pp. 269–284. ACM (2014)
4. Chen, Y., et al.: DadianNao: a machine-learning supercomputer. In: IEEE/ACM International Symposium on Microarchitecture, pp. 609–622 (2014)
5. Du, Z., et al.: ShiDianNao. ACM SIGARCH Comput. Arch. News **43**(3), 92–104 (2015)
6. Jia, Y., et al.: Caffe: convolutional architecture for fast feature embedding. arXiv preprint arXiv:1408.5093 (2014)
7. Liu, D., et al.: PuDianNao: a polyvalent machine learning accelerator. In: Twentieth International Conference on Architectural Support for Programming Languages and Operating Systems, pp. 369–381 (2015)
8. Liu, S., et al.: Cambricon: an instruction set architecture for neural networks. In: Proceedings of the 43rd International Symposium on Computer Architecture, pp. 393–405. IEEE Press (2016)

9. Reagen, B., et al.: Minerva: enabling low-power, highly-accurate deep neural network accelerators. In: ACM SIGARCH Computer Architecture News, vol. 44, pp. 267–278. IEEE Press (2016)
10. Zhang, S., et al.: Cambricon-X: an accelerator for sparse neural networks. In: IEEE/ACM International Symposium on Microarchitecture, pp. 1–12 (2016)

An Intelligent Parking Scheduling Algorithm Based on Traffic and Driver Behavior Predictions

Jiazao Lin[1], Shi-Yong Chen[2], Chih-Yung Chang[2(✉)],
and Guilin Chen[3]

[1] Peking University, Beijing 100871, China
Linjz84@126.com
[2] Tamkang University, New Taipei City 25137, Taiwan
dora@gms.tku.edu.tw, cychang@mail.tku.edu.tw
[3] Chuzhou University, Chuzhou 239000, China
glchen@chzu.edu.cn

Abstract. Smart parking is a common demand of citizen, especially for people living in a smart city. It is an important issue since it not only determines the required parking time of drivers but also impacts the urban population and traffic congestion. In this paper, an intelligent parking algorithm is presented based on the predictions of traffics and drivers' behaviors. The proposed parking algorithm analyzes the historical parking records, predicts the parking traffics and the driver's parking length and then schedules the vehicles to the parking grids such that the maximal benefits can be obtained. The proposed algorithm also dynamically allocates their reservations but guarantees the parking reservations for the VIP members. But based on the parking space resource. Performance analysis through extensive simulations demonstrates the efficiency and practicality of the proposed scheme.

1 Introduction

Parking lots are located all over the world. These parking lots were built in workplaces, sports centers, entertainment and tourist centers, shopping centers, airports, schools, family apartments and so on. The increments of cars are leading to more and larger parking lots, which increases efforts to deploy intelligent parking management systems. This also increases the motivation for developing an intelligent parking system for better managing parking space resources, providing a higher quality of parking service as well as increasing the benefits of the manager of the parking lots.

In the past few years, a number of researchers devoted themselves to improve the efficiency of parking systems. These studies developed new policies and algorithms, aiming for improving the utilization of parking grids or reduce the driver's parking time, creating advantages of the manager or drivers, respectively. These studies are generally partitioned into two classes. The first one [1–5] is free parking, which aims to provide parking information for drivers to easily park their vehicles to the parking grids of the street. The policy considered in this class is that the parking vehicle is free on the

© IFIP International Federation for Information Processing 2018
Published by Springer Nature Switzerland AG 2018
F. Zhang et al. (Eds.): NPC 2018, LNCS 11276, pp. 185–189, 2018.
https://doi.org/10.1007/978-3-030-05677-3_22

street. On the contrary, the second class is paid parking, which asked drivers to pay money for parking vehicle. Study [6] proposed an algorithm to allocate the incoming vehicles to available parking grids. It aims to improve the utilization of parking space such that the benefits of a manager can be maximized. However, most of them did not consider the predictions of parking traffics and drivers' behaviors based on parking history.

This paper proposed a new intelligent parking algorithm which considers the general needs of VIP members, drivers' service quality and the manager's benefits. Different from the previous works, the proposed algorithm predicts the traffics and the length of each driver's parking duration based on parking history. According to the predictions, the proposed parking algorithm selects the oncoming parking vehicles, schedules the parking grids and then allocates vehicles to the parking grids, aiming at maximizing the grid utilization and manager's benefits. The proposed algorithm not only guarantees the parking reservations for the VIP members but also improves the utilization of parking space.

To achieve this, the proposed algorithms consider two issues when developing the intelligent parking algorithm. The first one is the space reserved for VIP members. The VIP members have been usually maintained in the most parking management system. These members prepaid the money and expected to always have reservations of parking grids for their needs. To meet this requirement, the proposed algorithm considers the VIP members and dynamically reserves parking grids for them. The presented algorithm analyzes the behaviors of VIP members, predicts the starting parking time and length of time duration and then dynamically reserves the parking grids for them. In addition to the issue of VIP member, another important issue is the utilization of parking space. The proposed scheme aims to maximize the benefits for the manager of the parking lots.

The remainder of this paper is organized as follows. The assumptions, constraints and the design of the parking algorithm are proposed in the Sect. 2. The performance studies of the proposed algorithm and its improvements against the existing works are investigated in Sect. 3. Finally, the conclusions are drawn.

2 The Proposed Parking Algorithm

2.1 Assumptions, Goal and Constraints

This paper assumes that the information of drivers, their vehicles and their parking records have been collected in the parking management system. Each parking record contains the vehicle ID, starting parking time and end parking time. The parking time length of each parking record can be calculated based on this information. Given a parking lot which has k parking grids. A constant benefit can be created if the grid has been parked by vehicle for one basic time unit. Given a time period represented as $T = [t_1, t_2]$ where t_1 is a past time point and t_2 is a future time point. The overall benefits created by the parking lot is the summation of all benefits created by each parking grid in al he parking lot from t_1 to t_2. The goal of this paper aims to develop a parking schedule algorithm such that the overall benefits can be maximized. There are some constraints needed to be satisfied when finding the solution of the investigated issue. First, each parking grid can only have two states, the available state or the occupied state. Another constraint is that any vehicle can only occupy at most one parking grid at any given time in T. Similarly, each grid can only be occupied by at most one vehicle at any given time.

2.2   The Proposed Algorithm

The proposed algorithm is organized as three major parts. The first part mainly checks the validation of the input data and deletes the invalid ones existed in the historical parking records. After that, the designed algorithm further analyzes the history of parking records. This helps predict the parking traffic for a given specific day and time. Another important task in the second part is the behavior analysis, which aims to estimate the length of parking time for a certain driver. This analysis can help better schedule the parking grid and predict the time of an occupied grid to be released. Based on these predictions, the third part further selects proper vehicles from the incoming vehicles and then allocates them to the parking grids which are available.

There are three different policies proposed in the parking algorithm, namely Basic-Best-Fit, Basic-Worst-Fit and Parking Behavior Forecast. The designing concept of the Basic-Worst-Fit is to identify the starting time of each parking grid and guide the incoming vehicle to the grid with the largest available duration. The second policy, called Basic-Worst-Fit, guides the incoming vehicle to the parking grid whose available duration best matches the predicted length of the vehicle. The last part, called Parking Behavior Forecast (PBF) Scheme, predicts parking behavior based on parking history and the traffic for any given time of each weekday. The implementation of the Parking Behavior Forecast algorithm is separated into three parts. The first one is to fill in the VIP members to the empty parking grids. Then the method selects proper vehicles when the number of incoming vehicles larger than the number of available parking grids. The third one is to allocate the selected vehicles to the best-matched grids.

3   Simulation and Results

This section presents the performance evaluation of the proposed SPA method in terms of parking rates and the number of rejected vehicles. The proposed SPA is compared with traditional parking(TP) method [6]. The traditional parking method mainly adopted the strategy of FIFS (First comes First Serve). The proposed SPA adopts three policies, which are noted by BB-SPA, BW-SPA and PBF-SPA, respectively. The designing policies of the Basic-Best-Fit and the Basic-Worst-Fit have been presented in the previous section.

As shown in Fig. 1, 17 to 18 o'clock has peak traffics from Monday to Friday. Figure 2 shows that the weekends have peak traffic from 9 to 11 o'clock. However, the parking traffic of any given time points does not exceed 300.

Fig. 1. Daily traffic from Monday to Friday   **Fig. 2.** Daily traffic from Saturday to Sunday.

Figures 3 and 4 studies the accumulated parking rate of the parking lot with 300 grids. The parking traffic is created by scaling the real parking traffic, ranging from 75% to 95%. That is, the traffic is reduced ranging from 5% to 25%. The proposed SPA and the existing TP have a similar trend that the accumulated parking rate of them increase with time but decrease with the proportion of traffic reduction. This outcome is because of low parking traffic, which causes low parking rate. The proposed PBF-SPA has the best performance, as compared with the other three algorithms in all cases, because that PBF-SPA further predicts the vehicle arrival time and the parking length, and allows VIPs booking parking grids. The BB-SPA has a better performance than BW-SPA on both weekdays and weekends. This is because that BB-SPA predicts the duration of parking time and it always guides the vehicle to the grid with appreciate available time length. Consequently, the grid which is available for a long time can be reserved for the vehicle with the need for parking for a long time. The BW-SPA always guides the vehicle to the grid with maximal available duration and partitions the available duration into several small time segments. When a vehicle needs to be parked for a long time, the BW-SPA cannot support this requirement.

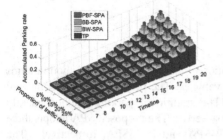
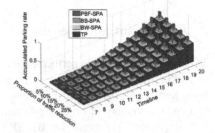

Fig. 3. Parking rate for different proportion of traffic reduction on weekdays.

Fig. 4. Parking rate for different proportion of traffic reduction on weekdays.

4   Conclusion

This work proposes an intelligent parking algorithm with three scheduling policies, aiming to improve the parking rate and obtain the maximal profits. The proposed BW-SPA and BB-SPA adopt the worst fit and best-fit policies, respectively. The proposed BB-SPA adopts predictions of parking traffic and parking length. Compared with the traditional parking mechanism, the proposed BW-SPA, BB-SPA and PBF-SPA significantly increase the utilization of parking space and hence improves the benefit of parking lots while guaranteeing the quality of parking services. Simulation results also verify the performance improvement in terms of accumulated parking rate and service quality.

References

1. Roman, C., Liao, R., Ball, P., Ou, S., de Heaver, M.: Detecting on-street parking spaces in smart cities: performance evaluation of fixed and mobile sensing systems. IEEE Trans. Intell. Transp. Syst. **19**(7), 2234–2245 (2018)
2. Shin, J.-H., Kim, N., Jun, H.-B., Kim, D.Y.: A dynamic information-based parking guidance for megacities considering both public and private parking. J. Adv. Transp. **2017**, 1–19 (2017)
3. Shahzad, A., Choi, J.-Y., Xiong, N., Kim, Y.-G., Lee, M.: Centralized connectivity for multiwireless edge computing and cellular platform: a smart vehicle parking system. Wirel. Commun. Mob. Comput. **2018**, 1–23 (2018)
4. Tilahun, S.L., Di Marzo Serugendo, G.: Cooperative multiagent system for parking availability prediction based on time varying dynamic markov chains. J. Adv. Transp. **2017**, 1–14 (2017)
5. Banti, K., Louta, M., Karetsos, G.: ParkCar: a smart roadside parking application exploiting the mobile crowdsensing paradigm. In: 2017 8th International Conference on Information, Intelligence, Systems and Applications (IISA), Larnaca, pp. 1–6 (2017)
6. Fang, J., Ma, A., Fan, H., Cai, M., Song, S.: Research on smart parking guidance and parking recommendation algorithm. In: 2017 8th IEEE International Conference on Software Engineering and Service Science (ICSESS), Beijing, pp. 209–212 (2017)

Author Index

Printed in the United States
By Bookmasters